W9-BRK-074

# VEGAN FOOD FOR THE REST OF US

## RECIPES EVEN YOU WILL LOVE

### ANN HODGMAN

ILLUSTRATIONS BY KATE BINGAMAN-BURT

A RUX MARTIN BOOK

HOUGHTON MIFFLIN HARCOURT   BOSTON   NEW YORK   2017

# TO HENRY, WORLD'S DOG

The recipes in this book include chocolate; coconut oil and other coconut products; corn; all-purpose (white) flour; lecithin; monosodium glutamate; peanuts; tree nuts; soy milk and other soy products; granulated (white) sugar; wheat gluten; xanthan gum; and meat. Oh, wait, not meat — that's the whole point!

No substitutes for the ingredients above have been tested, and none are recommended. If you are allergic or pretend-allergic to any of these items, avoid the recipes in which they appear.

Copyright © 2017 by Ann Hodgman
Illustrations © 2017 by Kate Bingaman-Burt

All rights reserved

For information about permission to reproduce selections from this book, write to trade.permissions@hmhco.com or to Permissions, Houghton Mifflin Harcourt Publishing Company, 3 Park Avenue, 19th Floor, New York, New York 10016.

www.hmhco.com

*Library of Congress Cataloging-in-Publication Data is available.*
ISBN 978-0-544-32449-7 (paperback); 978-0-547-52210-4 (ebook)

Book design by Melissa Lotfy

Printed in the United States of America
DOC 10 9 8 7 6 5 4 3 2 1

The expense is reckoned, the enterprise is begun;
it is of God; it cannot be withstood.
— Edmund Campion

Are you a hypocrite? Because I certainly am. I'm an animal lover who wears leather shoes; a vegetarian who can't resist smoked salmon. I badger my friends to see the Al Gore movie, but I also fly on fuel-gulping jets. Great clouds of hypocrisy swirl around me. But even a fraud has feelings. And I'm starting to think that our culture's frenzied and mindless assault on the last shreds of nature may not be the wisest course.
— George Meyer

# Contents

Don't Worry, EAT HAPPY ☺

# Introduction

"**I wouldn't mind never tasting this again,**" said my husband at supper one night.

"This" was my first try at seitan, a meat substitute based on wheat gluten. If you're new here, seitan is pronounced "*say*-tan." To make it, you wash flour over and over until it turns into a sort of rubber, knead in various flavorings meant to suggest meat, and cook it however you want. Or don't want, in the case of my first seitan, which ended up as a vaguely meat-tasting glob with a texture somewhere between Superball and hot dog.

Poor Dave. There's a steep learning curve when you suddenly adopt a plant-based diet, and for a year our food had been getting more and more horrible. One night, after an asparagus "paella" topped with a savory Rice Krispy treat had wrestled me to the ground, I dragged myself into David's office and announced, "I don't see a way around eating this. While we eat, I'll describe what it was supposed to be."

**Vegan props took over the kitchen, which began to look like a molecular gastronomy lab built by an orangutan.** Mesh bags filled with cooked soybeans drained into bowls in the sink. Gleaming pallid shapes loomed up in the refrigerator. I got a seed sprouter and a dehydrator and some cheese molds, along with twenty pounds of cashew pieces that I've never gotten around to using. They're still in the basement freezer.

Until the seitan night, David had been as nice as could be about all this. I could tell from his strangled politeness that he wasn't happy, but I kept thinking he just wasn't happy *yet*. It's hard to convert an omnivore to vegan food. It's even harder when that omnivore is originally from Kansas City, where people pick meat off the trees. And it's harder still when he's only giving voice to what you secretly agree with. I might have been able to convince myself that my seitan was okay. But I had already spent a year trying to master fake meat, fake dairy, and fake eggs, and David and I were tired out.

The seitan night was when I decided to stop trying to expect that all omnivore cooking could be perfectly replicated in a vegan version. There would be no more research on gelling agents. No more "So you ferment some seeds and add the ferment-juice to soy milk and stir in coconut oil and let it stand for six months and it ends up tasting exactly like spackling compound!" No more food that made us homesick for our former lives.

**No more Learning to Like Vegan Cooking.** Maybe you need to learn to cook vegan food, but whatever you make should be delicious.

NO MORE FOOD THAT MADE US HOMESICK FOR OUR FORMER LIVES.

I started over. My new rule was: No vegan recipe made the cut for this book unless David liked it enough to take a second helping or eat it as leftovers. Every recipe in the book would be Dave-tested and Dave-approved.

Whether you know Dave or not, you're going to thank him. But never as much as I do.

- - - - - -

"I want to become a vegan," my sister once said, "but I can't make myself watch the videos."

The horrifying videos, she meant. The ones that scald your eyes and sear your brain. The ones where you lurch away from your computer, sickened, and promise that this time you're really going to go vegan, or at least vegetarian. Because this time you've *seen*, you've really taken in — you recognize, deeply and permanently — the fact that the cows didn't somehow turn into flank steak, Cryovac themselves, and jump into the meat section at the supermarket on their own.

But then the next time you're at the supermarket, the images don't seem quite as powerful. Those packages of meat and poultry look so fresh and clean! And you've got to go out tonight, so you need a meal you can make fast, and probably you should educate yourself more before taking such a big step, and maybe this particular flank steak comes from one of the nice meat-packing plants. **There have to be *some* nice meat-packing plants** — look how much Temple Grandin has accomplished! And somehow the topic swims away.

I was like that for a long, long time. For most of my adult life, I was the one who ate whatever she wanted. Self-indulgence was my brand. *Life is too short! Leave the chicken skin on! Fat is our friend!* (I was right about that one, anyway.) *Everyone needs treats!* — those are the things I've told myself over and over. When people would ask me how to improve a recipe, I used to answer, "Double the chocolate and add bacon."

Then one day, while reading a book by James E. McWilliams called *Just Food*, I accepted the fact that everything about meat eating is wrong, and I became a vegetarian. This surprised a lot of people, but not me. **Like a cigarette smoker who knows she'll have to quit someday, I had always known that at some point I would stop eating meat.** I just hoped the change would come down the road — maybe after I was dead.

I've been pretty smug about this choice, but vegetarianism is a bowl of ice cream compared to veganism. As long as you still have dairy products and eggs, you can eat pretty much everything. But when you give up dairy and eggs? No cheese on your pizza. No butter on your English muffins. (No Thomas's English muffins, which contain milk and whey, either.) No cream in your coffee. No milk, no sour cream, no crème fraîche, no cream cheese, no Parmesan.

## Right Versus Wrong. Period.

Society doesn't encourage us to be vegans. So: Tell me again why I want to be one?

You don't actually have to tell me. Nor do you actually have to tell yourself why you should be a vegan. You already know why. Even if you choose not to know, you know. Hectoring people never works, but let me remind you of three things.

One is that if all the grain we feed to livestock was fed to people instead, there would be enough to sustain the populations of both China and India. The second is that factory farming is the biggest contributor to global warming and, according to the UN, one of the two or three top contributors to every single environmental problem on earth. The third — and, for me, the most important — is that no matter how nice you may be, eating animal products causes suffering on an unimaginable scale. The animals we eat are born into slavery, raised on slave ships, and set free by being killed.

I've always considered myself a friend to animals. I've shared my house with dozens of pets; I do wildlife rehab; I give money to Greenpeace; and for the last forty years, I've boycotted veal. Oh, wait — what I should say is that for my entire life, I've supported the veal industry without realizing it.

Dairy cows need to give birth once a year in order to supply enough milk for humans. In the world of dairy farming — even humane dairy farming — a cow's calf is generally taken from her when it's a couple of days old. Get back to making milk for humans, Mrs. Cow! Your calf can have formula.

Cattle being intelligent creatures, both mother and calf hate the separation. Female calves have a better chance of being kept alive than males because they're potential dairy providers. Male calves become veal. And we all know how bad the veal industry is! Haven't most of us been boycotting veal for decades?

Consuming dairy products is what keeps the veal industry in business. As one animal-rights writer put it, **there's a hunk of veal in every glass of milk we drink.**

No more onion dip, no more cheesecake, no more buttercream, no more croissants.

You try to reassure yourself that at least you won't miss eggs. You never eat eggs!

So what are you going to put into your pound cake — buttons? No eggs means no normal baked goods. No normal cakes, cookies, or chocolate mousse. No challah. No *pâte à choux*. No meringue on your lemon meringue pie, which also won't have a filling.

**SO WHAT ARE YOU GOING TO PUT INTO YOUR POUNDCAKE-BUTTONS?**

Every recipe that calls for eggs: gone. Also, no mayonnaise. Plus, **what the hell is up with the vegan ban on honey?** I agree that industrial honey making is cruel, but when the bees are well cared for, making honey does not exploit them. Bees make honey whether someone "owns" them or not. They can't help making honey! A worker bee who can't make honey is one sad bee. Besides, who pollinates so many of the plants in a plant-based diet? We need more bees making more honey. We do not need bees relaxing in tiny rocking chairs and buzzing about how much happier they are now that they're not following their instincts.

Anyway! At first, veganism seems like the land of No. But does it all have to be that hard? What if the process could be gentler?

"Now that you've made your decision," says one vegan writer, "start by throwing out all the nonvegan food in your house." *Why?* Will a single creature be helped by your wasting food that way? And will *you* be helped by plunging yourself helter-skelter into the world of nutritional yeast and rice bran syrup? No wonder you keep putting off becoming a vegan! Why not start more gradually and keep yourself happy?

**Going vegan doesn't have to be an instant change.** Nor does it need to be some kind of all-or-nothing line-crossing. If, one day, you snap at your kids,

## In PETA's Own Words

"Being vegan is about helping animals, not maintaining personal purity. Boycotting products that may contain trace amounts of animal products can actually be harmful to animals in the long run. For example, by refusing to eat a veggie burger from a restaurant because the bun may contain traces of milk or eggs, you are discouraging that restaurant from offering vegan options because it seems too difficult a task."
— People for the Ethical Treatment of Animals

you don't think, "That was a mean thing to do so I have no choice but to be constantly mean from now on." If you were planning to carpool somewhere but end up driving alone, you don't decide that saving fuel is hopeless. If you're a vegan who accidentally eats some real cheese in her salad, you don't have to stop being a vegan. And eating tofu does not have to mean you'll never again taste ice cream.

I wish I were a vegan instead of a vegetarian who eats a lot of vegan food. But I can't make the switch all at once. I just can't. So I eat as kindly as I can, donate to animal welfare causes, and hope to keep improving as I move along the path.

I will say, though, that **certain vegan foods *want* us to hate them.** I once saw a fake fried egg that had been made of God knows what and then wrapped in plastic to be reheated in the microwave. There's something called — truth! — "Dr. Cow's Aged Cashew Cheese with Blue-Green Algae." And tempeh, which is a stiff patty made from fermented soybeans that are "sewn" together by fungal filaments. Don't worry if your tempeh has black or gray spots! That's just spores. You can eat them fine.

When I first started this book, I assumed I had to learn everything about every aspect of vegan food. I taught myself to make tofu. (Easy but not worth it, at least not with the soybeans that are most readily available.) I went through all the different oils — expensive olive oil, cheap olive oil, peanut oil, coconut and hazelnut and grapeseed and, and, and . . . I studied the various dried seaweeds to see if

## Protein

Actually, some readers will think that this isn't enough information, but it's all you need: Most Americans eat twice as much protein as they require. If you are an adult and you're getting enough calories to maintain your weight, you're getting enough protein.

Truth.

any of them provided a "seagoing" taste that might replace fish. (No.) I ate some tempeh and hated it. I got more and more worked up. How could I learn to love this stuff? How could I persuade other people to even *try* it?

It took me a while to realize that I wasn't required to wander deeper and deeper into The Forest of Horror. No one was *forcing* me to eat fungus-covered fermented soybeans. Why not just come up with regular Ann-type recipes that happened to be vegan?

At the beginning, I wasn't sure there would be enough of those recipes to put into a cookbook. But there were!

# NOTE

In this book, you will notice a certain mild — or possibly insane-seeming — inconsistency in the ingredient measurements. For many people, weighing ingredients is annoying. For almost as many, using the metric system is infuriating. I've tried to cut readers as much slack as possible and have only used metric weights (and their feeble U.S. counterparts, pounds and ounces) when I think it makes a difference. Because anything less than ½ teaspoon is too hard to weigh, I've generally listed very small quantities by volume, not weight. I'm afraid I have to ask you to trust me on all this: Further explanation would be way too boring.

# OPTIONAL BUT NOT REALLY: PANTRY STAPLES

**You know the drill.** Every cookbook lists mandatory pantry ingredients and kitchen utensils. When you cast your eyes over the list, you see that each item falls into one of two categories. Either it's something *everyone* already has in her kitchen (Paper towels! Flour!), or it's something you've never heard of and have no intention of owning (Waxed Portuguese twine! Seed tweezers!).

If you're a beginning vegan, you may suspect that *all* of the following fall into the second category. But this list is actually pretty basic. Maybe we'll tackle Rejuvelac and agar-agar later. For now, here are the supplies you'll want to have on hand.

**Please don't cast your eyes over the list and slam the book shut because "these things are too hard to find."** Maybe that would've been true twenty years ago, but it's not *one bit* hard to find esoteric ingredients anymore. The internet makes it easy — much easier than driving to the supermarket. Powdered dried soy milk? Available on Amazon and on many natural foods websites. Soy lecithin granules? Available on Amazon and on many natural foods websites. Refined coconut oil — the kind that doesn't reek of coconut? Available on Amazon, on many natural

WAXED PORTUGUESE TWINE! SEED TWEEZERS!

foods websites, and at the grocery store in my 3,500-person town. A lot of vegan ingredients are becoming mainstream; the ones that are still rare are always available online. I would say "always on Amazon," but I don't want to sound (more) like a shill.

**Accent**  A brand of monosodium glutamate, also known as MSG, or **"the devil ingredient that made me think I was having a stroke in the Chinese restaurant that time."** I'm happy — or sorry, if you're a hypochondriac — to say that there's no evidence that MSG is harmful. Yes, it was created in a lab, but it's chemically identical to the glutamates in umami-rich foods, and it makes most plant-based dishes taste better. And vegans need every weapon they can add to the arsenal.

WAKES UP FOOD FLAVOR!

**aquafaba**  If only I had a time machine so that I could leap into the future and see what's happened to aquafaba between the time I'm writing this and the time you're reading it!

In 2015, aquafaba ("bean water" — another terrible vegan name!) changed vegan baking forever. I'm guessing that you who live in the future know what it is, but we who are stumbling around in the past have only just started working with it.

The fact that anyone even discovered aquafaba is as remarkable as anything else about it. How did an American software engineer named Goose Wohlt come to realize that the drained liquid from a can of chickpeas could be turned into a stable and 100 percent convincing meringue? A meringue that you can pipe and bake, or turn into utterly compelling buttercream and chocolate mousse? And use as an egg replacement in cakes and even in mayonnaise?

**Aquafaba seems like a gift from God to vegans** — a gift that we more than deserve, considering how long we've had to put up with crappy-tasting egg replacements. But I haven't used it in all my recipes that call for egg replacers. Flax cubes work better for anything baked above 300°F, which is most baking. But let's leave these matters to be sorted out by someone other than me. Instead, I'll show you how to make aquafaba.

Unfortunately, aquafaba hasn't been standardized as I write this; people still don't even know why it works. Yes, you can drain a can of chickpeas and get aquafaba, but are there brands that work better? Should the chickpeas be sodium-free? How much chickpea glop should you leave in? If you make your own aquafaba, how much should you reduce the liquid? Does it work better the thicker it gets? Why do chickpeas work so much better than other legumes?

That kind of thing. I'm certain that we'll be able to buy premade aquafaba soon, and then shall the lame man leap as an [sic] hart. In the meantime, you can join the many Facebook groups devoted to aquafaba if you want to try some of the recipes. And you can make the few recipes that call for aquafaba in this book, as long as you promise not to sue me if they don't work. They worked with my aqua-faba, which was made with the liquid drained from a can of *unsalted* chickpeas.

I hope that by the time this is published, Dole or Goya or some other legume processor will have gotten with the program and started selling standardized aquafaba. They've got the cans already! It wouldn't cost them anything!

Take a 15-ounce can of unsalted chickpeas. Pour them into a sieve set over a bowl and drain them. The drained-off liquid is aquafaba. Its beany taste will disappear when you use it.

**Bragg Liquid Aminos** Bragg Liquid Aminos looks just like soy sauce, comes in a soy-sauce-like bottle, can be used as a cup-for-cup soy sauce replacement, and . . . is made from soybeans, and contains more sodium than regular soy sauce. So what's the point?

Well, there are people who think Bragg's tastes better — probably because of the added sodium. And some believe that it doesn't contain soy, which is dumb.

But I suspect that the main value to Bragg's is that word "aminos." I myself always think "amigos" when I see it, but what's wrong with liquid amigos? I bet they're nice.

In sum, it doesn't really matter which one you use. But "All Purpose Seasoning from Soy Protein" is a pretty lame way to skirt the term "soy sauce." Also note that the Bragg family believes that fluoride in water is deadly poison.

**butter essence**  This is more embarrassing to recommend than MSG. For a while it was going to be my little secret, but then I decided to be upright and true. Butter essence smells so dreadful — like movie popcorn butter squared — that you'll reel backward the first time you sniff it. (I call that smell Butterine.) But you use it in insanely minuscule quantities. When people clean out your kitchen cupboards after you die, they'll say, "Why did she open this bottle of butter essence and not use any of it?"

The best brand I've found is L'Épicerie's Butter Aroma, which comes from the prestigious country of France (www.lepicerie.com/Butter-Melted.html). Steer clear of Lorann's, which is sold at craft stores and which tastes exactly like a flavoring you'd find at a craft store. **Hobby butter, you might call it.**

**citric acid**  *Every* kitchen, not just every vegan kitchen, needs a jar of citric acid. Citric acid, which is the source of the tartness in lemons, limes, and other citrus fruit, is one of the best taste-brighteners there is. If you like to sprout grains, citric acid will keep them fresh as they soak.

**cocoa butter, both regular and deodorized**  I buy regular cocoa butter in disk form; there's no chopping, and the disks melt more quickly than blocks or chunks. Regular cocoa butter adds a subtle chocolate note to many desserts and baked goods. Deodorized cocoa butter is mostly sold chopped into rough, irregular lumps. It has very little chocolate-y smell and is used primarily to improve the texture of vegan dairy replacements and baked goods. The deodorizing process involves forcing steam through the cocoa butter to drive out the volatile oils, which entirely removes the chocolate smell and taste, believe it or not.

COCOA BUTTER

To be honest, you probably don't need to keep cocoa butter on hand all the time. Just be aware that you may need both kinds from time to time.

**coconut vinegar**  While you may not welcome the suggestion that you add yet another vinegar to your crowded, sticky cupboard, coconut vinegar is worth it — and the bottles are usually small. Apple cider vinegar is made from fermented cider; coconut vinegar, which originated in the Philippines, is made from fermented coconut-flower sap. Maybe that's why it's sweeter and less pungent than most other vinegars.

*Why* buy a vinegar that's even sweeter and less pungent than rice vinegar? As if in explanation, one website points out that coconut vinegar has no calories, but get out of here; all vinegars are basically no-cal. The main advantage of coconut vinegar is that it imparts a slightly buttery note to homemade vegan butter. Like dairy butter, vegan butter needs a very, very, very, very, very slight acid note, but cider vinegar and lemon juice, even diluted, make it too sour. Coconut vinegar has the proper acidity. Even more than that, it has a faintly caramel/butter note that only Science can explain. Sniff it and you'll see what I mean! **(Come to my house if you want to sniff before buying.)**

I'll say this quickly before darting out of the way of your fist: Please buy coconut vinegar, not "coconut water vinegar." The latter is merely fermented coconut water, and buying it would truly be insane.

**flax cubes**  My cute name for "flax gel frozen in ice cube trays." The point is the flax gel, not the cubes. Flax gel is made from flax seeds that you, sigh, cook in boiling water until you've achieved a viscous liquid that you, sigh, stir through a sieve to separate the gel from the seeds. And since this is an annoying process, you make enough gel to fill at least one ice cube tray so that you can pull out a flax cube whenever you need one.

And when would that be, you're wondering? It would be when you need an egg substitute in vegan baking. Nothing can replace the magic of real eggs, but flax gel comes closer than many other suggested sub-ins: applesauce, yogurt, banana pulp. Flax gel is better than ground flax seed, which works pretty well as a binder but also contributes a distinctive (-ly bad) ground-flax taste and texture.

My flax-cube recipe is on page 203. Don't worry when the cubes turn out looking like scummy pond water. It won't affect the recipe, just your emotions.

**kelp granules** "Granules" is a terrible word, and when I'm the Vegan President, I'll change all those terms. But kelp granules (which are just dried, ground kelp — nothing granular about them!) are an okay way to add a very slight fishy note to recipes where you want The Kiss of the Sea. I use them in my Loxed Carrots (page 61) and Caesar Salad (page 74). Kelp granules come in a little shaker, like dried herbs, and if they're available at my small-town grocery store, I bet you can find them too.

**liquid smoke** All hail liquid smoke, one of nature's best vegan ingredients! It does so much to make up for the absence of meat, especially barbecued meat. Some vegans even claim that liquid smoke will convincingly replace bacon. That's far from true, but liquid smoke certainly adds a savory bacon quality wherever you use it.

What makes it so cool is that this isn't smoke flavor; the main ingredient is actual hickory smoke. (Or mesquite. Don't

bother with applewood liquid smoke, which has annoying additives like "red" and "green" apple flavoring.) Wood is burned in a magic chamber that captures the smoke in a condenser. As it cools, believe it or not, the smoke forms water droplets that are then collected, filtered, and bottled.

I've gone into detail here to prove that there's no reason you should be afraid of liquid smoke — at least no more afraid than you would be of any food that's grilled over charcoal.

. . . . . . . . . . . . . . . . . . . . . . . . . . . . . . . . . . . . . . . . . . . . . . . . . . . . . . . . . . . . . . . . . . . . . . . . . . . .

**macadamia nut pieces in bulk**  A lot of vegan cooking is based on nuts, most frequently raw cashews: They grind well and have a relatively neutral taste. But raw cashews are bitter compared to the mild sweetness of macadamias. Macadamias also have more fat than cashews, meaning that they carry more flavor and result in a better texture. This makes them the best nuts for vegan ice cream. **And no one should wade into veganism without the promise that good ice cream is out there waiting.**

BEST NUTS FOR VEGAN ICE CREAM

It's true that macadamia nuts are more expensive than cashews. But you can buy them in bulk or in pieces, both of which will cut down on cost. And gram for gram, they're not nearly as expensive as meat would be. One ten-pound bag, stored in the freezer, kept me supplied for almost three years.

. . . . . . . . . . . . . . . . . . . . . . . . . . . . . . . . . . . . . . . . . . . . . . . . . . . . . . . . . . . . . . . . . . . . . . . . . . . .

**miso**  By now, the theory of umami has been fully absorbed by the food world. Savory . . . the fifth flavor . . . meaty taste — you've heard all about it. Vegan cooking involves near-constant use of umami-rich ingredients, and miso — a Japanese seasoning paste made from soybeans — is one of the most potent sources. Miso comes in various strengths, but all you need for this book is white miso. Refrigerated, it keeps pretty much forever.

**olive oil** Both extra-virgin and "light," meaning light in flavor, not calories. Go to page 81 for an olive oil mini-lesson.

**powdered soy milk** Not mandatory, but it adds excellent texture to vegan breads.

**refined coconut oil — refined!** Remember when coconut oil was thought to be the devil, and they took it out of so many manufactured foods? Cracklin' Oat Bran and Pepperidge Farm Goldfish were never the same after that. Now, luckily, science has reversed itself, and coconut oil is back to being a *good* fat. I know some people who believe it's so restorative that they eat a tablespoon of straight coconut oil every day.

You don't need to go that far. But you do need to keep coconut oil around, especially for vegan baking and vegan dairy products. Because it becomes semi-solid at room temperature, it works better than regular oil in some recipes.

Coconut oil is available in two forms: "virgin," or unrefined, which tastes strongly of coconut, and refined, which has a completely neutral flavor. In this book, I only call for the refined kind. I like the taste of coconut fine, but it's thuggish and always hijacks other flavors if it gets a chance. And many people, such as everyone in my family but me, hate it.

**Soy Curls** I wish this were a generic name, but it's trademarked. Until someone invents Cutler Soi Kurlz, Butler Soy Curls have the monopoly. And they deserve it! As with so many vegan staples, though, I'm afraid that the instant I start describing them I'll hear your car door slamming, followed by the screech of wheels.

Still, I can't tell you to use them without telling you what they're like, can I? Let me soften the blow with the description from the Butler website:

"Butler Soy Curls are an all natural alternative to meat that are heart-healthy, delicious and easy to use. The exquisite texture, flavor and versatility of Soy Curls is unmatched."

Of course it should be "that IS heart-healthy"; the adjective is modifying the singular "alternative," not the plural "curls." And I might not use the word "exquisite" to describe the texture of *any* meat alternative. Still, the description is basically right.

Soy Curls are neutral-tasting morsels about the size of Cheez Doodles. For many vegans, they're the only acceptable chicken substitute. They soak up any flavor you want to give them, and they "chew" just like shredded chicken. After you reconstitute them in some kind of energetically seasoned stock, you can give them almost any chicken-y treatment you want. (Don't eat them plain, though. They're not *that* good.) They're great in fajitas, they're great in stir-fries, they're great deep-fried or baked.

I prefer Soy Curls to the much-praised chicken substitute that's currently sold at Whole Foods, and they're infinitely better than chicken-flavored seitan. As we know, seitan flunked the Dave Test bigtime, but he loves the things I've concocted with Soy Curls, especially Buffalo'd Soy Curls (page 160).

Soy Curls are sold in 8-ounce bags. They're very light, so they're cheap to ship and easy to buy in quantity. If you do buy more than a bag or two at a time, don't let their freeze-dried appearance fool you: *Soy Curls are perishable.* Any unused bags should be stored in the freezer.

**soy lecithin granules and soy lecithin powder**  See xanthan gum, page 27.

**soy milk and other nondairy milk**  . . . but preferably soy, which has more protein than rice milk or any of the nut-based milk replacements. This matters not because you need to eat more protein — if you're getting enough calories, you're getting enough protein — but because soy milk's protein approximates that of dairy milk. That means soy milk will behave more like cow's milk: It will set up better in yogurt, provide more stability in baked goods, and curdle more reliably when you're making vegan butter.

Now, I didn't say that soy milk tastes the best. The taste of cow's milk is veh-heh-ry hard to replicate, and as with many vegan dairy products, it can take a long time to get used to straight-up soy milk. The soyness shines through most mild-tasting desserts (and "shines" isn't really the word we want here). But vanilla soy milk doesn't taste in the least soyish, so I use it in a lot of dessert recipes and reduce the amount of sugar the recipe calls for.

There are currently three varieties of nonsweet soy milk: "original," "unsweetened," and "light." What you want is original, which was formulated to resemble dairy milk as closely as possible. Cow's milk has between 8 and 13 grams of various sugars per cup. Original soy milk has about 6 grams; unsweetened soy milk, only 1. Original is thus the one that will taste best to anyone who grew up drinking cow's milk.

### textured vegetable protein/textured soy protein — hereafter, tvp

Formerly TSP until Certain People started worrying about soy.

Textured soy protein and textured vegetable protein are the same thing. And they both sound awful, don't they? Like those "food pills" that, as children, we kept being told would one day replace actual food. "You'll just need to take one food pill a day!" people would say. "All the nutrition you need!" This prediction worried me. I couldn't see the point of replacing nice food with a single pill. And now that I'm a grownup, I realize that no one can see the point of doing that, and I don't have to worry that real food will be disappear in my lifetime. Similarly, I'm no longer quite as worried that one day I'll end up in jail.

But I digress, mostly because I don't want to describe TVP. Why would anyone want to describe a defatted granular soy flour product? That's what TVP is: dried soy flour, processed into little grains or pellets. The reason you should care about it is that once it's been reconstituted, TVP has an uncanny ability to mimic the texture of ground meat and to absorb any meaty flavor you want to give it. Then you can add it to things like lasagna and chili and sloppy joes and tacos and pizza sauce, and honest to God, no one will know it's not meat.

You want to use it in small amounts, though: A TVP meat loaf will not work, no matter how many websites try to persuade you otherwise. You don't need a lot. Just a few tablespoons will convey the necessary impression. Use the smallest-size flakes or chunks you can buy; the smaller the pieces, the less chance anyone will wonder what they're eating.

Let me add that TVP is very, very high in protein. It's also fat- and gluten-free. And it's cheap. If you've taken part in a school lunch program any time after 1971, you've had TVP; that was the year it began being added as a ground-beef extender at schools.

Remember bacon bits — Bac-Os? They're a primitive form of TVP. We can do a *lot* better than Bac-Os now.

**vanilla bean paste (versus vanilla extract)**  No one will laugh at you if you decide not to buy vanilla bean paste, but here's why you might want to: Because it has ground-up vanilla seeds, it proclaims "Vanilla!" louder in dessert recipes than ordinary extract. Vanilla desserts are probably the hardest to veganize convincingly, and a subtle visual reminder that you really *are* tasting vanilla can be helpful.

**vegan butter**  Contradiction in terms, yes! Something that dairy farmers think shouldn't be allowed to exist — or at least to be called "butter" — probably also yes! But you'd never try it if it were called Vegan Margarine, would you?

**Doing without butter is one of the biggest sacrifices vegans have to make, especially vegan bakers.** There *is* no perfect butter replacement. So what you have to do is sigh, reflect that you're still privileged, and try to find the best vegan butter you can.

I was all set to recommend only two kinds of vegan butter: Smart Balance (*not* Earth's Best), and my own homemade version. Then, while this book was being edited, the brilliant vegan chef Miyoko Schinner introduced her own "European Style Cultured Vegan Butter." This is the kind of timing writers must learn to accept.

Miyoko's butter is very, very good — possibly better, and certainly easier, than my homemade version. (Kite Hill, which makes excellent vegan cheese, must have a similar product in the works.) Now that it's here, a lot of previously closed doors will open. But at the moment, Miyoko's butter is expensive and hard to find. If you can find it and want to spend the money, use it! If not, use my two other recommendations.

Note that although Smart Balance lists no animal ingredients, it is not certified vegan. This is because it may contain trace amounts of whey. "*May* contain *trace* amounts" is not something that worries me (or PETA — see page 11), but I thought I should let you know.

Smart Balance is stable at room temperature; it won't separate into oil and substrate. Both my Vegan Butter (page 178) and Miyoko Schinner's separate as they reach room temperature. You need to use them cold.

**vegan sausage**  I'm guessing that it will take a long time before the vegan miracle-workers are able to duplicate bacon. The only people who might argue are lifelong vegans who have never tried real bacon. The taste isn't that hard to copy, but the texture? Forget it. Serious Eats has come up with a very good portobello substitute, but the recipe is so finicky that I can't bring myself to make it more than once a year.

Vegan sausage has evolved more successfully. Two kinds are worth keeping around: sausage-flavored textured vegetable protein (see page 22), and Gimme Lean "Ground Sausage Style." You can use a handful of TVP to flavor things like spaghetti sauce, and the Gimme Lean where you need actual sausage-y mouthfuls. The bulk kind is the most convincing. Chop it into half-inch pieces — or break it into crumbles — and fry till the pieces are good and brown; you want the exterior crusty. You can also fry thin slices till they're firm and *then* break them up and brown them.

Feel free to try other brands, though Gimme Lean tends to be the easiest to find. And *never* buy any vegan product marked "Light," "Lite," or "Reduced Fat." Low-fat pork sausage is bad enough; low-fat vegan sausage is a travesty.

**vegan semisweet chocolate and chocolate chips**  Both are easy to find in stores; just check the ingredients. Ghirardelli and Guittard both make excellent vegan chocolate chips and bar chocolate, even though they're not labeled as vegan.

You're safe with any brand of unsweetened chocolate — all unsweetened chocolate is vegan. And if you're craving milk chocolate to "eat out of hand," as they say, Rose City Chocolates has an excellent version made with rice milk (www .rosecitychocolates.com).

**vegan yogurt culture**  Right now, there isn't one mass-produced vegan yogurt on the market that's any good — at least not one plain unsweetened vegan yogurt. The creator of the excellent site VeganBaking.net, Mattie Hagedorn, is exactly right when he says that most vegan yogurts are just "glorified starch slurries."

Even if you never touched unsweetened yogurt in your omni life, you'll be using it as a vegan. This means finding a version that tastes better than starch

VEGAN
YOGURT
CULTURE

slurry, which inevitably means making your own, which in turn means using vegan yogurt cultures, at least when you start out. If you make yogurt regularly, you can use a few tablespoons from a previous batch to start the next one (and if you don't, a few tablespoons of Kite Hill's plain yogurt will do the trick). But the cultures seem to keep forever in the refrigerator and give consistently reliable results.

Cultures for Heath (www.culturesforhealth.com) and Thrive Market (www.thrivemarket.com) have vegan starters for plain, Greek, and Bulgarian-style yogurts. They also have good instructions for making your own yogurt. You don't need a yogurt maker, by the way — as long as you have a saucepan, a bowl, and an instant-read thermometer, you'll be okay.

**vital wheat gluten** Obviously, if you're gluten-sensitive (though, unless you have celiac, I bet you're fine), you'll want to skip this ingredient. Wheat gluten is exactly that: the protein (gluten) in wheat. Gluten is what gives wheat bread its texture and "spring." The more gluten, the more elastic the dough; the less gluten, the more tender the dough. Bagels have a lot of gluten; piecrust doesn't have much, or at least isn't supposed to.

Why do vegans have to know this? **Well, wheat gluten has a somewhat meaty texture and a vast flavor-absorbing capacity.** This is why it's the key ingredient in seitan, a meat replacement that, if you've read the introduction to this book, you already know I hate. But a little wheat gluten makes an enormous difference in vegan burgers (page 164). Without it, they tend to be too soft and pasty. For the perfect vegan burger, you'll want to use gluten.

If you take some wheat flour and rinse and rinse and rinse and rinse allllllll the starch out, you'll end up with an elastic lump of wheat gluten. But why go to all that trouble? Just buy a box of vital wheat gluten in the flour-and-grain section of your market and add some water. If you have space in the freezer, store it there or it may turn rancid.

**xanthan gum and lecithin powder** I'm bundling these because they're both used to improve the consistency of many vegan foods, especially dairy replacements. Both are plant-based, and both scare Chicken Little types who haven't done their homework. **(Every piece of chocolate you've ever eaten contained soy lecithin.)** If you suffer from ingredient fear, it will either cheer you up or annoy you to learn that lecithin and xanthan gum — and guar gum and carrageenan — are all perfectly healthy.

My one quibble about lecithin is that the liquid kind tastes and smells *hawrible*. Use soy lecithin granules or powder instead. I've tasted both kinds — there's nothing I won't do for my readers — and you should trust me on this.

IMPROVES
TEXTURE

# APPLIANCES, UTENSILS, AND MISCELLANY

The recipes in this book don't require a lot of specialized equipment, but the following will make your life much easier.

. . . . . . . . . . . . . . . . . . . . . . . . . . . . . . . . . . . . . . . . . . . . . . . . . . . . . . . . . . . . . . . . . . . . . . . . . . . . . . .

**bread thermometer or instant-read thermometer**  Useful if you bake a lot of bread. Testing for doneness by temperature is more accurate than guessing.

. . . . . . . . . . . . . . . . . . . . . . . . . . . . . . . . . . . . . . . . . . . . . . . . . . . . . . . . . . . . . . . . . . . . . . . . . . . . . . .

**candy/deep-frying thermometer and instant-read thermometer**
Some of the most delicious vegan food is deep-fried. Unfortunately, deep-frying is inevitably messy and arduous. Don't make it even harder by starting with oil that's too hot or cool — use a thermometer. If you make your own candy, you already know how important it is to heat sugar precisely.

An instant-read thermometer isn't quite as crucial, unless you plan to make your own yogurt (which I certainly hope you will), but I'll nag you more about it later.

**digital kitchen scale**   No more arguing—just get the damn scale. They're not expensive, and it's the twenty-first century, people! Even the *New York Times* has switched to listing ingredients by weight (and metrically). **Measuring by weight is light years more accurate than measuring by volume.** For baking, it's also easier. You don't have to wonder whether you've packed too much brown sugar into the cup; you don't have to level off your flour; you don't have to laboriously scrape peanut butter into tablespoon measures. You can just add an ingredient to the bowl, tare the weight back to zero, and add the next ingredient.

*Digital Scale*

Some of the best recipes in this book demand digital scales. *Demand.*

**food processor or blender**   . . . but preferably one of each, since one or the other works better for certain tasks. Food processors are better at chopping vegetables without pulverizing them; blenders are better for making utterly smooth liquids. I hate to say it, but if you want to do a lot of vegan cooking, you'll need a blender at some point. And I *really* hate to say *this*, but if you can afford a Vitamix or Blendtec blender, buy one. A high-speed heavy-duty blender laughs at jobs that would terrify a regular kind.

**FOOD PROCESSOR**

If you do spring for a Vitamix or Blendtec, spend a few cents extra and buy some earplugs. High-speed blenders are loud enough to impair your hearing if you use them a lot. Of course, so are stand mixers. And blow-dryers are worse, because people use them much more often. Maybe you should wear earplugs all day long.

**ice cube trays**   Food writers are a little too blithe about their readers' freezer space. *Buy extra for the freezer,* they carol, as though everyone keeps a stand freezer in her garage. If you live in an apartment, you're sometimes *lucky* to have a full-size refrigerator, let alone a freezer big enough to store a moose.

Still, a couple of extra ice cube trays won't take up much space, and they'll allow you to freeze individual small portions of ingredients that *always* come in a big container even though you *never* need more than a tablespoon at a time. Tomato paste is one of these, and chiles in adobo sauce are another.

You'll also need an ice cube tray or two if you plan to do vegan baking on a regular basis. Flax Gel Cubes (page 203), one of the best egg replacers, and aquafaba (see page 14) need to be measured out in egg replacement–size portions (one cube equals one egg) and frozen.

**immersion blender**  Not mandatory, but great to have for soups because it eliminates the need to slosh hot liquid from one container to another. When mine died, I replaced it with a secondhand industrial model I found on eBay. Now I can blend three gallons of liquid at a time if I want to.

**parchment cupcake liners (if you plan to bake a lot of cakes)**  This may sound like a weirdly specific purchase, but vegan cake recipes work much better as cupcakes than as full-size cakes. They can also be harder to get out of the pan than ordinary cakes. Paper cupcake liners are better than nothing, but you'll curse the whole world if you try to peel one off a cupcake and it takes a big chunk of cake with it. You'll never have that problem with parchment. **Do yourself a favor and treat yourself to a box of If You Care cupcake liners.** They'll improve not only your life but also your brain: Every time you open the box, you'll wonder anew about the company that thought "If You Care" was a good name.

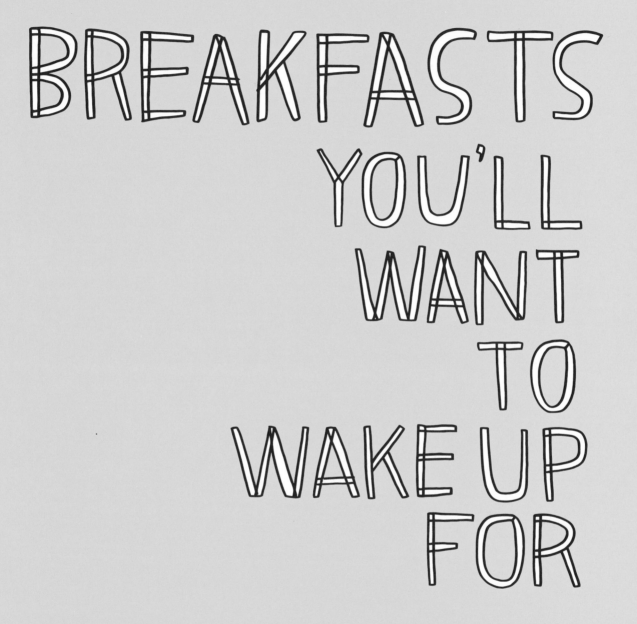

----- -

"Why can't humans hibernate?" howled a friend's son one school morning. I know so well what he meant! There's been only one morning in my adult life when I was happy to wake up: July 29, 1981, the wedding day of Prince Charles and Lady Diana. And look where *that* got us.

Most mornings, I think "Noooooooooooo!" as soon as I open my eyes. Dave and the dog have usually been up for hours by then, and their chipper energy blasts me in the brain when I finally lurch downstairs.

It's much easier to get out of bed when you know something good is waiting in the kitchen. Vegan breakfasts don't *have* to be things like Japanese pickled vegetables; they can just be familiar coffeecakes and muffins and so on. Even vegan scrambled eggs can be delicious.

Also, thank heaven, coffee is vegan.

----- -

# Laura's Granola

- - - - - - -▷ *Makes about 8 cups.*

I never believed in homemade granola until my daughter grew up and gave me this recipe. Although she's lived on this planet for twenty-eight fewer years than I, and although she works full-time, Laura runs a far more disciplined kitchen than I ever will. Everything in her cupboards is neatly lined up. She keeps a list of what's in the freezer. She composts, even though she lives in an apartment and has to walk the compost to a collection place a few blocks away. She makes all the sandwich bread for the family. And she makes her own granola. None of this stopped when she had her second child.

Homemade granola is really a lot better than store-bought, I have to say. And it keeps, in an airtight container, for up to a month. Naturally Laura has a dedicated container for hers.

Granola is a very flexible recipe. The rolled oats are generally a constant, but you can use whatever kinds of nuts and seeds you want as long as the measurements are the same. You can replace these dried fruits with others, or you can use all raisins. However, there's no real need to do any of that, because ***this* granola is the best.** Though I wonder what adding a cup of Rice Krispies would be like . . . ●

¾ cup real maple syrup or Lyle's Golden Syrup (8.8 ounces or 250 grams)

½ cup olive oil (3.8 ounces or 108 grams)

1 tablespoon vanilla extract

½ cup packed brown sugar (3.9 ounces or 110 grams)

½ teaspoon salt, or to taste (you probably won't want less)

Pinch of freshly grated nutmeg

4 cups old-fashioned rolled oats (13 ounces or 375 grams)

1 cup sliced almonds (5 ounces or 145 grams)

1 cup chopped walnuts or pecans (4 ounces or 117 grams)

1 cup flaked coconut (sweetened or not; 3 ounces or 83 grams)

1 cup hulled raw sunflower seeds (5 ounces or 140 grams)

2 cups dried cranberries or dried cherries (11 ounces or 320 grams)

1 cup chopped dried apricots (9.5 ounces or 270 grams)

1   Preheat the oven to 325°F. Line two rimmed baking sheets with parchment paper or silicone mats.

2   Combine the maple syrup, oil, vanilla, brown sugar, salt, and nutmeg over medium heat in a small saucepan and whisk constantly until the sugar has dissolved and the mixture is smooth. Take off the heat.

3   In a large bowl, toss together the oats, nuts, coconut, and sunflower seeds — using your hands is the best way to make sure they're evenly mixed. Pour the sugar mixture over the dry ingredients and toss until everything is coated.

4   Divide the mixture evenly between the baking sheets. Bake, rotating the pans every 10 minutes, for 30 minutes, or until the granola is golden. If you like clumpy granola, don't stir; if you like a more uniform mixture, stir when you rotate the pans.

5   When the granola is done, stir in the dried fruits. Let it cool on the pans completely before storing it — though there's no reason not to start eating it right away.

THIS GRANOLA IS THE BEST!

# Yogurt with Quinoa Muesli

*Breakfast for two!*

It's fun to say "muesli." Muesli. Muesli. **Make sure to purse your lips for the "ue" part!** Traditional muesli is like uncooked granola. Here the nuts and quinoa are toasted, making for a more refined result.

I don't see any point in making this with store-bought yogurt. Unless you have a brand you love, you'll need to make your own. But homemade is so good! ●

1 tablespoon red quinoa

2 tablespoons raw pistachios, chopped

2 tablespoons slivered almonds

1 teaspoon finely grated orange zest

¼ teaspoon vanilla extract

Pinch of salt

1½ cups homemade vegan yogurt (page 185)

5 dates, pitted and chopped

1   Preheat the oven to 350°F.

2   Put the quinoa in a small skillet and toast it over medium heat for 2 to 3 minutes, stirring constantly. When you start to hear popping sounds, transfer the quinoa to a small bowl or ramekin.

3   Toast the nuts in a small pan in the oven for 5 to 8 minutes, until they become fragrant and golden brown. Let cool completely.

4   Stir the orange zest, vanilla extract, and salt into the yogurt. Divide the yogurt between two shallow bowls, spreading it out to make a layer across the bottom of each bowl. Scatter the quinoa, toasted nuts, and chopped dates over the yogurt.

# PBB Oatmeal
## for Vegan Kids (or You)

*Serves 2 — or 3 or 4 if the children are small.*

One day a smart person realized that if you can make oatmeal in a slow cooker, why not make things even easier by just soaking the oats and not cooking them at all? Some overnight oatmealers like to eat the resulting cereal cold, but I can't go that far yet. I heat it up.

You want old-fashioned rolled oats — not steel-cut, which won't soften enough, and not instant, which will soften too much. Old-fashioned rolled oats have just the right heft for soaking overnight and retaining some texture.

As you look at the ingredient list, you'll see why **I think this recipe is best for kids — who, God knows, need plenty of treats if they have vegan parents.** But you'll also see that it can be adultified in all kinds of ways, depending on how creative you feel breakfast should be. You can also stir in some add-ins just before serving: berries, coconut, toasted almonds, chopped apple . . .
I suppose you could also replace the peanut butter with chocolate sauce or Nutella, but that might make the kids too optimistic about breakfast in general.

**2 very ripe bananas**

**1 cup soy milk — "original" or vanilla (8 ounces or 243 grams)**

**¾ cup old-fashioned rolled oats (2.6 ounces or 75 grams)**

**½ teaspoon ground cinnamon**

**Pinch of freshly grated nutmeg**

**Pinch of salt**

**¼ cup peanut butter (0.75 ounce or 21.5 grams; if it's unsalted, you might want to add 2 more pinches of salt)**

**A few drops of vanilla extract**

**1 tablespoon packed light brown sugar, or to taste**

VEGAN FOOD FOR THE REST OF US

**36**

1  Puree the bananas in a food processor or blender. Transfer them to a large bowl, add everything else except the brown sugar, and mix well. Taste for sweetness and add the brown sugar if you want to. Cover the bowl and refrigerate overnight.

2  The next morning, heat the oatmeal in the microwave—or don't. Toss any add-ins on top (see headnote) and slap it down in front of your sleepy children.

## NOTES

If you want, you can replace some of the soy milk with homemade or store-bought vegan yogurt. In that case, use ⅔ cup soy milk and ½ cup yogurt.

For maximum adorableness, make this in individual servings in Mason jars.

# Breakfast Scramble

*Serves 3 or 4.*

Because eggs are outside my comfort zone to begin with, and because I don't like the drab 1970s name "tofu scramble," **it took me a long time to venture into the tofu-scramble swamp.** Not every vegan eats toast and cereal for breakfast, though, so I gritted my teeth. David, who eats eggs every day, gritted his teeth even more strongly. When we actually ungritted our teeth enough to let the scramble enter our mouths, we were both surprised at how good it was. "Much better than real eggs in motels," said David.

Plain tofu scramble would be as discouraging as motel eggs; you need add-ins. I like mushrooms and vegan sausage the best, but obviously they're just a starting point. Anything you'd put into scrambled eggs can go into tofu scramble. I also use silken tofu. For me, big curds in eggs *or* tofu . . . no. Silken tofu gets the point across without making you think about it so much.

Very earnest vegans like to color their tofu scramble with turmeric, which does make the tofu a cheery scrambled-egg yellow. On the other hand, anyone who says you won't taste the turmeric is a cheery scrambled-egg dreamer. I would much rather use a drop of yellow food coloring than eat turmeric at breakfast.

One cool thing, though: black salt. When you add activated charcoal to rock salt (and really, when *don't* you add activated charcoal to rock salt?), you get Indian black salt, or *kala namak* — which is actually pink or purple, but let's not get into technicalities. Kala namak has a lot of sulfur, the element that makes eggs taste and smell eggy. Am I doing a bad job of selling this product? Let's start over. **"Black salt adds the magic touch!"** is what I really meant to say. But regular salt and a ton of black pepper also work well. ●

¼ cup vegetable oil, plus more if necessary

½ package (about 6 ounces) Gimme Lean Veggie Sausage

8 ounces white or cremini mushrooms, trimmed and sliced

Kosher salt, plus more to taste

One 14- to 16-ounce container silken tofu, drained

1 or 2 drops yellow food coloring (optional)

¼ teaspoon black salt (kala namak; see headnote; optional)

A TON of freshly ground pepper to taste

1   Heat a large, heavy skillet and add the vegetable oil. When the oil shimmers, plop in the hunk of Gimme Lean and break it into chunks with a wide spatula. Continue breaking it up as well as stirring and scraping it up: You want the chunks small, crusty, and well browned. Don't worry if some of the tofu sticks to the bottom of the skillet. The moisture in the mushrooms will help with that.

2   And here come those mushrooms! When the sausage is brown, add the mushrooms to the skillet. Sprinkle kosher salt over them. Cook, continuing to stir and scrape, until the mushrooms have first given up their liquid (how I wish there were a better expression) and reabsorbed it. *It is very important that all the liquid be cooked away.* Add more oil to the skillet if you need to.

3   When the liquid is gone and the mushrooms are as brown as you like them, add the tofu to the skillet. If you're using the food coloring, drop it onto a piece of tofu. Stirring constantly, blend the coloring into the tofu, and the tofu into the sausage-mushroom mixture. Add the black salt, if using; it's salty, so if you use it, check the tofu for salt before you add regular salt and pepper to taste.

4   Stirring frequently, cook the scramble until the tofu liquid is gone. (Tofu liquid is just as unwelcome as mushroom liquid.) Check the seasoning and serve immediately.

# *NOTE*

If there are mushroom-haters in your household — children, say — this recipe is also excellent without the 'shrooms.

# Basic Vegan Pancakes

*Makes about 24 pancakes, which you may top however you want.*

**Aren't we lucky that maple syrup is vegan?** And blueberry syrup and probably anything else named "syrup"? But we mustn't ask syrups to *disguise* vegan pancakes. The pancakes need to be good enough to eat syrup-free — with a sprinkling of confectioners' sugar, say. This is extra-important since we can't slather them with dairy butter but must timidly apply the vegan kind and hope no one notices.

2 cups all-purpose flour (8.8 ounces or 240 grams)

1 tablespoon granulated sugar (12 grams)

1 tablespoon light brown sugar (12.5 grams)

1 tablespoon plus 1 teaspoon baking powder (20 grams)

¼ teaspoon salt

Pinch of ground cinnamon

2 cups "original" soy milk (16 ounces or 486 grams)

4 tablespoons vegan butter, homemade (page 178) or store-bought, melted (2 ounces or 57 grams)

½ teaspoon vanilla extract or vanilla bean paste

Vegetable oil for cooking the pancakes

1   Sift the flour, sugars, baking powder, salt, and cinnamon into a large bowl. (This amount of baking powder requires sifting, not just stirring. Baking powder lumps are icky.) Add the soy milk, melted butter, and vanilla and whisk until the batter is mostly smooth. A few little lumps are okay.

2   Heat a large skillet or griddle until very hot. Brush lavishly with oil; vegan pancakes stick more easily than the regular kind. (I don't use nonstick pans, but this might be a good place for one.) It's best to make a little test pancake before you really get going.

(That one is for you, of course.) Then form pancakes by evenly spacing ¼-cup dollops of batter in the skillet; a spring-operated ice cream scoop is good for this if you own one. Let the pancakes cook until bubbles appear all over the surface — not just a couple of bubbles here and there, but really all over. Then flip them and cook for another 2 minutes. Serve immediately if you can; otherwise, keep the pancakes warm in a 200°F oven until they're all ready. You may need to turn the heat down after the first batch so the skillet doesn't get too hot. Regrease the skillet before each new batch.

# Gingerbread Pancakes

*Makes about 24 pancakes, which you may top however you want.*

These magnificently solve the problem of **"can people tell that I used vegan butter instead of the real thing?"** Any kind of syrup might be overkill here; I'd use confectioners' sugar or applesauce. ●

2 cups all-purpose flour (8.8 ounces or 240 grams)

2 teaspoons ground ginger (4 grams)

2 teaspoons ground cinnamon (4 grams)

⅛ teaspoon freshly grated nutmeg

1 tablespoon plus 1 teaspoon baking powder (20 grams)

1 teaspoon baking soda (5 grams)

¼ teaspoon salt

2 cups "original" soy milk (16 ounces or 486 grams)

2 tablespoons molasses (1.5 ounces or 42 grams)

4 tablespoons vegan butter, homemade (page 178) or store-bought, melted (2 ounces or 57 grams)

Vegetable oil for cooking the pancakes

1  Sift the flour, spices, baking powder, baking soda, and salt into a large bowl. Whisk in the soy milk, molasses, and melted butter, mixing until the batter is mostly smooth. (A few little lumps are fine.)

2  Heat a large skillet or griddle over medium heat until very hot. Lavishly brush it with oil; vegan pancakes tend to stick more easily than the regular kind. (I don't use nonstick pans, but this might be a good place for one.) When the oil is hot, make a little test pancake so you'll have a sense of what your "frying conditions" will be, then form pancakes by evenly spacing ¼-cup dollops of batter in the skillet. (A spring-operated ice cream scoop works well for this, if you've got one.) Cook until the entire surface of the pancakes is pocked with bubbles, then flip them and cook for 2 minutes on the other side. Serve immediately if you can; otherwise, keep the pancakes warm in a 200°F oven until they're all ready. You may need to turn the heat down after the first batch so that the skillet doesn't get too hot. Regrease the skillet for each new batch.

# Apple-Cranberry Bran Muffins

*Makes 12 muffins.*

Bran muffins have been known to taste punitive even when they're not vegan. These are delicious, period — partly because the bran is so well disguised. **What did we do before dried cranberries came along?** ●

¾ cup "original" soy milk (6 ounces or 182 grams)

½ teaspoon apple cider vinegar

1 cup unsweetened applesauce (255 grams)

3 tablespoons vegan butter, homemade (page 178) or store-bought, melted (1½ ounces or 42 grams)

½ cup packed light brown sugar (3.9 ounces or 110 grams)

1½ cups all-purpose flour (7.5 ounces or 200 grams)

2 teaspoons baking powder (9 grams)

½ teaspoon baking soda (2 grams)

½ teaspoon salt (2.5 grams)

1 teaspoon ground cinnamon (2 grams)

1 teaspoon ground ginger (2 grams)

½ teaspoon freshly grated nutmeg (1 gram)

¾ cup oat bran (2.8 ounces or 80 grams)

½ cup dried cranberries (2.8 ounces or 80 grams)

1  Preheat the oven to 350°F, with a rack in the middle. Line a 12-cup muffin pan with cupcake liners.

2  In a large bowl, whisk the soy milk with the vinegar. Let this mixture stand for 10 minutes to curdle (which is a good thing here), then whisk in the applesauce, melted butter, and brown sugar, mixing well.

3  In a medium bowl, sift the flour, baking powder, baking soda, salt, and spices. Stir the bran into the sifted ingredients. Then fold this mixture into the wet ingredients, stirring only to mix. Fold in the dried cranberries.

4  Scoop the batter into the cupcake liners, filling them three quarters of the way. Bake the muffins for 28 to 30 minutes; a toothpick stuck into one of them should come out clean. Let the muffins cool in the pan for 10 minutes, then transfer them to a wire rack to finish cooling.

# French Toast Bread Pudding

*Serves 4 to 6.*

When I taste silken tofu, I always think, "Tastes like salad," which is why I don't use it very often. But in this recipe, it works great, probably because **the horrid eggy taste isn't lurking behind the door.** You could probably serve this as a dessert, but — well, I mean, it's got the words "French toast" right in the name.

You'll need to put this together the night before so that the bread can soak up all the flavors before baking. 

**12 ounces crusty baguette, cut into 1-inch-thick slices**

**6 ounces silken tofu (not low-fat; 162 grams)**

**½ cup packed light brown sugar (3.9 ounces or 110 grams)**

**2 teaspoons vanilla extract (0.3 ounce or 9 grams)**

**1½ teaspoons ground cinnamon (3 grams)**

**½ teaspoon ground ginger (1 gram)**

**½ teaspoon freshly grated nutmeg (1 gram)**

**½ teaspoon salt (2.5 grams)**

**2½ cups vanilla soy milk (20 ounces or 608 grams)**

**¼ cup maple syrup (5.9 ounces or 166 grams)**

**2 tablespoons vegan butter, homemade (page 178) or store-bought (1 ounce or 28 grams)**

**⅓ cup chopped walnuts (1.4 ounces or 40 grams), lightly toasted**

1  Preheat the oven to 300°F.

2  Tear the bread into bite-size pieces. Arrange the pieces on a rimmed baking sheet. Bake for 20 minutes, or until golden brown.

3  Grease a 3-quart baking dish and pack the bread cubes into it.

4  In a blender or food processor, blend the tofu, brown sugar, vanilla, spices, and salt until smooth. Add the soy milk and maple syrup and blend for a few more seconds. Pour this mixture over the bread pieces. Top the dish with plastic wrap and press down a few times so the liquid starts soaking into the cubes, then refrigerate the pudding over-night.

5 The next morning, preheat the oven to 350°F. Peel the plastic wrap off the pudding. Sprinkle dots of the butter over the pudding, then sprinkle the walnuts evenly over the top. Cover the dish tightly with foil.

6 Bake the pudding for 30 minutes. Remove the foil and bake for another 30 minutes until nicely browned on top.

7 You can serve this with more maple syrup if you want, but I think it's sweet enough already. And if *I* say that . . .

FRENCH
TOAST
BREAD
PUDDING

# Chocolate-Almond Swirl Bread

*Makes 1 large loaf.*

For new vegans, the first year of vegan holidays can be tough. At no other time do traditional foods feel more important. As you watch your relatives cramming in the Christmas stollen, it hurts to think that you may never taste it again. It's Christmas! **Don't Santa and the Baby Jesus want you to eat what you've always eaten on Christmas morning?** Isn't skipping the kuchen kind of a diss to them? I am not equipped to answer these questions for you.

But if you track down vegan holiday foods that are exactly as good as the omnivore kind, the anguish abates, and you might be able to remind yourself that eating animal products isn't all *that* festive. With recipes like this one, you may not even remember what the kuchen tasted like. Chocolate and marzipan (well, almond paste) are candy, after all. How can it not be a treat to eat them at breakfast?

Most yeasted bread recipes will benefit from less yeast, a longer rising time, and an overnight stay in the refrigerator. The bread will taste better, the crust will have a better texture, and the dough will be easier to handle — a benefit for you, at least. So start this recipe the night before. I say that a lot, don't I? But at least it protects you from having to do industrial-strength recipe deciphering first thing in the morning.

Bread flour versus all-purpose plus vital wheat gluten: your call. The dough won't know the difference and neither will you. I have both of them in the house because I use the gluten in vegan main dishes and I have an extra freezer with space for both. If you do a lot of bread-baking, you might want to keep bread flour handy; if you don't, the gluten comes in a smaller package that will take up less space.

If you'd like to finish baking the bread the night before your festive breakfast, it's fine to let it cool overnight. After 12 hours, though, it should be frozen. Thaw before slicing. ●

### BREAD

1¼ cups warm water (10 ounces or 300 grams)

⅓ cup plus 1 teaspoon granulated sugar (2.75 ounces or 78 grams)

1½ teaspoons dry yeast

3 to 4 cups bread flour, or 4 cups all-purpose flour plus 2 tablespoons vital wheat gluten (19.3 ounces or 550 grams)

2 tablespoons soy milk powder (see page 20; 0.47 ounce or 13 grams; optional)

1 teaspoon salt

2 tablespoons vegan butter, homemade (page 178) or store-bought (1 ounce or 28 grams)

1½ teaspoons vanilla extract or vanilla bean paste

### FILLING

2 ounces bittersweet chocolate, chopped (60 grams)

2 tablespoons vegan butter, homemade (page 178) or store-bought (1 ounce or 28 grams)

6 ounces almond paste (170 grams)

⅛ teaspoon almond extract

Pinch of ground cinnamon

Pinch of salt

1 to 2 tablespoons nondairy vegan milk or water (0.5 to 1 ounce or 15 to 30 grams), if necessary

### GLAZE

1 cup confectioners' sugar (4 ounces or 113 grams)

1 to 2 tablespoons water (0.5 to 1 ounce or 14 to 29 grams)

¼ teaspoon vanilla extract

½ cup sliced almonds (1.5 ounces or 43 grams), lightly toasted

1 **Bread:** In a small bowl, combine ¼ cup of the water and 1 teaspoon of the sugar. Stir on the yeast and let the mixture bubble for 10 minutes. Or, if you're using a bread machine (which is what I do), pour in the water-sugar mixture and then sprinkle the yeast over the water.

2 Put 3 cups of the flour, the remaining ⅓ cup sugar, the soy milk powder, and the salt into the bowl of a stand mixer fitted with the paddle attachment. Add the remaining 1 cup warm water, the butter, yeast mixture, and vanilla. (Or, if you're using a bread machine, just dump in all the dough ingre-

dients.) Beat with the paddle attachment until everything's combined and the dough is beginning to form. Switch to the dough hook and knead the dough for 10 to 15 minutes, until it's smooth and no longer sticky. If it's too stiff, add a tablespoon or so of water; if it's too liquid, add more flour 2 tablespoons at a time. The dough should be firm but malleable.

3   Grease a big bowl and put in the dough. Flip the dough around a couple of times to grease the surface. Cover the bowl with plastic wrap or a kitchen towel. Let the dough rise in a warm place until it has doubled in bulk, 2 to 3 hours.

Gently punch down the dough. Transfer it to a smaller bowl if the space in your refrigerator is limited. Cover the bowl with plastic wrap and refrigerate it for 2 hours; then check to see if it needs deflating again. If it does, gently punch it down, re-cover the bowl, and chill the dough for 12 to 24 hours.

4   **Filling:** Melt the chocolate and butter in a double boiler or microwave. Scrape them into a medium bowl and add the almond paste, almond extract, cinnamon, and salt. Mash these ingredients like Play-Doh until everything is combined. (I use my hands.) If you need to, add a tablespoon or two of milk or water to ensure that the mixture is smooth.

5   Grease a baking sheet or line it with baking parchment (which is what I do). When the dough has finished chilling, take it from the refrigerator and gently punch it down if you need to; it may have risen some overnight. Flour your rolling pin and your rolling surface. Roll out the dough, stretching it with your hands if necessary, until you've got a rectangle about 13 by 16 inches. If necessary, turn the rectangle so a long side is in front of you.

6   Spread the filling evenly over the dough, leaving a 1-inch border. Dip your finger into water and lightly "paint" the border; theoretically, this will help seal it. Then tightly, tightly, tightly roll up the dough the long way. Press down hard, pinching to seal the loaf tightly. Transfer the rolled-up dough to the baking sheet, seam side down. Let the dough rise for about 90 minutes. It's ready to bake when you stick a finger into it and the dent remains without filling in.

7   Preheat the oven to 425°F, with a rack in the bottom third. Put the bread into the oven, turn the oven temperature down to 350°F, and bake the bread for about 45 minutes, or until a bread or instant-read thermometer stuck into the center reads 190°F.

8  **Meanwhile, prepare the glaze:** Whisk together the confectioners' sugar, water, and vanilla.

9  When the bread is done, carefully transfer it to a rack and let cool for 10 minutes. Spread the glaze over it. (Don't worry if some of the glaze drips off.) As soon as you've spread the glaze, sprinkle the almonds evenly over the top of the loaf.

10  Cool the bread completely before slicing it. Cutting it while the center is still warm will mash down the loaf irreparably.

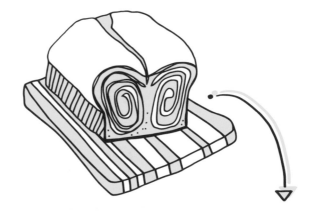

CHOCOLATE-ALMOND
SWIRL BREAD

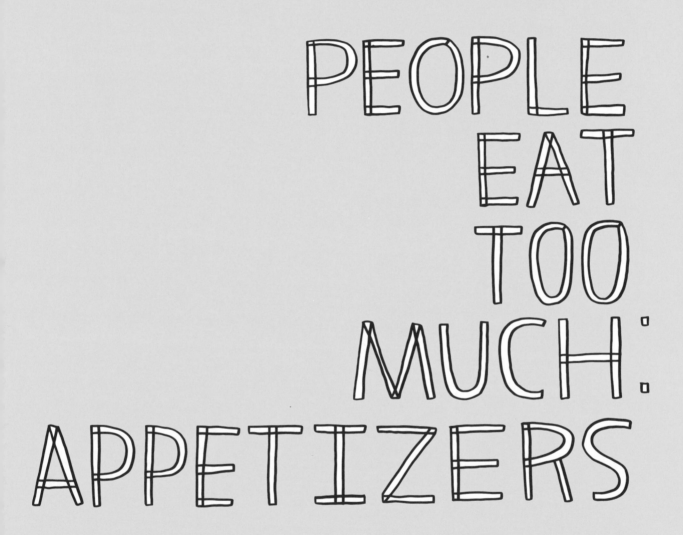
PEOPLE
EAT
TOO
MUCH.
APPETIZERS

— — — — —

I went *insane* over appetizers back in the dinner-party days. "How often do you enter-tain?" my mom asked me recently. "Never," I said. But back when we still gave dinner parties, I was all, "Make your own filo!" and, "Top each square with a single caviar egg rolled in platinum leaf."

It was Peg Bracken's fault. In *The I Hate to Cook Book*, she says, "A dish of maca-damia nuts is usually emptied faster than the plateful of bread-rounds fancied up by loving hands at home." I read this with a sinking heart, knowing it to be true — about bread rounds, at least. *My* appetizers, I vowed, would be better than bread rounds. I would put just as much effort into them as into the dessert. Perhaps the fact that hors d'oeuvres and desserts are my favorite parts of the meal had something to do with this; in any case, it didn't occur to me until I stopped entertaining that why *not* just put out some macadamia nuts? I want people to focus on the whole meal, not just the beginning of it.

I also stole one of Peg Bracken's titles, to punish her. She has a chapter called "Desserts, or People Are Too Fat Anyway."

But you have to have an appetizer chapter in a cookbook like this, and I can't say, "Oh, just put out some popcorn." The point is to *sell* people on plant-based eating, not make them think, "I guess she's saying that popcorn is better than any other vegan appetizer."

So here are a cherished few vegan appetizers. There's so much overlap in vegan cooking that you can also find several appetizer-ish recipes in other chapters. Just cut them into smaller pieces or serve tiny portions on little plates: Loxed Carrot Spirals, Crispy Tofu with Peanut Sauce, Endive Tarte Tatin . . . You see where I'm going with this. It depends on what else you'll be serving. And on whether you're still in your dinner party stage.

— — — — —

# Classic Hummus
## and Three Edgy Modern Variations

*Makes about 2 cups.*

Let's start with some terrible news: For the best hummus, you must peel the chickpeas — one at a time.

Don't blame me! Blame my friend Polly Roberts, who brought a batch of her hummus to dinner at my house. **You wouldn't normally call hummus astonishing, but hers was.** If there had been an SAT test, the question would have been:

Polly's hummus is to Ann's hummus as . . .

. . . and the correct answer would have been C: velvet is to scrunched-up foil.

I had no choice but to ask Polly how she'd made it. This is a tiny town, and we try not to poach each other's recipes; it's not fun to bump into your mom's Apricot Tiddles at someone else's house when you thought there were still a few of your own friends left to stun with them. But I still asked Polly, who said that the ingredients were ordinary. It was peeling the chickpeas that had made the difference.

So let's find something to binge-watch and park ourselves on the sofa, because we're going to be here for a while. ●

## Polly's Super-Classic #1 Best A+ Hummus

2 garlic cloves, sliced

¼ cup reserved chickpea cooking liquid or water

2 tablespoons fresh lemon or lime juice, or more to taste

1½ cups well-cooked chickpeas, peeled, or one 15-ounce can chickpeas, drained, rinsed, and peeled

½ cup tahini

¼ cup extra-virgin olive oil, plus more for drizzling

2 teaspoons ground cumin

1½ teaspoons Sriracha, or ¼ teaspoon cayenne, or more to taste

¾ teaspoon salt, or to taste

1   Put the garlic, cooking liquid or water, and lemon or lime juice in a food processor or blender and process until the garlic is finely dispersed throughout the liquid. Add the chickpeas, tahini, oil, cumin, Sriracha or cayenne, and salt and process until the mixture is utterly smooth. If the consistency seems too stiff to you, add a little more water. Check the seasonings, adding more lemon or lime juice, salt, and/or Sriracha if you think the mixture needs it.

2   Transfer the hummus to a serving bowl. Ideally, you should cover the bowl with plastic wrap and let the hummus rest at room temperature for an hour or chill it for at least 2 hours. But no one's going to complain if you serve it right away. (You can make it up to 48 hours ahead of serving.)

3   Drizzle with olive oil and serve with crudités and pita chips. But you knew that.

## The Roasted Red Pepper Version

*Makes about 2½ cups.*

**2 red bell peppers**

**2 garlic cloves**

**3 tablespoons fresh lemon or lime juice, or more to taste**

**1½ cups well-cooked chickpeas, peeled, or one 15-ounce can chickpeas, drained, rinsed, and peeled (see headnote)**

**3 tablespoons tahini**

**2 tablespoons extra-virgin olive oil**

**1 teaspoon smoked paprika**

**¾ teaspoon salt, or more to taste**

**¼ teaspoon granulated sugar**

**Water or reserved chickpea cooking liquid, if needed**

1   Preheat the oven to 450°F, with a rack as close to the top as possible. Line a rimmed baking sheet with foil.

2   Cut the peppers in half, remove the seeds and stems, and put them skin side up on the baking sheet. Wrap the garlic cloves in a double-thick twist of foil and put them on the baking sheet as well.

3   Roast the peppers for 10 to 15 minutes, until their skin is blackened in many places. Use tongs to lift them into a plastic bag or a snap-top lidded container. Knot the bag to close it, or snap the top onto the container. Let the pepper halves cool, all sealed up, until you can handle them without burning your poor, poor fingers.

4   When the peppers are cool enough, peel off the blackened skin and pull the peppers into pieces. (A pleasantly violent act.) It's okay if a little bit of skin sticks here and there. Put the peppers in a food processor. Squeeze the garlic out of the skins and add it to the bowl, along with the lemon juice; process till smooth. Add the rest of the ingredients except the water or cooking liquid. Process until the hummus is as smooth as you want. If you need to, you can thin it with a couple of tablespoons of water or cooking liquid. Check the seasoning, adding more salt, pepper, and/or citrus juice if you want.

## The Squashed Version

*Makes about 3 cups.*

1 small butternut squash

3 garlic cloves, sliced

1 tablespoon fresh lemon juice

1 tablespoon balsamic vinegar

2 tablespoons water or vegetable stock, homemade (page 177) or store-bought

2 tablespoons olive oil

1½ cups well-cooked chickpeas, peeled, or one 15-ounce can chickpeas, drained, rinsed, and peeled (see headnote)

2 tablespoons tahini

½ teaspoon granulated sugar

1 teaspoon salt, or more to taste

1 teaspoon ground cumin

½ teaspoon smoked paprika

½ teaspoon freshly ground pepper, or more to taste

Pinch of ground cinnamon (optional)

1   Preheat the oven to 350°F, with a rack in the middle. Line a rimmed baking sheet with foil.

2   Cut the squash in half the long way and scrape out the seeds and stringy glop. Put the squash skin side up on the baking sheet. Bake for an hour, or until it's very tender. Let cool until you can scoop out the flesh without burning yourself.

3   Scoop out enough squash flesh to pack into a 1-cup measure. "Reserve the rest for another use," such as feeding your Hermann's tortoise. My own tort, Susie (who is actually a male), *loves* squash.

4   Same drill as for Polly's Hummus: Process the garlic, lemon juice, vinegar, water or stock, and olive oil until the garlic is dispersed. Add the chickpeas, tahini, squash, sugar, and seasonings and whir everything until it's as smooth as you like. Taste for seasoning. Before serving, let the hummus sit at room temperature for an hour, or chill it for 2 hours.

# The Rapturously Gorgeous Beet Version

*Makes about 2½ cups.*

2 garlic cloves

One 2- to 4-ounce beet

1½ cups well-cooked chickpeas, peeled, or one 15-ounce can chickpeas, drained, rinsed, and peeled (see headnote)

¼ cup olive oil, or 2 tablespoons *each* olive oil and walnut oil

2 tablespoons fresh lemon juice, or more to taste

2 tablespoons tahini

1 tablespoon finely grated lemon zest

1 teaspoon salt, or more to taste

1   Preheat the oven to 400°F.

2   Wrap the garlic cloves in a double-thick twist of foil. Stick them on a small rimmed baking sheet, along with the unpeeled beet, and put in the oven. After ½ hour, remove the garlic cloves; leave them wrapped for the moment. Roast the beet for another ½ hour, or until it's tender. Let it cool until you can handle it, then peel and dice it.

3   Put the beet in a food processor. Squeeze the garlic pulp out of the skins and add it to the bowl. Now — you got it! — add the other ingredients and process until they're as smooth as you want. Check to see if the hummus needs more salt or lemon juice.

4   Before serving, let the hummus sit at room temperature for an hour or chill it for 2 hours.

# Fantastic Roasted Eggplant Dip
## (It Could Also Be a Side Dish)

*Makes 2 generous cups.*

Long prized for its deeply purple, glossy beauty as well as its unique taste and texture, eggplants are now available in markets throughout the year — **wait, I'm plagiarizing!** I couldn't think of anything good to say about eggplant, so I inadvertently stole some copy from the World's Heathiest Foods website, www .whfoods.org! I would never use "its" and "are" in the same sentence like that.

I do agree when the description continues, "One can generally describe the eggplant as having a pleasantly bitter taste and spongy texture." I can't get past that texture: watery and dry at the same time. So I go for recipes that concentrate the eggplant's umami-packed flavor while transforming its texture entirely. This dip is a perfect example.

Serve with pita wedges. You can also serve this as a side. ●

½ cup walnut pieces

1 batch Roasted Eggplant Puree (page 170)

1 cup homemade vegan yogurt (page 185)

2 tablespoons flavorful olive oil

1 or 2 garlic cloves, crushed (optional)

2 to 4 tablespoons minced fresh cilantro, mint, basil, or parsley, or a mixture of all four

Fresh lemon juice to taste

1 teaspoon ground cumin

Salt and freshly ground pepper to taste

1  Turn the oven on to 300°F. No need to preheat!

2  Scatter the walnut pieces on a rimmed baking sheet and stick 'em into the oven for about 10 minutes, until they're fragrant and slightly darker. Let them cool while you do the rest of the stuff.

3  The rest of the stuff is pretty simple: Whisk everything together. Check for lemon juice and seasoning. Stir in the walnuts. Eat.

# White Bean Aioli

*Makes about 1½ cups.*

I don't know why this is called aioli. You could just as easily call it White Bean and Garlic Dip. Or Spread. It's creamier than the average bean dip, though, and certainly more garlicky. And come to think of it, what else do you use aioli for besides dipping or spreading? So I guess "White Bean Aioli" is truth in advertising.

It's rare for me to prefer a lower-fat version of a classic, but I find this recipe much more versatile than real aioli, and I like the texture better. Even I can't eat an unlimited quantity of aioli, but this? **I could eat the whole recipe with a spoon.**

One 15-ounce can white beans, drained and rinsed

2 tablespoons fresh lemon juice, or more to taste

¼ teaspoon salt, or more to taste

½ teaspoon freshly ground pepper, or more to taste

1 or 2 "shakes" of cayenne

⅓ cup olive oil or other vegetable oil

6 garlic cloves, cut into 8 to 10 pieces each

1   Put the beans, lemon juice, salt, pepper, and cayenne in a food processor or blender and blend until smooth, which may mean a few scrape-downs, because this is a stiff mixture. (Leave the mixture in the processor or blender.)

2   Heat a small skillet over low heat and add the oil. Add the garlic and cook for 3 to 5 minutes; don't let it brown.

3   Add the oil and garlic to the bean mixture and blend until everything is smooth. Taste for seasoning, adding more lemon juice, salt, pepper, and/or cayenne if you want.

4   Let the aioli stand at room temperature for an hour before you serve it, to blend the flavors. Or store it in the fridge and bring it to room temperature before serving. It will keep, airtight, for 3 days or so.

# Spinach Bites

*Makes about 16 spinach bites.*

Remember those spinach bites we used to make with Pepperidge Farm Stuffing? (They were usually called spinach balls, but I don't like that.) You knew they were declassé, but whenever you served them, people vacuumed them up! What were you supposed to do, be mean to your guests?

In the future, where we live now, Pepperidge Farm Stuffing isn't as much of a thing; also, we like our foods to have texture. But with this recipe, which I'm sure derives from the spinach balls of yore, the basic bite-size deliciousness still applies, and **using garbanzo flour instead of crushed stuffing cubes turns these into World Food instead of just some Middle-American thing.** ●

### BITES

4 tablespoons vegetable oil

1 small onion, minced

1 teaspoon freshly ground pepper, or more to taste

½ teaspoon dried thyme

1 garlic clove, minced

½ cup quinoa, rinsed

1 cup vegetable stock, homemade (page 177) or store-bought

½ teaspoon salt, plus more as needed

One 10-ounce package baby spinach

1 teaspoon Dijon mustard

⅛ teaspoon cayenne, or more to taste

2 Flax Gel Cubes (page 203), thawed

½ cup garbanzo flour

### DIPPING SAUCE

1 cup orange juice

¼ cup whole-grain mustard

2 tablespoons honey

1 tablespoon soy sauce

1 teaspoon grated or minced fresh ginger, or to taste

WHENEVER YOU SERVED THEM, PEOPLE VACUUMED THEM UP!

1   Preheat the oven to 400°F. Grease a rimmed baking sheet or line it with parchment paper.

2   **Bites:** Heat 2 tablespoons of the oil in a small saucepan over medium heat. When it shimmers, add the onion and cook, stirring frequently, until it begins to brown. Add the pepper, thyme, and garlic and cook, stirring, for about 30 seconds. Add the quinoa and stir for a couple of minutes. Stir in the vegetable stock and salt, turn the heat to medium-low, and cook, covered, for 15 minutes, or until all the liquid has been absorbed. Transfer the quinoa to a big bowl and let cool while you cook the spinach.

3   Heat the remaining 2 tablespoons oil in a pot or large saucepan over medium heat. When it shimmers, dump in the spinach, add a pinch of salt, and stir-fry the spinach until completely wilted. If the leaves are biggish or stem-y, use kitchen shears to cut them up in the pot.

4   Stir the spinach into the quinoa mixture, then add the mustard, cayenne, and flax cubes, mixing well. Your hands may work best for this, but make sure the mixture's not too hot before you jam them into the bowl. Mix in the flour thoroughly. Taste a bit of the mixture to see if you want to add more salt, pepper, and/or cayenne.

5   Use your hands to shape the mixture into 1-inch balls and arrange them evenly on the baking sheet. Bake the bites for 20 to 25 minutes, until the bottoms are brown.

6   **Meanwhile, make the dipping sauce:** In a small saucepan, bring the orange juice to a boil over medium heat. Reduce it to ¼ cup, checking frequently. Add the rest of the sauce ingredients and cook, stirring, until the mixture thickens slightly. Remove from the heat.

7   When the spinach bites are done, let them stand on the baking sheet for 10 minutes, then transfer to a cooling rack. Serve hot, warm, or at room temperature, with the dipping sauce.

SPINACH BITES

# Cocktailers

*Makes a lot — 10 to 12 dozen at least.*

A long time ago, a friend from Alabama brought us a red-and-white tin of tiny, tiny cocktail snacks called Cannonballs — super-spicy pastry spheres flavored with sesame and poppy seeds. That same year, *Gourmet* published a recipe for them. (Come back, *Gourmet*. We miss you so much!) I made them once or twice, everyone loved them, and then I lost the recipe.

**The last time I thought about Cannonballs, I suddenly realized that they were vegan.**

Vegans need nice cocktail snacks too, so I jumped aboard the internet to look for a recipe. Amazingly, I couldn't find one. Had I only dreamed about them? I asked my friend Sumner Jenkins, a true-blue Southerner, if he'd ever heard of Cannonballs. Almost before I'd sent the email, Sumner had fired back a recipe from the *Charleston Junior League Cookbook*:

> One recipe of pie crust, add 1 cup of parched benne seeds,
> & 2 t cayenne pepper. Roll into balls, bake in a hot oven, salt while hot.

"We think 'parched' means toasted," Sumner added. (He was correct.) Later he turned up a second recipe, this one originally from *Texas Monthly*, called Benne Seed Cocktailers. The recipe's headnote said, "This is the original benne seed biscuit of which the *New York Times* says, 'A cocktail biscuit that should revolutionize cocktail parties.'"

**Thing is, though, I no longer have the patience to roll balls of dough the size of chocolate chips.** I roll out the dough and cut it into little cubes. That's why I call them Cocktailers instead of Cannonballs. Also, I'm a peacenik. ●

¾ cup sesame seeds (3.75 ounces or 108 grams)

2 cups all-purpose flour (8.8 ounces or 240 grams)

1 teaspoon salt, plus more for sprinkling (6 grams)

1 teaspoon freshly ground pepper (2 grams)

1 teaspoon cayenne (2.3 grams)

Pinch of granulated sugar

¾ cup cold solid vegetable shortening, such as Crisco (5.4 ounces or 154 grams)

5 tablespoons ice water, plus more as needed (2.6 ounces or 75 grams)

½ cup poppy seeds (2.5 ounces or 70 grams)

1 Preheat the oven to 300°F, with a rack in the middle.

2 Spread the sesame seeds on a rimmed baking sheet and bake for 7 to 10 minutes, until they're fragrant and honey colored. Let cool completely.

3 Pulse the flour, salt, both peppers, and sugar in a food processor. Slice the shortening into eight pieces. Scatter the pieces over the flour mixture and pulse just until the mixture is the texture of coarse cornmeal. (You can also do this in a regular bowl with a pastry blender or your fingers.)

4 Dump the flour-shortening mixture into a bowl (unless it was already in one). Sprinkle the ice water over it, then mix with a fork until you have a dough that holds together. You may need an extra tablespoon of ice water. Use your hands to mix in the cooled sesame seeds and the poppy seeds.

5 On a lightly floured surface, with a floured rolling pin, roll out the dough until it's about ¼ inch thick. Use a sharp knife to cut it into ¼-inch cubes. If you prefer, you or your children can roll the cubes into tiny balls.

6 Line two rimmed baking sheets with parchment paper. Carefully transfer the cubes to the baking sheets and bake for 15 to 20 minutes, until they're golden brown, rotating the pans halfway through the baking period so the Cocktailers will cook evenly.

7 Lavishly sprinkle the cubes with salt when they come out of the oven. Cocktailers are too small to transfer to a cooling rack — just slide the sheets of parchment onto the counter and let them cool. When they're cool, store them in an airtight container. These will keep for up to 2 weeks.

# Loxed Carrots

*Makes about 12 ounces — enough for 4 to 6 bagels or a batch of Loxed Carrot Spirals (page 64).*

I know several vegetarians who make an exception for smoked salmon. The number of vegan smoked-salmon recipes suggests that a lot of vegans at least *wish* they could make an exception. Many of these recipes are the "I'll add anything" type; my favorite lists store-bought vegan lox as one of the ingredients, which seems like adding chopped pancakes to a pancake recipe. **I don't know who first thought of subbing carrots for the fish;** it doesn't seem like an intuitive choice. But it sure works! Carrots taste good right from the start, and you don't have to add a lot of trickery to disguise them. Just realize that salt, smoke, and, above all, *time* are what really make the difference. The carrots need to bake for 90 minutes and then marinate for at least 2 days. For me, this amount of effort exactly equals the exorbitant cost of real smoked salmon, so it's a fair trade. Besides, roasting things in a bed of salt is fun!

Most vegan cream cheese is hateful. As of this writing, the best brand by far is made by Kite Hill; also as of this writing, Kite Hill products are only available at Whole Foods, though General Foods has just bought the company. That should make for a wider distribution. Maybe something even more wonderful and more accessible will have come along by the time you read this. ●

1 pound kosher salt

5 carrots (the biggest you can find), unpeeled and untrimmed

2 tablespoons olive oil

4 teaspoons liquid smoke

1 teaspoon coconut vinegar (see page 17) or apple cider vinegar

½ teaspoon kelp granules (see page 18; optional)

¼ teaspoon Accent (optional)

Bagels and Kite Hill Vegan Cream Cheese for serving

Capers, sliced red onion, snipped fresh dill, lemon wedges, and whatever else you used to have when you could eat smoked salmon

1 Two to three days before you plan to serve the loxed carrots: Preheat the oven to 375°F, with a rack in the middle.

2 Pour half the salt into a 9-by-13-inch baking dish, preferably one that's nonreactive. Wash the carrots and, while they're still wet, arrange them in the dish so that they're all on the salt and not touching one another. Pour the rest of the salt over the carrots, making sure they're completely buried.

3 Bake the carrots, uncovered, for 90 minutes.

## TMI

### More of PETA'S Own Words

"It is important to realize that if one accepts a process-based definition of vegan, then many other familiar products would also not be considered vegan. For instance, steel and vulcanized rubber are produced using animal fats and, in many areas, groundwater and surface water is filtered through bone charcoal filters. Under a process-based definition of veganism, even a simple box of pasta that contains no animal products but has been transported to the store in a steel truck on rubber wheels and then cooked in boiling water at your home may not be considered vegan. According to such a definition, it would be difficult to find any product in this country that is 100 percent vegan.

"We recommend that vegans concentrate their attention on the most obvious animal ingredients and the true meaning of veganism, helping animals. In our experience, concentrating on processing or on trace ingredients can make a vegan diet exceedingly difficult and dissuade people from adopting it."

Other unavoidable items containing animal products:

- Insulin
- Plywood
- Rubber
- Foam rubber
- IV bags
- "Collagen" and "elastin" in cosmetics (they don't work anyway)
- Most mouthwashes, toothpastes, and chewing gum
- Transmission and brake fluid
- Silk
- Soap

4   Meanwhile, whisk together the oil, liquid smoke, vinegar, kelp granules, and Accent, if using.

5   Remove the pan from the oven and carefully upend it onto a rimmed baking sheet. Use a heavy knife or ice pick or some such gadget to crack the salt crust and free the carrots. When they're still warm, but cool enough to handle, gently pry each carrot loose. Working one at a time with a knife and your fingers, remove the skin as best you can; this is an annoying and finicky task that won't be completely successful. If only a vegetable peeler worked! But little bits of left-on skin won't matter. (To make for somewhat easier peeling, you can also chill the carrots, tightly wrapped, for up to a day.)

6   When you've peeled all the carrots, use a mandoline or sharp knife to slice them lengthwise into strips that are as thin as you can make them. Another finicky chore! Maybe you should listen to an audiobook or binge-watch an HBO series that everyone in the world but you has already seen. If it's the latter, watch your fingers.

7   Transfer the carrot strips to a locking container, the kind you can turn upside down without anything leaking out. (If you don't have a container like that, put the strips into a zipper-lock bag.) Then pour the marinade over all and seal the vessel you're using.

8   Marinate the carrots in the refrigerator for 48 to 72 hours, turning them every few hours to give them all their fair share of marinade. If you want, take a little nibble occasionally to taste what happens as they transform. At the end of the marinating period, the carrots will have taken on an unexpectedly lush texture, very different from the way they started out.

9   Bring the carrots to room temperature before serving with the bagels, cream cheese, and various accompaniments.

LOXED CARROTS

# Loxed Carrot Spirals

*Makes about 48 spirals.*

I used to make this recipe with smoked salmon. In an earlier cookbook, I said that **people "bolt them down without even chewing, like seals catching fish."** Still true with these wonderful appetizers, although it would be a mistake to try to pass off the smoked carrots as fish.

As of this writing, Kite Hill's vegan cream cheese is the only one I can recommend. And I recommend it one jillion percent. ●

16 ounces Kite Hill Cream Cheese–Style Spread (plain or chive-flavored)

1 tablespoon finely grated lemon or lime zest

2 tablespoons fresh lemon or lime juice, or to taste

3 scallions, minced, with some green

3 tablespoons minced fresh dill, plus small sprigs for garnish

2 teaspoons sweet paprika (not hot or smoked)

2 tablespoons drained small capers

6 large flour tortillas (10 to 12 inches in diameter)

1 recipe Loxed Carrots (page 61)

1 Blend the cream cheese, lemon zest, lemon juice, scallions, dill, and paprika. (I do this in a food processor.) When these ingredients are well mixed, remove from the processor and stir in the capers by hand.

2 Spread each tortilla with about ¼ cup of the cream cheese mixture, leaving a ¼-inch margin. Arrange one sixth of the smoked carrots over the cream cheese. Roll up the tortillas tightly, pressing down hard as you roll.

3 Wrap each finished tortilla in plastic wrap, like a Tootsie Roll. Chill for at least 3 hours, but no more than 12.

4 To serve, use a serrated knife to cut the rolls into ½-inch-thick slices. The uneven ends of the rolls are for you, of course. Arrange the slices on a serving plate and garnish with sprigs of dill.

VEGAN CHEESE PLEASE

## Cheese

More than five thousand years ago, near the Tigris and Euphrates Rivers, the civilizations of Sumer and Urim were invaded and destroyed by armies from Elam and Sua. "The Lament for Sumer and Urim," one of the world's oldest written records, recounts the aftermath of the battles.

The "Lament" begins, "The storms [invading armies] gather to strike like a flood, to overturn the divine powers of Sumer." Everything is gone — cities leveled, waterways turned brackish, fields overrun by weeds, mortar and pestle lying idle. And this:

> *The reed huts were overrun, their walls were*
> *breached.*
> *The cows and their young were captured*
> *and carried off to enemy territory.*
> *The cows took an unfamiliar path in an*
> *open country that they did not know.*
> *Gayau, who loves cows, dropped his weapon*
> *in the dung.*
> *Cuni-dig, who stores butter and cheese, did*
> *not store butter and cheese.*
> *Those who are unfamiliar with butter were*
> *churning the butter.*
> *Those who are unfamiliar with milk were*
> *curdling the milk.*
> *The sound of the churning vat did not*
> *resound in the cattle-pen.*

The "Lament" gives milk, butter, and cheese a lot of ink — okay, cuneiform, but you know what I mean. Thousands of years ago, dairy products had the same emotional resonance they do now.

"Cheese is part of our patrimony," says Noella Marcellino, an American Benedictine nun who has devoted her life to perfecting the cheese made at the Abbey of Regina Laudis in Bethlehem, Connecticut.

"Cheese is magical," says Barb Stuckey, an executive vice president at Mattson (the nation's biggest packaged food development company). "What's that old saying? It's milk immortalized. And it's very, very hard to duplicate."

It turns out that our attachment to cheese may be physical as well as emotional. Scientists at the University of Michigan recently discovered that the casein in cheese can trigger the brain's opoid receptors and spark euphoria — a mild version of what hard drugs do for the brain.

Stuckey promised me that Mattson is working on fake cheese that will fool everyone. But for now, you can't satisfy your cheese cravings with fake cheese. Don't even try, I say. If you *have* to have some cheese, for God's sake just eat some once in a while! Ideally it will be a high-quality humanely produced variety, but don't obsess over that. Savor the cheese — and then make a donation to a humane farming or animal-advocacy group. You'll be helping the cause more than if you just sit around yearning for cheese.

# Vodka Tomatoes

*Makes 60 to 70 vodka tomatoes.*

What with these and Cocktailers (see page 59), we're getting awfully retro. **But retro is something that vegan foods never get to be!** And I guess vodka tomatoes can't be *that* retro, since so few people know about them. Guests always fall onto the floor with joy when they first taste them. Then they ask for the recipe, which came from my friend Zemma.

You need to make these a day in advance so they'll get properly liquored up. But surely that's not a problem! No one makes appetizers once their friends are already in the house.

**3 pints firm small red and yellow cherry tomatoes**

**1 cup vodka**

**6 tablespoons white wine vinegar**

**2 tablespoons granulated sugar**

**1 teaspoon finely grated lemon zest**

**1 garlic clove**

**3 tablespoons kosher salt**

**1½ tablespoons coarsely ground pepper**

1 Some recipes say you have to peel the cherry tomatoes. No way! Just use a toothpick or skewer to pierce each one of them in about a dozen places. Then put them in a medium bowl.

2 Stir together the vodka, vinegar, sugar, and lemon zest in a small bowl until the sugar has dissolved. Pour this mixture over the tomatoes, drop in the garlic, and stir so that they all get coated, then refrigerate them, covered, for 24 hours. Stir them a few times if you think of it.

3 When it's time to serve the tomatoes, drain them well and put them in a lovely bowl or whatever. Stir the salt and pepper together and put them in a lovely ramekin or clamshell or something. Serve with toothpicks for spearin' and dippin'.

THINGS THAT START WITH S:

SOUPS AND SALADS

(OH, AND BREADS)

— — — — — —

"Soups, Sips, Sides, and Snacks," or something like it, was the chapter title of a fund-raising cookbook put out by the board of my kids' preschool. David was the only man on the board then, and perhaps the only man ever. He brought John, then three weeks old, to a meeting. "The moms all helplessly rushed over," he reported afterward.

When he got home from the first cookbook-planning meeting, Dave reported that there had been a certain amount of fuss about what the title of the cookbook should be. One board member suggested "Nursery Nuggets," which the head of the board solemnly wrote down with all the other suggestions. They ended up calling the book *Family Favorites*, but Dave and I always called it *Nursery Nuggets*.

You do have to have a catch-all chapter for the things no one cares about as much. My *Nursery Nuggets* assignment was two vegetable recipes — "because we don't have any interesting ones," said the board chair. So Green Beans with Tomatoes and Spinach-Mushroom Casserole took their place alongside Crumbled Cream of Wheat, Salami Chips, and something called, simply, Chicken. I'm sure no one ever looked at them again.

Since vegan cooking can't rely on a big hunk of protein in the middle of the plate, soups and sides and so on end up being pretty important. Traditional vegan writers will tell you that you don't need a dinner entrée; make a meal out of five or six side dishes. To this I want to shriek, "Five or six? What is this, Thanksgiving?" Isn't it hard enough that vegans always, always have to be thinking about how to replace that big hunk of protein?

— — — — — —

# Black Bean Soup → *Serves 6.*

It's almost cheating to feature black bean soup in a vegan cookbook. But the rules state that I must include one.

This soup is already plenty hearty, but I've been known to add a handful of reconstituted ham-flavored TSP (see page 22) when I'm serving it to omnivores. **How terribly *vegan* that sounds:** "reconstituted ham-flavored textured soy protein!" And yet a little bit provides a subtly meaty effect. ●

2 tablespoons vegetable oil

2 medium onions, chopped

2 large carrots, scrubbed and sliced into ⅛-inch-thick coins

1 celery stalk, minced

4 garlic cloves, minced or crushed

1 tablespoon ground cumin

2 teaspoons chili powder

¼ teaspoon cayenne, or to taste

Four 15-ounce cans black beans, drained and rinsed

4 cups vegetable stock, homemade (page 177) or store-bought

1 cup frozen corn kernels (don't waste fresh corn on this!), thawed

One 15-ounce can crushed tomatoes

2 tablespoons fresh lemon or lime juice, or more to taste

Salt and freshly ground pepper to taste

Optional garnishes: diced avocado, chopped fresh cilantro, crumbled tortilla chips, and/or minced onion

1   Heat the oil in a large, heavy "soup type" pot over medium heat. When the oil is shimmering, add the onions, carrots, and celery, and cook for 5 minutes, stirring frequently. Add the garlic and spices and cook for 3 to 5 more minutes, stirring, until the onion is soft and translucent and the carrots start to soften. Add half the beans, along with 3 cups of the vegetable stock and the corn. Stir the mixture well and bring to a boil.

2   Meanwhile, in a food processor or blender, process the remaining beans, the tomatoes, the remaining 1 cup vegetable stock, and the citrus juice until quite smooth.

3   Stir the contents of the food processor (or blender) into the pot and reduce the heat to maintain a simmer. Simmer for 15 minutes. Add salt and pepper to taste. Serve with any or all of the optional garnishes.

# Creamiest Tomato Soup

*Serves 6 to 8.*

I realize that 4 cups of raw macadamias is a lot. Since we're going the trad-vegan route here, **feel free to use raw cashews if you'd rather.**

4 cups raw macadamia pieces (see page 19) or raw cashews

8 cups water or vegetable stock, homemade (page 177) or store-bought

2 tablespoons vegetable oil

2 large onions, chopped

1 celery stalk, chopped

1½ teaspoons salt, or more to taste

1 teaspoon freshly ground pepper, or more to taste

3 or 4 garlic cloves, minced or crushed

1 tablespoon dried basil

1 teaspoon ground cumin

½ teaspoon curry powder

Two 24- to 28-ounce cans chopped tomatoes

1 tablespoon honey, packed brown sugar, or granulated sugar

3 tablespoons fresh lemon or lime juice, or more to taste

1　Half an hour before you want to start cooking, put the nuts and 4 cups of the water or stock into a large saucepan. Bring to a boil, then lower the heat and simmer for 15 minutes. Turn off the heat and let the nuts sit for another 15 minutes.

2　Drain the nuts and put them into a blender, along with the remaining 4 cups water or stock. Blend, blend, blend, blend, blend until the mixture is as smooth as possible. Let it sit in the blender while you go on to the next step.

3　Heat the oil in a large saucepan over medium heat until it shimmers. Add the onions, celery, salt, and pepper. Cook the vegetables, stirring frequently, for 8 to 10 minutes, until the onions are soft and translucent. Add the garlic and cook, stirring, for a minute or so. Stir in the basil, cumin, and curry powder and cook for another minute.

4   Add the tomatoes, sweetener, and blended macadamia mixture. (Don't wash the blender. You'll be using it in a minute.) Bring the mixture to a simmer over medium-low heat. Simmer for about 15 minutes, or until it's beginning to thicken slightly. Then *carefully* blend it in batches until smooth and *carefully* pour each blended batch into a heatproof vessel.

5   When all the soup is blended, return it to the pan and add the citrus juice. Check the seasoning, adding more salt, pepper, and/or citrus juice if you like.

6   Reheat the soup over low heat, stirring constantly so as not to scorch the bottom of the pan, until it's as hot as you want it. Why do recipes always say, "Ladle into bowls and serve"? Obviously you're going to ladle it into bowls.

CREAM of TOMATO SOUP

# Ribollita

I was telling one of my nieces that I didn't want a lot of vegan soup recipes in this book because I'm not really a soup person. You have to wade through so much liquid to get to the good stuff! But my niece disagreed. *"I'm* a soup person! You should have a *lot* of soup recipes," she said. So I decided to put in a couple more.

Niece or no niece, I like this soup. **It proves my theory that bread equals meat,** or at least it proves that adding bread to soup gives it a lot more body. Without the bread, this would just be vegetable soup; with it, you can think, "This is how peasants added substance to their meager fare." Most ribollita recipes want you to use untoasted bread, which I guess is traditional. But how can that be right when toasting the bread adds a whole 'nother layer of flavor to the soup? Get real. ●

7 tablespoons extra-virgin olive oil, plus more for drizzling

4 cups sourdough bread cubes

1 large onion, chopped

3 carrots, scrubbed and sliced into coins (no need to peel them)

3 celery stalks, chopped

6 garlic cloves, minced

1 bay leaf

1 teaspoon salt, or more to taste

1 teaspoon freshly ground pepper, or more to taste

½ teaspoon red pepper flakes, or to taste

One 28-ounce can plum tomatoes in thick puree, chopped

8 cups chopped stemmed kale

3 cups cooked or canned white beans, with their liquid, if you have it

6 cups vegetable stock, homemade (page 177) or store-bought

½ cup dry white wine (optional)

½ cup chopped fresh basil

1  Preheat the oven to 350°F.

2  Pour 2 tablespoons of the oil onto a large rimmed baking sheet and smear it all around. Scatter the bread cubes over the baking sheet and scumble them around with your hands to gloss them with the oil. Bake the cubes for about 15 minutes, stirring them a couple of times so they cook evenly. They should be golden brown and crisp in many places when done. Set aside.

3  Heat the remaining 5 tablespoons oil in a large, heavy pot over medium heat. When the oil is shimmering, add the onion and turn the heat to medium-low. Cook, stirring frequently, until the onion is soft and translucent, about 10 minutes. Add the carrots, celery, garlic, bay leaf, and seasonings and cook for 10 minutes, or until the carrots and celery give a little when poked with a fork. Add the tomatoes, along with their puree, and the kale. Cook for — yes! — another 10 minutes.

4  In a blender or food processor, puree half the beans with a little of their cooking liquid if you still have it, or a little water. Add the bean puree to the pot, along with the whole beans. Add the vegetable stock and the wine, if using. Bring the mixture to a boil, then turn the heat to low. Simmer the soup, uncovered, for 20 minutes, stirring occasionally.

5  Stir the toasted bread cubes and basil into the soup. Simmer for 10 more minutes. Check the seasoning and serve, letting people drizzle olive oil over their soup at the table if they want (and if you want them to).

RIBOLLITA

# Yes! Caesar Salad!

The original Caesar salad, the one created in the 1920s by Caesar Cardini, was an alien being. For one thing, it was bristling with anchovies. And right before you served it, you were supposed to break an egg over it — an egg that had been coddled for one minute. Pure translucent blobular runniness! Horrible.

These days, most Caesar salads can be summarized as "romaine with a lemon-garlic dressing, grated Parmesan, and lots of croutons." The dressing is surprisingly easy to veganize, and homemade croutons are so much better than the boxed kind that you won't even notice there's no cheese.

This is one of the very few recipes in which I use nutritional yeast, a traditional umami-booster that you might believe tastes cheesy only if you've never tasted cheese. The first time I tried nooch, as we professionals call it, I threw the jar away in a fit of rage. "I'll never use this for *anything!*" So of course I ended up having to buy more.

I realize that **these ingredients look *awfully* vegan, but somehow they alchemize beautifully.**

### CROUTONS

**5 tablespoons olive oil**

**3 garlic cloves, minced**

**1 teaspoon dried basil**

**8 ounces sourdough or French bread, cut into ¾-inch cubes**

**Salt and freshly ground pepper**

### DRESSING

**½ cup raw macadamia nuts, soaked in water overnight in the refrigerator or boiled for 20 minutes**

**3 tablespoons fresh lemon juice, or more to taste**

**1 tablespoon white miso**

**1 teaspoon Dijon mustard**

**2 tablespoons nutritional yeast**

**½ teaspoon kelp granules (see page 18; optional, but they add some good umami)**

**1 large garlic clove, minced**

**½ teaspoon salt**

**2 heads romaine**

1 **Croutons:** At least 2 hours before making the salad, put the oil in a little bowl, add the garlic and basil, and let the mixture stand.

2 When you decree that the oil has finished steeping, preheat the oven to 300°F and line a rimmed baking sheet with parchment paper.

3 Put the bread cubes in a big bowl. Pour the garlic oil through a fine sieve onto the bread. (You don't want the actual garlic or basil, just the infused oil.) Toss the cubes to coat them with the oil. Lavishly salt and pepper them and toss again.

4 Transfer the croutons to the baking sheet, spreading them into a single layer. Bake for 20 minutes, then turn them over and bake for another 20 minutes. The croutons should be thoroughly crisp and golden brown. Let them cool completely.

5 **Dressing:** Drain the nuts well. Put them in a blender. Add all the remaining dressing ingredients and blend until you have a completely smooth dressing. Check the seasoning, adding more lemon juice and/or salt if you want.

6 Wash and dry the romaine, then tear it into bite-size pieces or cut it into ribbons. Toss with about two thirds of the dressing and the croutons, then add more dressing if you think the salad needs it.

YES! CAESAR SALAD!

# Farro, Fennel, and Radicchio Salad

*Serves 3 or 4 as a main dish, or 6 as a side.*

On an old *Simpsons* episode, Reverend Lovejoy asked, "Have you thought about any of the other world religions? They're all pretty much the same." This is the case with most of the new/old grains that have resurfaced over the past twenty years. Amaranth, Kamut, teff, freekeh — they're all fine. For the most part, they're high in protein, pleasantly chewy, and **more interesting than mashed potatoes** or Minute Rice. Farro's probably my favorite, for no other reason than that it's the first I tried after quinoa. (If you're buying it in bulk instead of in a package, as I do, the general method is to cook it in a 2:1 ratio of liquid to grain for 25 to 40 minutes, until all the liquid's been absorbed and the grains are tender but chewy. If you need to add more stock during the cooking, go ahead. If there's any remaining liquid once the farro is tender, drain it off.)

Farro and toasted walnuts mean this can be a main-dish salad if you want. If you haven't yet tried pomegranate molasses, which is actually a syrup made by reducing pomegranate juice, it works wonders in grain-based salads. If you can't stand to buy one more ingredient, lemon juice and honey are an okay substitute. But don't try real molasses! It's not *at all* what you want! ●

¼ cup extra-virgin olive oil

2 tablespoons pomegranate molasses (or 1 tablespoon fresh lemon juice plus 1 tablespoon honey)

1 teaspoon finely grated orange zest

2 scallions, sliced, or 2 tablespoons chopped Bermuda or Vidalia onion

1 cup farro, cooked in vegetable stock according to the package directions and then drained well

⅓ cup dried currants

1 medium fennel bulb, trimmed, halved, and sliced into thin rounds, plus 2 tablespoons chopped fennel fronds

½ cup fresh mint leaves, chopped

½ head radicchio, cored and slivered

½ cup chopped walnuts, lightly toasted

Salt and freshly ground pepper to taste

1 Whisk together the olive oil, pomegranate molasses, and orange zest in a bowl, then add the scallions or chopped onion. Let the dressing stand while you do the other stuff.

2 As soon as you've drained the farro, stir in the currants.

3 When the farro has cooled, transfer it to your salad bowl. Toss in the sliced fennel and fennel fronds, then the mint and radicchio. Add the dressing and chopped walnuts and toss well. Add salt and pepper, check the seasoning, and serve.

# AMARANTH, KAMUT, TEFF, FREEKEH— THEY'RE ALL FINE

*TMI*

## Amaranth

Hopeful food writers keep trying to bring amaranth aboard — May is Amaranth Month, for instance — but it never quite seems to take hold. I myself don't care about amaranth as a supergrain. What I care about is that the little bitty seeds pop like little teeny bitsy tiny popcorn that's so *damn* cute. The fact that it tastes nowhere near as interesting as popcorn doesn't matter in this case because it looks so adorable.

Heat a skillet or medium saucepan until a drop of water flicked onto the hot metal instantly sizzles and disappears. Amaranth will scorch almost as quickly, so pop just a tablespoon at a time. Drop the spoonful into the skillet and stir constantly, and in 20 to 30 seconds it will have popped. (You may have to do a couple of test batches before you get the procedure down.) The seeds are so little that they (mostly) won't fly out of the skillet as popcorn would. Pour/scrape it into a bowl, and keep going until you have as much popped amaranth as you want. It's prettiest as a soup garnish.

Amaranth won't pop in oil, sad to say, and the popped grain is too small to stir oil into. But you can add salt and seasonings to it after it's popped.

# Roasted Carrot and Orange Salad

*Serves 4.*

This is an adaptation of a fancy recipe created by the chef Ludo Lefebvre. **It has one of the happiest tricks in the food universe:** two very different-tasting components that look very similar. Take the time to plate the salad, rather than tossing all the ingredients together. When the carrots and oranges are tossed with the dressing, the salad looks a little *too* vegan — indistinct and blobby. When they're arranged on top of the cumin dressing, the dish becomes a rustic *salade composée*. In either case, scattering chopped herbs on top is an important part of the presentation, so don't skip that step. ●

### CUMIN DRESSING

1 cup homemade vegan yogurt (page 185)

2 tablespoons fresh lemon juice, or more to taste

2 teaspoons ground cumin

Salt to taste

### SALAD

1½ pounds carrots, scrubbed and trimmed

2 navel oranges

¼ cup slivered almonds

½ teaspoon ground cumin

8 garlic cloves, cut in half

1 bay leaf

¼ cup extra-virgin olive oil

Salt and freshly ground pepper to taste

### ORANGE VINAIGRETTE

6 tablespoons fresh orange juice

1 tablespoon balsamic vinegar

1 tablespoon granulated sugar

½ teaspoon salt

⅓ cup extra-virgin olive oil

2 tablespoons minced fresh parsley

1 tablespoon chopped red onion or thinly sliced scallions

1 Preheat the oven to 400°F.

2 **Cumin Dressing:** In a small bowl, whisk together the yogurt, lemon juice, cumin, and salt to taste. Chill the dressing while you prepare the salad.

3 **Salad:** Cut the carrots on the diagonal into 1½-inch chunks. Peel the oranges, separate the segments, and cut each segment crosswise in half. (You're actually supposed to prepare the orange so that each segment emerges without its membrane, but it's a finicky task and I always skip it.)

4 Roast the almonds on a small rimmed baking sheet for 5 minutes, or until they begin to change color. They'll keep cooking for a minute or so after you take them out of the oven, so don't let them get too brown in there. Set the almonds aside. (Leave the oven on.)

5 In a small skillet, toast the cumin over medium heat for 2 to 3 minutes, until it turns a shade darker and begins to smell good. Transfer to a small plate.

6 Put the carrots, garlic, and bay leaf in a bowl. Pour in the olive oil and toss well. Add the toasted cumin and re-toss. Transfer the carrots and their friends to a rimmed baking sheet and spread them out evenly. Lavishly salt and pepper them. Bake for 35 to 45 minutes, stirring every 10 minutes or so, until the carrots are soft and caramelized in many places. When they are done, fish out and discard the garlic cloves and bay leaf. Let the carrots cool.

7 **Orange Vinaigrette:** In a large bowl, whisk together all the vinaigrette ingredients. Add the carrots and toss well.

8 Spread the cumin dressing evenly over a large serving plate. Arrange the carrots over the dressing. Sprinkle the chopped red onion or scallion over the carrots, and then the almonds. Artfully place the orange segments here and there. Finally, sprinkle the whole thing with the minced parsley.

9 No matter how you serve this, make sure everyone gets enough cumin dressing.

# Green Bean Salad
## with Fried Almonds and Fennel

This is one of those salads you could serve along with an interesting bread and another side dish, and there you go: a delightful and charming ladies' lunch. I mean, the lunch is delightful. I can't speak for the ladies.

The recipe is adapted from Deb Perelman's *Smitten Kitchen*, also known as the *Silver Palate Cookbook* of our day.

½ fennel bulb (about 8 ounces), trimmed

½ Granny Smith or other tart apple, cored (no need to peel it)

1 small red onion

1 tablespoon fresh lemon juice

¼ cup balsamic vinegar

¼ cup water

1½ teaspoons salt, plus more to taste

1½ teaspoons granulated sugar

2 tablespoons plus 2 teaspoons olive oil

1 pound green beans, trimmed and sliced on the diagonal into 1-inch pieces

½ cup chopped or slivered almonds

Freshly ground pepper to taste

1 Slice the fennel, apple, and onion as thin as possible. Put the fennel and apple into a medium bowl and toss thoroughly with the lemon juice.

2 In a small microwavable bowl or a small saucepan, whisk together the vinegar, water, salt, sugar, and 2 teaspoons of the oil. Bring the liquid to a boil, then stir in the onion slices. Remove from the heat.

3 Steam the green beans for 5 minutes. Rinse them under cold, cold water to stop the cooking. Drain them very well and spread them out on a paper (or kitchen) towel to dry.

4 Heat a small heavy skillet over medium heat and add the remaining 2 tablespoons oil. When the oil is shimmering, add the almonds and stir constantly for 2 to 3 minutes, until golden brown. Remove the skillet from the heat and season the almonds and their oil with salt and pepper.

5   Drain the red onions, but SAVE the pickling liquid.

6   Toss together the green beans, fennel, apple, and drained onions in a medium bowl. Then toss with the almonds, their oil, and 2 tablespoons of the reserved onion pickling liquid. Add salt and pepper to taste, along with more pickling liquid if you think the salad needs it. Give the salad a final stir and serve.

**THE LUNCH IS DELIGHTFUL. I CAN'T SPEAK FOR THE LADIES.**

TMI

### Olive Oil

Oil is one of the main *things* in vegan cooking. If we can't use butter, then we need the best oil possible. But what many people consider the best-tasting oil — extra-virgin olive oil — doesn't always taste best after being heated.

Extra-virgin olive is a great "condiment oil": perfect for vinaigrettes, bread-dipping, and drizzling over soups and other cooked foods right before you serve them. But for searing or sautéing, using EVOO is pointless. In skillet-cooked foods, the difference in taste between EVOO and a lower-quality olive oil — or even another kind of vegetable oil, like canola — is so small as to be undetectable to most people. I use extra-virgin olive oil as a condiment and "light" ("neutral-tasting") olive oil or peanut oil when I'm sautéing.

It may be my imagination, but vegan baked goods made with olive oil seem to have a nicer consistency than ones made with other oils. For oil-based vegan baking, I use a light olive oil.

Olive oil turns rancid faster than many other oils. Whether you're buying extra-virgin or a light oil, buy it in small bottles, preferably dark ones, and store it in a closed cupboard. Light is not olive oil's friend.

# Fresh Corn, Basil, and Potato Summer Salad

*Serves 4.*

After your ten-millionth serving of corn on the cob, it's nice to use fresh corn for other things — like this potato salad, which is much more interesting than the usual gummy mayonnaise kind. **That's a very disloyal thing for me to say about both regular potato salad *and* corn on the cob,** and I wouldn't do it if I didn't think this one wasn't so perfect for summertime.

**SALAD**

8 ounces small red potatoes, scrubbed

3 cups fresh corn kernels (from about 4 ears corn)

2 cups cherry tomatoes, halved

1 medium red bell pepper, finely diced

**DRESSING**

3 shallots, minced

3 tablespoons balsamic vinegar

1 tablespoon Dijon mustard

¼ teaspoon salt, or more to taste

¼ teaspoon freshly ground pepper, or more to taste

3 tablespoons extra-virgin olive oil

6 cups arugula or baby spinach, stems trimmed

½ cup torn fresh basil leaves

2 ounces Tofu "Feta" (page 187), crumbled

1 **Salad:** Put the potatoes in a medium saucepan with enough water to cover. Bring the water to a boil and boil the potatoes for 15 to 20 minutes, until tender. Drain the potatoes and cool them to lukewarm, then chill them thoroughly.

2 Slice the cold potatoes into quarters. In a large bowl, gently stir them together with the corn, cherry tomatoes, and bell pepper.

3 **Dressing:** Put the shallots, vinegar, mustard, salt, and pepper in a small bowl and toss to combine. Slowly whisk in the oil. Check the seasoning, whisking in more salt or pepper if you want.

4 Drizzle the dressing over the corn mixture and toss thoroughly. Add the arugula and basil and toss again. Sprinkle the tofu feta over the top. Serve within an hour or so.

# Anne's Southwest Salad

*Serves 8 to 10 (Anne says 12, but I always eat 3 cups of this at a time).*

This is a wonderful summer recipe if you've got fresh corn on hand, but it also works well with frozen corn. **It would be a shame to deprive yourself in the winter.**

Anne is Anne Sontag Karch, my college roommate and lifelong friend. Didn't we make life complicated for all our friends by having the same name! ●

**SALAD**

One 15-ounce can black beans, drained and rinsed

2 large tomatoes, halved, deglopped, and diced (about 1 cup)

1 large cucumber, peeled, halved lengthwise, seeded, and sliced (about 2 cups)

4 or 5 scallions, chopped, with some green

1 red, orange, or yellow bell pepper, diced

1 jalapeño pepper, seeded and minced

Kernels from 3 medium ears corn, or about 1½ cups frozen corn kernels, thawed

**DRESSING**

3 tablespoons apple cider vinegar (actually, I use balsamic — sorry, Anne!)

Juice of 1 lime (about 2 tablespoons)

1 tablespoon extra-virgin olive oil

1 garlic clove, minced

1 teaspoon ground cumin

½ teaspoon chili powder

Salt and freshly ground pepper to taste

1 **Salad:** Toss all the salad ingredients together in a large bowl, as you probably guessed you'd need to do.

2 **Dressing:** Whisk the dressing ingredients together in a small bowl.

3 Pour the dressing over the salad and toss well. Check the seasoning. Let stand at room temperature, or in the fridge, for at least 2 hours before serving chilled or at room temperature.

# Sliced Sugar Snap Salad

*Serves 6.*

Yes, this is a very good recipe. But it's also here for another reason: You should know that sugar snap peas look much more interesting in slices. Thin slices, that is, cut on the diagonal. If the little peas stay put, **the slices look a lot like eyes.** It's a great presentation, and it's the only way I serve sugar snaps now. ●

2 tablespoons extra-virgin olive oil

1 tablespoon vinegar — any kind you want

1 teaspoon fresh lemon or lime juice, or more to taste

1 pound sugar snap peas, trimmed, stringed, and sliced diagonally into ¼-inch-wide pieces

4 ounces red radishes (about 8), trimmed and thinly sliced

3 ounces Tofu "Feta," (page 187), crumbled (about ½ cup)

Salt and freshly ground pepper to taste

1 tablespoon coarsely chopped fresh mint, plus more to taste

1 tablespoon dried barberries (optional; see Note)

1   Whisk the oil, vinegar, and lemon juice in a small bowl.

2   Toss the peas, radishes, and feta in a large bowl. (You can do this up to 1 day ahead. Cover the dressing and the salad separately and chill.)

3   Add the dressing to the salad and toss everything around. Season with salt, pepper, and more lemon juice, if you want. Stir in the mint and sprinkle with the dried barberries, if using.

**NOTE**   Dried barberries are something Yotam Ottolenghi told me about, although not to my face. He mentioned them in *Plenty*, one of the most important cookbooks of the past decade. They look like tiny red currants but are more tart. Barberries are starting to make inroads into stores, but you can also, of course, get them online.

# Kitchen Sink Chickpea Salad

*Serves 4 as a main dish, or 6 as a side.*

"Kitchen sink" because, as you may have figured out, it has a lot of ingredients — too many, you may think at first. But they all work so well together! I never thought much of radishes until I started using them chopped. **They impart a mysterious water chestnut quality that's much better than actual water chestnuts.**

## SALAD

3 cups cooked or canned chickpeas (drained and rinsed if canned)

1 Vidalia or other sweet onion

1 cup diced celery

1 cup diced cucumber

1 cup diced deglopped tomatoes

½ cup chopped radishes

½ cup dried currants

3 tablespoons sunflower seeds

## DRESSING

⅓ cup vegan mayonnaise (I like Vegenaise)

3 tablespoons fresh lemon or lime juice, plus more to taste

1½ teaspoons apple cider vinegar

2 tablespoons granulated sugar

2 tablespoons sunflower seeds

¼ cup packed fresh basil leaves

1 garlic clove

⅓ cup "original" soy milk

¼ teaspoon salt, or more to taste

¼ teaspoon freshly ground pepper, or more to taste

¼ teaspoon cayenne, or to taste

1 **Salad:** In a large bowl, toss all the salad ingredients together.

2 **Dressing:** In a blender or food processor, process all the dressing ingredients until smooth.

3 Toss the salad with the dressing; check the seasoning. Let the salad rest for at least 2 hours, stirring occasionally, before serving. Serve chilled or at room temperature. If you're not serving it when the 2 hours are up, refrigerate it. Eat within a day for the best texture.

# Lentil Salad
## with Roasted Vegetables

*Serves 6 as a main dish, or 8 to 10 as a side.*

Lentils are adorable. The trouble is that too often they're served in a big meaningless clump that diminishes their charm and keeps other ingredients from speaking up. A few handfuls of lentils: excellent! A huge glop of lentils: terrible! So this recipe: excellent! Vegetables star and lentils back them up by adding substance. **And because there's not a glut of lentils, you can appreciate their dear flat roundness.**

2 pounds fennel bulbs

1 pound carrots, scrubbed and diced (no need to peel them)

1 large onion, diced

¼ cup olive or vegetable oil

Salt and freshly ground pepper to taste

4 cups vegetable stock, homemade (page 177) or store-bought

2 cups dried French green lentils, picked over, rinsed, and drained

4 garlic cloves, finely chopped

1 bay leaf

¼ cup extra-virgin olive oil

2 tablespoons grainy Dijon mustard (or other "country-style" mustard)

1 tablespoon balsamic or sherry vinegar

1 tablespoon honey

½ teaspoon Accent (optional)

2 teaspoons minced fresh thyme

1   Cut the stalks off the fennel bulbs and slice them like celery. Snip the fennel fronds and set aside. Thinly slice the trimmed fennel bulbs.

2   Preheat the oven to 425°F.

3   Toss the sliced fennel, carrots, and onion with the olive or vegetable oil in a 10-by-15-inch (or similar size) ovenproof pan. Lavishly salt and pepper the vegetables and toss them again. Roast, uncovered, for 30 to 45 minutes, until the vegetables are tender and browned in spots. Set aside.

4   Put the stock, lentils, garlic, and bay leaf in a large saucepan. Bring to a boil, then lower the heat until the mixture is simmering

and let the lentils simmer for 25 minutes, or until tender. Drain them thoroughly and stir in ½ teaspoon salt. Fish out the bay leaf and toss it (or compost it or whatever).

5 In a large bowl, whisk together the extra-virgin olive oil, mustard, vinegar, honey, and Accent, if using. Add the thyme and snipped fennel fronds and whisk again.

Carefully dump in the lentils and cooked vegetables and mix everything thoroughly. Taste for seasoning, re-mixing if you add more salt and pepper. (The salad can be made a day or two ahead and stored in the refrigerator until you need it.)

6 Serve the salad warm, at room temperature (which is my favorite), or cold.

TMI

### Still More of PETA's Own Words

"Some packaged foods have a long list of ingredients. The farther an ingredient is down the list, the less of that ingredient is in the food. People who have made the compassionate decision to stop eating animal flesh, eggs, and dairy products may wonder if they need to read every ingredient to check for tiny amounts of obscure animal products. Our general advice is not to worry too much about doing this. The goal of sticking to a vegetarian or vegan diet is to help animals and reduce suffering; this is done by choosing a bean burrito or a veggie burger over chicken flesh, or choosing a tofu scramble over eggs, not by refusing to eat an otherwise vegan food because it has 0.001 grams of monoglycerides that may possibly be animal-derived."

EAT KIND

## *Heartbreakingly Good*
# Fried Rice Salad --------▷ *Serves 4.*

Not the kind of fried rice you used to get in Chinese restaurants. This is brown rice that's deep-fried until it's puffed and crackly — **"puffed, crackly, and phenomenal," a weaker person would write.** The process takes so little time that it barely counts as deep-frying. Also, you can fry the rice up to 5 days in advance and store it in an airtight container at room temperature. So that's another time-saver. I'm emphasizing this because I SO want you to make this salad and serve it to all your friends and watch them die of happiness.

Getting back to earth: You need to cook the rice at least 12 hours ahead so that it can dry thoroughly. Cooking it the night before you make the salad is probably the easiest way to accomplish this. ●

1 cup short-grain brown rice

2 cups vegetable stock, homemade (page 177) or store-bought

¼ cup dried cranberries, or 3 tablespoons dried currants

2 tablespoons balsamic vinegar, or more to taste

2 tablespoons fresh orange juice

2 cups broccoli florets

2 cups peanut or vegetable oil

Salt and freshly ground pepper

2 scallions, thinly sliced, with some green

⅓ cup extra-virgin olive oil

½ teaspoon red pepper flakes, or more to taste

1 tablespoon finely grated orange zest, or to taste

½ cup sliced almonds, toasted

1  Cook the rice according to the package directions, using the vegetable stock instead of water. When it's done, spread it evenly on a rimmed baking sheet. Let the rice dry, uncovered, for at least 12 hours, stirring it occasionally if you think of it (and if you're awake). You don't need to refrigerate it. If you're worried that mice or something will get at it, you can let it dry in a turned-off oven.

2  When you're ready to make the salad: In a small microwaveable bowl or small saucepan, stir together the cranberries or currants, vinegar, and orange juice. Bring the mixture to a boil, then let cool while you prepare the rest of the ingredients.

3  Steam the broccoli florets for 2 to 3 minutes, until very, very, very slightly cooked. Let them cool until you can handle them, then separate them into the tiniest itsy-bitsy florets you can.

4  Put the peanut oil in a medium saucepan and bring it to 350°F over medium heat.

5  Meanwhile, line a rimmed baking sheet with paper towels. Working in four batches, deep-fry the rice for about 1 minute, until it's puffed and golden. Using a fine-mesh sieve, transfer to the towel-lined baking sheet to drain. Sprinkle the rice with salt and pepper to taste and let cool.

6  Transfer the cooled rice to a bowl. Stir in the cranberries or currants and their soaking liquid, then stir in the broccoli, scallions, olive oil, red pepper flakes, and orange zest. Then toss well, add the toasted almonds, and toss again. Check the seasoning and add more vinegar, orange zest, red pepper flakes, salt, and/or pepper if you want.

# NOTE

This recipe is also excellent if you replace the broccoli with 2 cups coarsely chopped broccoli rabe that you've cooked and drained well.

# Roasted Potato Salad with White Beans

*Serves 4 as a main dish, or 6 as a side.*

Serving potatoes and white beans in the same dish may seem like buttering your bread and then dipping it into olive oil. They're oddly similar, yet it's hard to imagine that they can work together. English doesn't have the words for explaining that they actually combine beautifully, so **what can I say but "Try them"?**

Start soaking the dried beans the night before. ●

**SALAD**

1½ cups dried white beans

Salt

1 garlic clove, minced

2 bay leaves

¼ cup vegetable oil

1¾ pounds Yukon Gold potatoes, scrubbed

¼ teaspoon freshly ground pepper, or to taste

**DRESSING**

2 tablespoons drained capers

1 garlic clove, minced

2 tablespoons balsamic vinegar, or more to taste

1 tablespoon chopped fresh rosemary

⅛ teaspoon red pepper flakes, or more to taste

Salt and freshly ground pepper to taste

½ cup extra-virgin olive oil

20 cherry tomatoes, halved, deglopped, and quartered

1  **Salad:** Rinse the beans in a colander, making sure there aren't any little pebbles or twigs in there. Put the beans into a large bowl, cover them with 8 cups water, and stir in 1 tablespoon salt. Soak the beans for 12 hours.

2  Drain the beans and put them in a large saucepan. Pour in enough water to cover them by 2 inches. Add ½ teaspoon salt, the garlic, one of the bay leaves, and 2 table-spoons of the vegetable oil. Bring to a boil over medium heat, then lower the heat so the beans are simmering. Simmer the beans for 45 minutes, stirring them when you think of it. Then break one in half to see how they're doing. If they're creamily tender, drain them and check the seasoning; if not, cook them for another 15 to 30 minutes, then drain. Fish out the bay leaf.

3   While the beans are boiling, get the tates ready: Preheat the oven to 425°F, with a rack in the middle.

4   Slice the potatoes into ½-inch chunks. Pour the remaining 2 tablespoons vegetable oil onto a rimmed baking sheet, dump on the potatoes, and sprinkle them with salt and the pepper. Flip/stir them around until they're evenly coated with oil, then spread them out in a single layer. Slide the second bay leaf somewhere under a corner of the potatoes.

5   Roast the potatoes for 15 minutes, then flip/stir them around. Cook for another 10 minutes, then test for doneness. If the potatoes aren't quite tender enough, flip/stir

them around again and cook for 5 to 10 more minutes. Fish out and toss the bay leaf. Set the potatoes aside.

6   **Dressing:** Put all the dressing ingredients except the olive oil in a blender. Blend until smooth, then blend in the oil. Check the seasoning, adding more vinegar and/or salt if you want. Pour the dressing into whatever (large) serving dish you plan to use.

7   Add the beans, tomatoes, and potatoes to the dish. (It's fine if either is still warm.) Carefully toss them together until well mixed. Check the seasoning once more. Serve warm or at room temperature.

## TMI

### Salting Bean Water

There have always been arguments about whether to put salt in the water when you cook dried beans. *Maybe it will toughen them!* seems to be the main issue. Also, you may have noticed that people will argue about anything. Anyway, you should always salt the water in which you soak and cook beans. Here's why:

- Salting the water is the only way to flavor the whole bean. The difference between a bean cooked in salted water and a bean cooked in plain water is instantly noticeable. Adding salt after cooking will mainly flavor whatever sauce you added to the beans, not the beans themselves.

- Beans that have soaked in salted water will have a better texture after cooking.
- It really won't toughen them, I swear. In fact, the salt helps to break apart the calcium and magnesium ions in the outer skin, and it's these ions that make the skins tough.

# Tomato-Watermelon Salad *with "Feta," Almonds, and Mint*

One minute, the notion of combining tomatoes and watermelon was inconceivable. The next minute, there they were, cuddled up together in one of the world's best summer salads.

**Part of this recipe's genius is the visual joke of using two ingredients that look so similar.** You can use a melon baller on the watermelon; conversely, you can substitute full-size tomatoes cut into cubes and cube the watermelon. And what about *yellow* tomatoes and *yellow* watermelon? That would be almost *too* great, but it reminds me that peaches and tomatoes also make a great salad. Good old wonderful summer produce . . .

**8 cups 1-inch chunks or balls seedless watermelon**

**3 pounds cherry tomatoes, halved**

**½ teaspoon salt, plus more to taste**

**¼ cup extra-virgin olive oil**

**1½ tablespoons red wine vinegar**

**1 cup crumbled Tofu "Feta" (page 187)**

**½ cup sliced almonds, toasted**

**2 tablespoons packed shredded fresh mint leaves**

**Freshly ground pepper to taste (optional)**

1 Combine the melon and tomatoes in a large bowl. Stir in the salt and toss to mix. Let rest for 15 minutes.

2 Add the oil and vinegar to the salad and toss to mix. Gently mix in the tofu feta, toasted almonds, and mint. Taste for seasoning, adding salt and pepper if you want.

I never do. There's enough going on here already.

3 The salad can be made a couple of hours ahead of time and kept at room temperature. It fades fast, so leftovers won't be something you want your friends to see — but they'll still taste good the next day.

# Smashed Lemon Potatoes ------▷ *Serves 4.*

**These are a dressed-up, much sprightlier version of regular mashed potatoes.** If you like, though, leave the potatoes chunky and serve this as a potato salad that's also much sprightlier than the usual. ●

### VINAIGRETTE

2 tablespoons fresh lemon juice, or more to taste

1½ teaspoons Dijon mustard

⅛ teaspoon granulated sugar

Pinch of dried oregano

¼ cup extra-virgin olive oil or vegetable oil

Salt and freshly ground pepper to taste

### POTATOES

2 pounds small red or Yukon Gold potatoes

Salt

½ cup homemade vegan yogurt (page 185)

1 tablespoon finely grated lemon zest, plus more to taste

2 tablespoons minced fresh parsley

2 tablespoons minced fresh chives

Freshly ground pepper to taste

1 **Vinaigrette:** In a medium bowl, whisk the lemon juice, mustard, sugar, and oregano together. Add the oil in a slow stream, whisking constantly until the mixture has emulsified. Add salt and pepper to taste.

2 **Potatoes:** Dice the potatoes and put them in a medium saucepan with enough water to cover them by a couple of inches. Add 1½ teaspoons salt. Bring the water to a boil over medium-high heat. Turn the heat to medium-low and simmer the potatoes, covered, until tender, 15 to 20 minutes.

3 Drain the potatoes well. Return them to the hot saucepan and dry them out over very low heat, stirring frequently. This won't take more than a couple of minutes.

4 Take the pan off the heat. Add the yogurt, lemon zest, parsley, chives, and pepper to taste. With a potato masher or the bottom of a sturdy glass, smash the potatoes until they're the consistency you want. Rewhisk the vinaigrette and toss the potatoes with it.

5 Serve the potatoes hot, at room temperature, or chilled.

# Roasted Grape—Rosemary Flatbread

*Makes 1 large flatbread.*

Here's an ancient Roman-seeming bread that's good with any meal. **It's also wonderful as an appetizer.** We (well, I) like it spread with Kite Hill ricotta.

The dough must be started at least 24 hours before you bake it. The grapes can be roasted up to 2 days ahead and stored airtight in the refrigerator.

**1½ cups lukewarm water (12 ounces or 355 grams)**

**1 teaspoon active dry yeast**

**3 tablespoons granulated sugar (1.3 ounces or 38 grams)**

**3½ to 4 cups all-purpose flour (15.4 to 17.7 ounces or 438 to 500 grams)**

**¼ cup extra-virgin olive oil (2 ounces or 55 grams)**

**2 teaspoons salt**

**2 tablespoons snipped fresh rosemary (0.23 ounce or 6 grams)**

**1 teaspoon olive oil, plus more for brushing**

**1½ pounds seedless, stemmed red or black grapes — the smallest you can find (680 grams)**

**Maldon or other flaky salt for sprinkling**

1   Depending on your lifestyle, the bread can be prepared with a stand mixer, in a food processor, or in a bread machine. Dump the lukewarm water into the appropriate container. Sprinkle the yeast evenly over the surface and stir in the sugar. Add the flour, extra-virgin olive oil, salt, and rosemary and mix until all the flour is incorporated. Do not knead the dough!

2   Grease a large bowl and transfer the dough to it. Brush the top with a little olive oil. Cover and refrigerate for 24 to 72 hours.

3   Take the dough out of the fridge and let it stand, covered, until it reaches room temperature and doubles in bulk. This may take 3 to 4 hours if your kitchen is chilly, so plan accordingly.

4   Preheat the oven to 350°F.

5   Spread the 1 teaspoon olive oil over a large rimmed baking sheet. Plop the grapes all over the baking sheet and flip them around until they're coated with oil. Roast the grapes for about an hour, turning them

every 20 minutes or so. When they're done, they'll be wrinkled, browned in spots, and collapsed-looking — somewhere between grapes and raisins. Let cool.

6   Preheat the oven to 500°F, with one rack in the middle and the other in the lower third. Spread a tablespoon or so of oil across the bottom of a 17-by-12-inch rimmed baking sheet.

7   Punch down the soft, annoying dough and cut it into two equal pieces. On a well-floured surface, with a well-floured rolling pin, roll the first piece into a rectangle that's as thin as you can make it — ideally, ¼ inch thin and almost as big as the baking sheet. Gingerly transfer the rolled-out dough to the baking sheet: This is easiest to do with both your hands spread out under the dough. Don't worry if the dough tears en route — just patch it together as best you can once it's on the baking sheet. Sprinkle half the grapes evenly over the dough.

8   Reflour the rolling surface and rolling pin. Roll out the second rectangle of dough, trying to make it the same size, shape, and thickness as the first one. Carefully place the second piece of dough over the graped piece. Use your fingers to press the two rectangles together, pushing out as much air as possible. Then dip your fingers into cold water (or oil

them) and punch little dents all over the dough. Then stretch the dough an inch at a time so that it fills the pan. It doesn't matter if you tear small holes in it; in fact, you should do that here and there. As you can imagine, this is a random process; what you want is to make little craters and holes all over the dough so you can see the pan here and there. When you're done, you should have a rough rectangle about 12 by 16 inches.

9   Brush the dough with more olive oil. Arrange the rest of the grapes evenly on it, pushing them in. Sprinkle the dough with a little flaky salt and let stand for 15 minutes.

10   Bake the bread on the middle oven rack for 5 minutes. Turn the oven temperature down to 400°F and transfer the baking sheet to the lower rack. Bake for another 20 minutes or so, until the bread is golden brown. Use a wide spatula to lift it so you can make sure the bottom is browned enough.

11   Slither the spatula under the bread to loosen it, and cool it on a wire rack. Serve warm or at room temperature, cut into strips. (I use kitchen shears for this.)

# Chipotle Bread

------▷ *Makes 1 large or 2 smaller loaves.*

**A good crusty bread is the only food that "chews" almost like meat and tastes great without needing a lot of things done to it.** A couple of slices, grilled and brushed with olive oil, can stand in for a main course as long as the bread is interesting enough; one way to make it interesting enough is to use some of the seasonings we usually associate with meat.

As with most breads, this one will taste better if you let the dough chill overnight, or for up to 24 hours. Because I hate kneading almost as much as I hate having flour spill across the counter, I always mix the dough in a bread machine and then bake it in a conventional oven. You can make this bread by hand or use a food processor, a stand mixer with a dough hook, or a bread machine. I'm going to give you "by hand" directions.

1 canned chipotle pepper in adobo, chopped

1½ teaspoons salt

2½ to 3 cups bread flour (10.6 to 12.8 ounces or 317 to 381 grams)

½ teaspoon instant yeast

1 teaspoon freshly ground pepper

½ teaspoon dried oregano

1 to 1½ cups water (8 to 12 ounces or 237 to 355 grams)

Flour or cornmeal, for dusting the baking sheet

1   Lavishly flour a work surface. Grease a medium bowl.

2   Stir the chipotle and salt together in a little bowl or cup.

3   Put 2½ cups of the flour, the yeast, pepper, and oregano in a large bowl. Stir these ingredients for a few seconds, then add 1 cup of the water. Mush everything around with your hands until somewhat combined. Dump in the chopped chipotle and salt. (I had you put them into a cup so that you wouldn't have to stop and wash your hands at this point.) Mush in these ingredients with your hands until you have a shaggy dough.

Transfer the dough to the floured surface. Cover it with a damp towel and let it rest for 20 minutes.

4   Flour your hands and knead the dough for about 10 minutes, until it feels smooth and elastic. If you need to, add up to ½ cup more flour or water to the dough.

5   Put the dough in the greased bowl and cover the bowl with plastic wrap. At this point, I transfer the bowl to the refrigerator and chill it overnight. If you decide to do the same, check on the bread a couple of times at the beginning to see if it's started to rise. If so, keep gently punching it down. When it's cold enough, the dough will stop rising. Then, to use the dough the next day, take it out of the refrigerator and let it sit at room temperature for 2 to 4 hours, until it's doubled in bulk.

6   If you don't want to do the overnight step, let the covered dough rise in a warm place for 2 to 4 hours, until it's doubled in bulk. (The small amount of yeast in this recipe makes it rise more slowly than some doughs.) Then gently punch it down, form it into a ball, cover the bowl, and let the bread rise for another 1 to 2 hours, or until it has doubled once again.

7   Line a baking sheet with parchment paper. Sprinkle some flour or cornmeal evenly over the parchment. With floured hands, roll the dough into one or two long baguette-type loaves. (Now that there are only two people living in this house, boo-hoo, I always make two loaves and freeze one. For simplicity's sake, I will refer to one loaf here.) Put the loaf on the prepared baking sheet. With a sharp knife or a baker's *lame*, cut four or five diagonal slashes across the top. Brush the loaf with cold water. Let it rise in a warm place for another hour or so, until it's almost doubled in size.

8   Preheat the oven to 400°F with a rack in the bottom third.

9   Bake the loaf for 20 minutes (15, if making 2 smaller loaves). Then move the pan to a middle rack and bake for 20 to 25 more minutes. (The 2 smaller loaves may be done after 15 more minutes or so.) You can do the thing about rapping the bottom of the loaf and seeing if it "sounds hollow," but a bread or instant-read thermometer is more reliable and will read 185°F when the bread is done.

10   Cool the bread on a rack for at least 2 hours before cutting it.

# Peanut Satay Bread

*Makes 1 loaf.*

**It would be insulting Thai cuisine to call this "Thai Peanut Bread,"** but some of its ingredients come from recipes for Thai peanut sauce. It works well as a main-course bread and makes delicious sandwiches.

This recipe calls for making the dough by hand, but if you own a bread machine, stand mixer, or a food processor, feel free to use it. ●

1 tablespoon vegetable oil

4 scallions, thinly sliced, with some green

⅔ cup lukewarm water

2½ teaspoons active dry yeast

⅓ cup coconut milk (not low-fat; 80 grams)

2 tablespoons brown sugar (0.9 ounce or 25 grams)

1 to 1¼ cups bread flour (6¾ to 8 ounces or 191 to 239 grams)

½ cup whole wheat flour (2¼ ounces or 64 grams)

2 tablespoons soy sauce (1.1 ounces or 32 grams)

1 tablespoon fresh lime or lemon juice

½ teaspoon Thai red curry paste (or, in a pinch, ¼ teaspoon cayenne)

½ teaspoon ground ginger

¼ teaspoon salt

½ cup extra-chunky peanut butter (4.6 ounces or 129 grams)

1  Heat the oil in a small skillet over medium heat. When it's hot, scatter in the scallions and cook, stirring, for 2 minutes, then take the skillet off the heat.

2  In a small bowl, stir the yeast into the water. Let stand for 10 minutes or until it bubbles, then stir in the coconut milk and brown sugar.

3  Meanwhile, put 1 cup of the bread flour and the whole wheat flour in a large bowl. Stir them together, then make a well in the center. Add the soy sauce, lime or lemon juice, curry paste, and ginger to the yeast mixture. Pour the liquid ingredients into the flour and mush them in with your hands until you've achieved a big, gloppy mess.

4  Transfer this mess to a floured work surface. Sprinkle the salt over the mixture. Then "sprinkle" — i.e., drop blobs of — the peanut butter over the mixture and start kneading. After everything is incorporated and the dough looks cohesive, cover it with a damp towel and walk away for 20 minutes. (As a three-year-old I know once told his hovering mom, "Why don't you go make some lunch or something?")

5  Knead the dough for about 10 minutes, until it becomes smooth and elastic. If you need to, add up to ¼ cup more flour or a little water to the dough; if you *really* need to, add more flour to the kneading surface.

6  Put the dough in a clean bowl and cover the bowl with plastic wrap. (The peanut butter will "oil" the inside surface of the bowl,

so there's no need to grease it.) At this point, I transfer the bowl to the refrigerator and chill the dough overnight: This resting period improves the taste and texture of almost any bread. If you decide to do the same, check on the bread a couple of times at the beginning to see if it's started to rise. If so, gently punch it down. When it's cold enough, the dough will stop rising. Then, to use the dough the next day, take it out of the refrigerator and let it sit at room temperature for 2 to 4 hours, until it's doubled in bulk.

7  If you don't want to do the overnight step, let the covered dough rise in a warm place for about an hour, until it's doubled in bulk. Punch it down — always fun — and form it into a ball. Cover the bowl and let the bread rise for another 30 to 40 minutes, or until it has doubled once again.

LIME JUICE

CURRY PASTE

SOY SAUCE

8 This bread looks way more authentic and interesting if you bake it free-form rather than jailing it in a bread pan. Line a baking sheet with parchment paper. Sprinkle some flour evenly over the parchment. With floured hands, shape the dough into an oval or disk and put the nascent loaf on the baking sheet. Cover the loaf with plastic wrap and let it double again, which will probably take about 30 minutes this time. You'll know it's risen enough when you poke it with your finger and the indentation stays there instead of bouncing back.

9 Preheat the oven to 400°F, with one rack in the lower third and the other in the middle.

10 With a sharp knife, make a few slashes across the top of the dough. Bake the bread on the lower oven rack for 20 minutes. Then move it to the middle rack and bake for 20 to 25 more minutes, or until well browned; if you knock on it, it should sound hollow. (What an annoying, arbitrary way to test something!) If you have an instant-read thermometer, it will read 185°F when the bread is done.

11 Cool the bread for at least 2 hours before slicing.

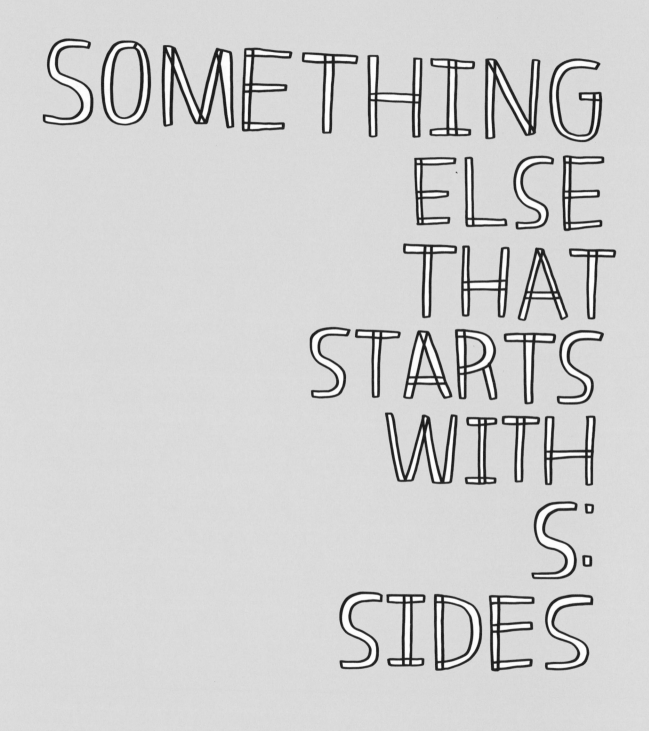

— — — — — —

"... The best part of the meal."

Everyone says that about Thanksgiving side dishes, but for vegans it should be true about *all* sides. When there isn't a big hunk of animal protein soaking up everyone's attention, "accompaniments" have to be more than a scoop of Minute Rice and some carrot sticks. Ideally, a vegan dinner would be like Thanksgiving but without the turkey: ten or twelve great sides arranged on your plate like a William Morris tapestry.

Vegan and vegetarian food writers are always urging us to cast away the notion that a dinner plate has to have the Basic Three — a protein, a starch, and a vegetable. Okay, done! Consider it cast away! But on ordinary occasions, most of us still don't have the time or inclination to make more than three things for dinner — not unless one of them is, like, steamed broccoli or something else we don't need a recipe for.

On the other hand, it can be freeing to make a meal that doesn't center around that big hunk of animal protein. When you know that you're already getting enough protein (and if you're getting enough calories to keep you going, you're getting enough protein), you don't have to think of side dishes as something that "goes along" with the main event. They can be the main event their own little selves!

And really, two sides and a salad make a *very nice dinner*.

— — — — —

# Artichoke Hearts Amandine

*Serves 4.*

**Anything you can do with a scallop, you can do with an artichoke heart** — or "arti heart," as I always write it on my shopping list. I don't often buy frozen vegetables, but artichoke hearts are different. Unlike, say, spinach, they hold up nicely when frozen. And my lord, think of how many whole artichokes you'd have to trim and cook to get as many hearts as you want here!

You panfry the artichoke hearts, then make a lemon-almond sauce in the same skillet. MAXIMUM results — better than scallops, whose texture I never loved back in the day because it raised too many questions. ("Is this fully cooked? Is it really scallop?") Here everything is straightforwardly perfect. ●

2 cups all-purpose flour (more than you'll need, but it makes things easier)

1 teaspoon salt

1 teaspoon freshly ground pepper

1 teaspoon paprika

1 "shake" of cayenne

Two 10- or 11-ounce packages frozen artichoke hearts, thawed, well drained, and patted dry with paper towels

¼ cup vegetable oil

¼ cup olive oil

1 large shallot, finely chopped

½ cup sliced almonds

¼ cup fresh lemon juice

Chopped fresh parsley for sprinkling (optional)

1 Line a rimmed baking sheet with parchment paper. Put the flour and spices in a large bowl and whisk to combine. Carefully place the artichoke hearts in the flour mixture and gently roll them around until they're well coated — doing this a few hearts at a time may make it easier. Set the floured hearts on the baking sheet.

2 Heat a large skillet — or two large skillets, if you want to work faster, in which case you'll want to divide the oils between the two. Add the oils and heat over medium-high heat. When it shimmers, use tongs to set the artichoke hearts into the skillet(s) and cook, carefully turning the hearts to brown them on all sides, 8 to 10 minutes.

3 Transfer the artichoke hearts to a plate. If you used two skillets, pour any remaining oil from one into the other. Scatter in the shallot and stir-fry for a few seconds, still using medium-high heat. Scatter in the almonds and cook, stirring constantly, until golden brown. Whisk in the lemon juice, jumping nimbly out of the way as it sizzles and steam rises, then whisk hard for a few seconds to combine everything. Pour the sauce over the artichoke hearts and serve immediately.

4 I would suggest topping these with chopped parsley, but does anyone still do that?

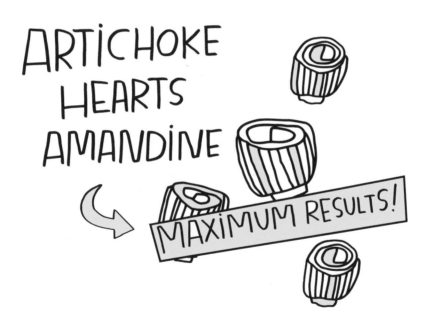

ARTICHOKE HEARTS AMANDINE

MAXIMUM RESULTS!

# Three-Hour Green Beans

*Serves 6 to 8.*

Bygone generations would be shocked that we cook our green beans for such a short time. An hour, minimum, used to be standard. Of course, their green beans may have been more "horsey" than ours, but they were certainly right that long simmering makes green beans taste totally different from steaming them for 10 minutes. **If this were a women's magazine, I would add, "And *deliciously* different!"**

There's even a science reason for this. Corby Kummer, the great food writer and author of *Slow Cooking* (and Close Personal Friend of Mine), did a lot of research after tasting the marvelousness of long-cooked green beans. What he learned matters enough that I'm going to squander two of my treasured bullet points to summarize it:

- The flavor compounds in green beans don't emerge until the beans have been cooked for hours.
- Green beans are packed with something called lignin — a woody, indigestible substance that doesn't break down. If you eat green beans too early, you'll taste plenty of green but not much bean.

As another Corby fan, the food writer Ed Bruske, said, "Sorry, the compounds that govern flavor and color in green beans are completely different. You have to choose between one and the other, and I choose flavor." I'm not quite that binary about it. But at least I feel a pang when I *don't* cook green beans for a long time.

Let me show you why. This is a recipe of Corby's that was adapted by Ed and first published in the *Washington Post*. I've toyed with it a little.

3 tablespoons extra-virgin olive oil

1 medium onion, cut into thin strips

1 pound green beans, trimmed

2 shallots, minced

One 14.5-ounce can diced tomatoes, with their juice

1 teaspoon freshly ground fennel seeds (see Notes)

½ teaspoon salt, or to taste

Freshly ground pepper to taste

1 to 2 tablespoons bacon-, ham-, or pepperoni-flavored TVP granules, reconstituted (optional; see Notes)

1  Heat the oil in a heavy pot or Dutch oven with a tight-fitting lid. Add the onion and cook over medium heat until tender, about 8 minutes. Add the remaining ingredients, toss together, and bring to a simmer. Cover the pot, reduce the heat to very low, and simmer for about 3 hours, stirring and tasting the beans occasionally.

2  When the beans are tender and flavorful, adjust the seasoning and serve.

## NOTES

Having raised the issue of slow-cooking suddenly made me realize: What about using a slow-cooker? I tried it and found that it does work, but you end up with a lot of unreduced liquid. But THAT made me wonder if you could cook the beans in the oven if you set it at 200°F and left them in there for 8 hours. I don't have 8 hours to spare at the moment, but I don't see why it wouldn't work.

**Crushing the fennel seeds:** You can't just leave them whole; the texture will be too distracting even after long cooking. If you don't have a spice grinder or a mortar and pestle, you can put the seeds on a cutting surface and pulverize them with the bottom edge of a heavy pan or with a heavy rolling pin. To keep the seeds from scattering, it's helpful to put them in a sandwich-size zipper-lock bag.

**The question of the TVP:** This is a dish that was made for TVP. As always, you want to use it as a flavoring, not a full-blown ingredient. And, as always, you want to use granules, not a larger size. If you're not opposed to TVP (I like it!), reconstitute the granules the way the package tells you to and add them along with everything else.

# Yes, <u>That</u> Green Bean Casserole

*Serves 4.*

When I was seven, our street had a block party. I remember nothing about it except for being allowed to walk in the middle of the street — that, and the green bean casserole with canned French's Fried Onions on top, which I remember *extremely* well. I was bowled over by love for it.

**But the time makes itself to go along, as the French say. (The France French, not the onions kind.)** One day you start to feel ashamed of using cream of mushroom soup. Soon afterward, you decide you don't even *like* cream of mushroom soup anymore. It's so processed-tasting, with its little mushroom cubes! Besides, it's not vegan. With a sigh, you take the recipe card out of your Thanksgiving file.

And although you still secretly love those canned fried onions, you figure you'll never taste them again. BUT YOU WILL! They make much fancier brands of the same thing now — fancier, but they still taste the same. Trader Joe's, among other places, sells them. And you can sprinkle them over a vegan green bean casserole that's miles better than the kind I first ate on Cobb Terrace in Rochester, New York. ●

Salt

1 pound green beans, trimmed

2 tablespoons vegetable oil

2 shallots, minced

1 garlic clove, minced

4 ounces white or cremini mushrooms, trimmed and sliced

2 cups Béchamel/Velouté Sauce (page 181)

1½ cups canned crisp fried onions

1  Preheat the oven to 400°F.

2  Bring a large pot of water to a boil. When it boils, add salt in about a 1-tablespoon-to-1-gallon ratio. Toss in the green beans and cook for 10 minutes; they shouldn't be aggressively crisp for this dish. Drain the beans, rinse them under cold running water, re-drain, and set aside.

3  In a large ovenproof skillet, heat the oil over medium-high heat until it shimmers. Scatter in the shallots and garlic and cook, stirring, for 3 to 4 minutes. Add the mushroom slices and a shake or two of salt. Cook, stirring frequently, until the mushrooms give up their liquid.

4  Whisk the sauce into the mushrooms, then stir in ½ cup of the fried onions, along with the beans. Mix well. Top the bean mixture with the remaining 1 cup fried onions.

5  Bake for 20 minutes, or until brown and bubbling. FOR GOD'S SAKE, use a pot holder to take it out of the oven — don't grab the handle. It's so easy to forget this with a skillet!

## ALTHOUGH YOU STILL SECRETLY LOVE THOSE CANNED FRIED ONIONS, YOU FIGURE YOU'LL NEVER TASTE THEM AGAIN.

# "Barbecued" Cabbage

*Serves 6.*

**One time I always feel Sorry For Self is when David brings home barbecue** from a great place called Big W's Roadside Bar-B-Que. It's near the Wingdale, New York, train station. Big W has *such!* great barbecue that it's hard to remind myself that even the best burnt ends in the universe still come from cows.

Lucky for me that Big W also sells barbecued cabbage that's 100 percent as good as any of their meats. I was astonished the first time I tried it — not only at how good it was, but at the mere fact of its existence. Who knew?

Lots of people, it turns out. Barbecued cabbage is fairly common worldwide; it's just not called *barbecued* cabbage in most places, mainly because it's stir-fried. Which is also lucky for me, because I've always sat back and let the men in the family be in charge of barbecuing. My *dainty* little self just wouldn't know what to do with a charcoal grill! Anyway, there are too many mosquitoes out there. ●

½ cup peanut or olive oil

2 large onions, halved lengthwise and sliced

1 head green cabbage, cored and coarsely chopped

½ teaspoon salt, plus more to taste

2 tablespoons soy sauce

1 tablespoon balsamic vinegar

1 tablespoon light brown sugar

½ teaspoon freshly ground pepper, plus more to taste

¼ teaspoon liquid smoke

Accent to taste (optional, but please use it!)

1  Heat the oil in a large saucepan or skillet over medium-high heat. When it's shimmering, add the onions, turn the heat to medium-low, and cook for 20 minutes, stirring frequently. The onions should be gently browned — about the color of honey — in many places.

2  Add the cabbage and salt, then turn the heat to medium. Stirring frequently, cook the cabbage-onion mixture for 10 minutes. Add the soy sauce, vinegar, brown sugar, pepper, liquid smoke, and Accent to taste, if using. Turn the heat to low and cook the mixture for 20 to 30 more minutes, stirring from time to time. The cabbage should be limp and almost lacquered-looking by the time you're done.

3  Check the seasoning before serving.

# Corn Fritters

*Makes about 2 dozen fritters.*

I don't know that I've ever eaten even a spoonful of canned creamed corn straight up, but I know I love it. It's vegan, but it tastes so 1950s! Coziness is its theme, not freshness — cozy memories of a time I never saw even though I was *born* in the 1950s. What I mostly remember from those pastoral days is knocking over Dwight Jacobs's snowman and having to apologize to his mother. She wasn't very gracious, as I recall. Maybe she should have apologized to *me*.

**Because vegans don't get to eat the centerpiece of Thanksgiving dinner, they should be allowed to have something deep-fried.** Ideally, you'd bring these fritters to an omni Thanksgiving and there would only be enough for the vegans.

Since we're using these as a side dish, please don't drench them in maple syrup. Instead, serve them with the fritter sauce, which actually has a little maple syrup (or honey) in it.

**SAUCE**

1 cup vinegar (any kind is fine)

½ cup pure maple syrup or honey

½ to 1 teaspoon red pepper flakes

1 teaspoon salt, plus more to taste

2 scallions, thinly sliced

About 4 cups corn or peanut oil (not olive oil)

**FRITTERS**

2 cups all-purpose flour

1 tablespoon granulated sugar

2 teaspoons baking powder

¾ teaspoon salt

¾ teaspoon freshly ground pepper

2 cups canned creamed corn

2 Flax Gel Cubes (page 203), thawed, or 6 tablespoons aquafaba (see page 14)

½ cup nondairy milk, preferably soy

**OPTIONAL INGREDIENTS (IF YOU WANT THE FRITTERS TO TASTE "EXOTIC")**

1 teaspoon ground cumin

2 scallions, thinly sliced

½ cup chopped fresh cilantro

1 Unless you plan to serve these fritters straight into people's hands, preheat the oven to 200°F. Have two baking sheets ready: one for draining the fritters and one for keeping them warm in the oven. Cover the "draining" sheet with a ¼-inch thickness of newspaper, then cover the newspaper with a paper towel or two. If you don't have newspaper handy, it's fine to use all paper towels. I'm just trying to Save The Earth.

2 **Sauce:** Put all the sauce ingredients except the scallions in a small saucepan. Bring the mixture to a slow boil over medium heat, stirring frequently. Boil for 10 minutes or so, until the sauce has thickened slightly. Take the pan off the stove, stir in the scallions, and serve the sauce warm or at room temperature.

3 **Fritters:** Heat the oil to 350°F in a large pot, remembering that this usually takes longer than you expect. If you don't have a deep-fry thermometer (tsk, tsk!), you can tell if the oil is ready by pressing a bamboo chopstick or skewer against the bottom of the pot. When a swirl of tiny bubbles immediately streams from the juncture of pot and implement, the oil is hot enough.

4 **Meanwhile, make the batter:** Sift the dry ingredients into a large bowl. Mix in the cumin if you're using it.

# CORN FRITTERS

5 In another bowl, vigorously beat together the corn, flax cubes or aquafaba, and milk. Add the corn mixture to the flour mixture. Mix thoroughly. If you're using the scallions and/or cilantro, add them now.

6 When the oil is hot enough, *carefully* use two serving spoons or an ice cream scoop to drop 2-tablespoon–sized blobs of batter into the oil. No matter how careful you are, there will still be some spatters, so be even *more* careful. Cook the fritters until they're medium brown — about the color of a pancake. If they don't flip their little selves, turn them with tongs to make sure both sides will be equally brown. Then use those tongs to transfer the cooked fritters to the paper-lined baking sheet. When they've drained, put them on the second baking sheet and then into the oven. (No harm in having someone help with this trotting back and forth, by the way.) Cook the remaining fritters. Serve hot.

# Seared Endive
## with Pistachio Gremolata  — — — — — ▷  *Serves 4 to 6.*

**Cooking does great things for endive.** Somehow, braising and then searing alchemizes the leaves into meat, burnishing the flavor and refining the texture to something simultaneously silky and firm.

And gremolata! Traditionally, this sparkling sprinkle-on is made from lemon zest, herbs, garlic, and, in this recipe, browned bread crumbs. Delicious, but definitely a "topper" — but if you substitute pistachios for the bread crumbs, you'll get a layer of flavor and texture that elevates your *ahnd-eev* to full entrée status. ●

1 garlic clove, peeled

¼ cup shelled salted pistachios

2 tablespoons minced fresh parsley

2 teaspoons finely grated lemon zest

¼ teaspoon salt, plus more to taste

4 large, compact, heavy heads Belgian endive

2 tablespoons vegetable oil (don't bother with expensive olive oil here)

Freshly ground pepper to taste

1 tablespoon walnut oil

1 tablespoon fresh lemon juice

1  Drop the garlic clove into a microwaveable cup filled with water and put the cup into the microwave. Once it boils, cook on 100% power for 2 minutes. (This can also be done in a small saucepan on the stovetop, of course.) Drain the garlic and let it cool.

2  Turn on a food processor or blender and drop in the garlic clove. Buzz it around for a few seconds, then turn off the machine. Add the pistachios, parsley, lemon zest, and salt.

Pulse the mixture a few times until you've got bread crumb–sized pieces. Don't let it turn into a paste — it needs to be sprinkleable.

3  Trim the bottoms off the endives, then slice each head in half the long way. Heat a skillet that's large enough to hold all the endive halves in a single layer. Add the vegetable oil and heat over medium-high heat until shimmering. Set each endive half in the skillet cut side down. Lavishly sprinkle the

halves with salt and pepper, then cover the skillet. (If the skillet doesn't have a dedicated cover, you can use a baking sheet or foil.) Cook the endive over medium-high heat for 6 to 8 minutes, until the cut sides are well browned.

4 Flip over each half head of endive and carefully transfer to a serving dish. Sprinkle evenly with the gremolata.

5 In a little bowl, whisk together the walnut oil and lemon juice, then drizzle this evenly over the gremolata'd endive. Serve warm or at room temperature.

*TMI*

### Bread Crumbs Treated Right

Seasoned or not, depending on the "fare." (Bad word, fare. So is "provender.") And they don't have to be made from scratch if you use panko, the super-crisp bread crumbs originally from Japan. Panko is made from crustless bread. According to Wikipedia — the deepest I feel like going into this — "Panko is made from bread baked by passing an electric current through the dough, yielding bread without crusts." I'd like to know more about what the hell that means, but not right now.

Anyway, panko! Good as it is right out of the box, that's not enough. For a Parmesan-quality topping, you need to sauté the crumbs in oil with some seasonings. A flavorful olive oil, a little minced garlic, and some flaked salt make a great start. Or red pepper flakes, crumbled nori, snipped fresh herbs . . . Ground almond meal! Ground hazelnut meal! A few mashed capers! Chopped salted peanuts! A minced onion sautéed until brown in the oil before the panko is added! The possibilities aren't endless, but almost.

But let's not forget good old regular bread. Toast a couple of slices, pulverize them in a food processor or blender, and treat them to the same olive oil/seasonings romp. I save homemade bread for this, or the heels of good purchased bread — olive-rosemary, for instance. Pumpernickel makes a nice change; you could even add a few more caraway seeds to the skillet.

Although fried bread crumbs are technically less important than what they're garnishing, I recommend preparing them before you start the rest of the dish. The closer you get to mealtime, the less you'll feel like pulling out a skillet just for a garnish. If you're up for it, you can make a big batch of fried crumbs and freeze the rest. Later the crumbs can be recrisped on a sheet of foil in a 350°F oven. Though they won't have quite their original fervor, they'll be way better than nothing.

# "Oh My Lord" Potatoes

*Serves 4, but this recipe is infinitely expansible.*

It would be nice if only vegans were allowed to make this recipe. That way, people would envy us instead of heaping calumny upon us.

This is an adaptation of Susie Middleton's recipe, which my sister-in-law Mimi and I discovered in *Fine Cooking* in the same month. Both of us immediately started making the potatoes all the time. When I first served them to my mother-in-law, she said, "Oh, these are the ones Mimi makes!"

**I oomphed up the recipe a little bit.** It was already so easy that a tiny bit more prep was almost welcome — the way adding something extra to a cake mix makes it seem more homemade.

If you're using new potatoes that come prebagged, get them as small as possible. If you're choosing them individually, choose ones that are not only as small but also as round as possible. The rounder they are, the easier to smush.

2 quarts vegetable stock, homemade (page 177) or store-bought

1 garlic head, cloves separated and peeled

20 small round new potatoes

Salt and freshly ground pepper to taste

½ to ¾ cup extra-virgin olive oil

8 scallions, finely chopped (include a lot of the green part)

1 Bring the stock and garlic cloves to a boil in a large pot. Add the potatoes and simmer until they're thoroughly tender, at least 40 minutes. The long cooking time is crucial. They shouldn't be falling apart, but they should definitely be easy to pierce with a skewer and should "give" when pressed.

2 Spread out a double layer of clean dish towels on the kitchen counter. (Why do I feel compelled to say "clean"?) Use tongs to take the potatoes out of the pot and set on the towels. Let the potatoes cool for 3 to 5 minutes.

3   Now take another dish towel — yes, a clean one — and fold it into quarters. Using it as a sort of mitt/potholder, gently press on each potato, flattening it into a disk slightly less than ½ inch thick. Press about as hard as you would when pressing dirt over seeds (as if I know what I'm talking about). This is a fun task that you won't want to share.

4   Line a rimmed baking sheet with parchment paper. With a wide spatula, gingerly move the potatoes, and any broken bits, onto the parchment. Let them cool completely, to firm them up. (If you're doing this a few hours — or up to a day — ahead, cover and refrigerate them.)

5   Preheat the oven to 450°F, with a rack in the middle.

6   Salt and pepper the potatoes liberally. Then pour the oil over them, making sure to hit the top of each potato. Add more oil as needed. With that good old wide spatula, turn each potato gently so that both sides are coated and some of the oil travels underneath.

7   Roast the potatoes for 10 minutes. Sprinkle them with half the scallions, return to the oven, and roast for 10 minutes more. Take them out of the oven and carefully turn them over. Salt and pepper the turned-over disks again. Return to the oven and roast for 10 minutes. Sprinkle the remaining scallions over the potatoes and roast for 10 *more* minutes, for a total cooking time of 40 minutes. The potatoes should be brown and crispy-looking, especially around the edges. Serve as soon as they're done.

IT WOULD BE NICE IF ONLY VEGANS WERE ALLOWED TO MAKE THIS RECIPE.

# "Oh My God" Potatoes

*Serves 8.*

**I can't make good French fries, but hey! — that means one less vat of hot oil to contend with.** In any case, there are shockingly good oven-fried potato recipes. This one is like the reverse of the "Oh My Lord" Potatoes on page 114. Those you cook in broth and then bake; these you bake and then add some broth and bake some more. (I did say it was "like" the reverse, not the *exact* reverse.)

These wedges are beautifully browned on the outside and creamy, almost melted, on the inside, and they're easier than French fries. ●

6 tablespoons olive oil

3 pounds (about 6) russet potatoes, peeled

1 teaspoon coarse salt

1 teaspoon freshly ground pepper, or more to taste

2 cups vegetable stock, homemade (page 177) or store-bought

1  Preheat the oven to 500°F, with a rack in the upper third. Pour the olive oil onto a rimmed baking sheet around 12 by 17 inches.

2  Cut the potatoes in half the long way, then cut them crosswise in half. Now you have four quarters, each of which should be cut into three wedges. Put the cut potato wedges onto the baking sheet and scumble them around to coat them evenly with the oil. Season with the salt and pepper.

3  Roast the tates for 15 minutes, then take them out and turn them with a wide spatula or pancake turner, making sure they're all turned onto an unbrowned side. Back to the oven they go, to be roasted for another

10 minutes. Then turn them again and bake for another 10 minutes. THEN take them out of the oven.

4  Pour the vegetable stock over the potatoes, return them to the oven, and bake them for 15 more minutes. The total cooking time is 50 minutes. But you can also prepare the potatoes up to this point, stash them at room temperature for up to 6 hours, and roast them for another 5 to 15 minutes, depending on how warm they were to start with.

5  When the potatoes are done, get them off the baking sheet immediately so they don't stick. Check the seasoning and serve.

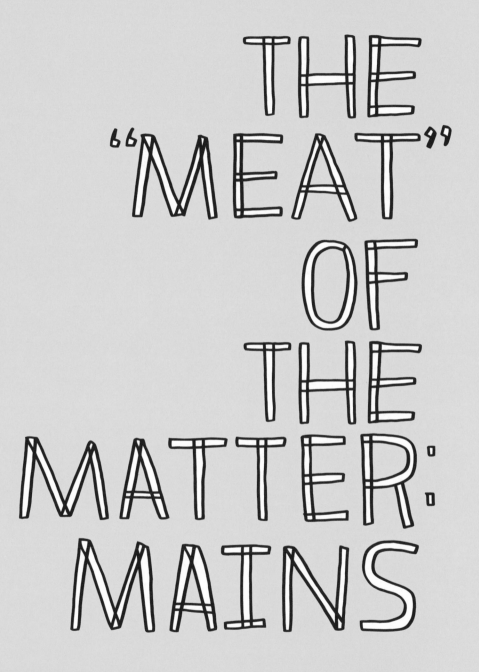
THE "MEAT" OF THE MATTER: MAINS

–  –  –  –  –  –

"I could be a vegetarian, but not a vegan. I wouldn't be able to manage without cheese."

That's the commonest thing I hear about vegan cooking: that maybe it's possible to produce a main dish without meat, but without cheese —? Can't be done.

But think of the cuisines that don't rely on dairy at all. You don't eat Thai food and miss the cheese. Same with Chinese food. In fact, the many-splendored world of Asian food immediately "puts paid" (whatever the derivation of that phrase is) to the notion that cheese is essential in a dish that contains no meat.

Okay, but you don't *want* Asian food every night. You don't require daily steak, but there are going to be times when you want regular food: the kind of food you grew up with, assuming that you didn't grow up with Asian food.

When you veganize a cherished dish, you need to ask what exactly it is that you cherish. Fried chicken, for instance. Is it the chicken you care about, or the "fried"? For me, it's the fried. Well, a deep-fried exterior is absolutely doable with vegan food. Is it the cheese you miss in lasagna, or the creaminess? There are many ways to make food creamy without dairy — really creamy, not just whitish. Is it meat you miss, or meat's browned-umami quality? Or its texture? These can both be duplicated, and in ways you don't have to get used to: You'll like them from the start.

Vegan main dishes are without a doubt the most challenging form of vegan cooking you'll — oh, no, wait. Vegan cakes are harder. But you're going to be eating a lot more vegan main dishes than cakes. Don't panic! This chapter will show you how it's done.

Admittedly, I'm saying this from the far side of a river that you may just be beginning to wade into. But remember that David is a main-course-type guy and that all the recipes in this book had to pass the David test. He had to like them enough to take seconds and then to eat as leftovers. And I mean "choose to eat as leftovers," not "eat something again because Ann served it a second night." Would Dave voluntarily eat a vegan entrée for lunch the next day?

With some of these recipes, he couldn't even wait for lunch. He had them for breakfast.

–  –  –  –  –  –

# *Much More Interesting* Lentils!

*Makes 4 servings.*

Lentils — eh. **They're fine, and individually they're cute,** but they seem so . . . mandatory for vegans that I find myself resenting them. One more brownish pile of glop for the vegan plate! That's how I felt until I learned about recipes where the lentils were treated like rice in a pilaf — stir-fried with spices and aromatics before being cooked. ●

¼ cup vegetable oil

10 scallions, thinly sliced (include a lot of the green part)

2 garlic cloves, minced

1 tablespoon Madras curry powder

1 teaspoon ground cumin

1 teaspoon freshly ground pepper

¼ teaspoon cayenne, or to taste

2 cups lentils

2 tablespoons tomato paste

One 15-ounce can diced tomatoes with their juice (I use Pomi)

1 teaspoon salt, plus more to taste

About 4 cups vegetable stock, homemade (page 177) or store-bought

1 cup dried unsweetened flaked coconut

2 tablespoons black or yellow mustard seeds

2 tablespoons extra-virgin olive oil

Chopped fresh cilantro (optional)

1   Heat a large, heavy pot and add the vegetable oil. When it shimmers, add the scallions, garlic, and spices. Cook over medium heat, stirring, for 5 minutes.

2   Add the lentils and tomato paste to the pot. Stir constantly for 5 minutes. Add the diced tomatoes and the salt; stir well. Pour in enough stock to cover the lentils by about ½ inch; if you somehow don't have enough stock, make up the difference with water.

Bring the lentils to a boil, then lower the heat and simmer for 25 to 35 minutes, until the lentils are soft. Add more water or stock if the mixture starts to look dry during this period.

3   Heat a small skillet. Add the coconut and mustard seeds along with a pinch of salt. Stir constantly over medium heat until the coconut is a pale golden-brown. Pour this mixture into a small heatproof bowl or ramekin.

4   Stir the olive oil into the lentils. Serve them hot, passing the chopped cilantro and toasted coconut mixture at the table.

THE "MEAT" OF THE MATTER: MAINS

# Tomato Tart
## with "Feta"

*Makes 1 large tart, about 12 by 16 inches. I'd say that as a meal, it would serve 4 people, because they might want seconds. If you want to use it as an appetizer, the size and number of pieces is up to you.*

**We are very, very lucky that Pepperidge Farm Puff Pastry is vegan,** readily available, and easy to work with. Sure, you could make a tart with a regular pastry crust, but the puff pastry is so festive and beautiful and delicately flaky that *for heaven's sake,* please pull a box or two out of the frozen pastry section in your supermarket and make this! ●

1 sheet (10 by 15 inches) Pepperidge Farm puff pastry, thawed in the refrigerator for 24 hours

½ cup Béchamel/Velouté Sauce (page 181), whisked with 1 tablespoon Dijon mustard

2 big tomatoes, halved, deglopped, and thinly sliced (it's nice to have two different colors)

½ cup crumbled Tofu "Feta" (page 187)

1 tablespoon honey, warmed

Freshly ground pepper to taste

2 tablespoons fresh oregano leaves or ½ cup chopped fresh parsley

1 Preheat the oven to 350°F, with a rack in the bottom third.

2 On a floured surface, with a floured rolling pin, roll out the puff pastry sheet until it's about 12 by 16 inches. Gently transfer the rolled pastry to a large rimmed baking sheet. Prick it all over with a fork.

3 Bake the puff pastry according to the package directions. If it starts to rise in the middle, pat the bulges down with your oven-mitt-covered hand. (While the tart shell is baking, you can prepare the other ingredients. Then, as Peg Bracken said in *The I Hate to Cook Book,* "Light a cigarette and stare sullenly at the sink.")

4 When the crust is baked, remove it from the oven. Turn the oven temperature down to 350°F and move a rack to the middle.

5 Spread the béchamel sauce over the crust as evenly as possible, leaving a 1-inch border. Then arrange the tomato slices over the sauce. You'll probably need to overlap

them slightly to get them to fit. Sprinkle the crumbled tofu feta evenly over the tomatoes. Then, using an offset spatula, a pastry brush, or the back of a spoon, paint the honey evenly over the tart. Oh, sure! Paint feta with honey! Well, you can just clumsily dab the feta. The point is to get a small amount of honey evenly spread, not to have each tomato evenly covered. Grind some pepper over everything. If you're using fresh oregano, sprinkle it over the tart.

6   Bake the tart for 20 to 25 minutes, until the tomatoes and cheese are starting to brown. Let it cool for 10 minutes.

7   If you're using parsley, sprinkle it over the tart. Serve. A sharp serrated knife works best for cutting this.

TOMATO TART with "FETA"

# Savory Onion Squares

Not quite a quiche, not quite a tart, not quite a flatbread. Well, more like a tart than anything else. These are nonsweet pastry bars baked with a delicious onion-tomato topping. When you serve them depends on what size you make them. Big squares work for supper or lunch; little ones work as an appetizer or snack. Why not just make them and figure out that part later? ●

**CRUST**

2 cups all-purpose flour (8.8 ounces or 240 grams)

1 teaspoon salt (6 grams)

1 teaspoon freshly ground pepper (2 grams)

1 teaspoon dried thyme (2 grams)

1 teaspoon granulated sugar (2 grams)

1 cup (8 ounces) solid vegetable shortening, such as Crisco (205 grams)

5 to 7 tablespoons ice water (2.6 to 3.5 ounces or 74 to 104 grams)

**TOPPING**

¼ cup olive oil, plus more if needed

2 pounds onions, thinly sliced

2 garlic cloves, minced

½ teaspoon dried rosemary

Salt and freshly ground pepper to taste

1 cup Béchamel/Velouté (page 181) or Cauliflower Cream (page 183)

12 oil-packed sun-dried tomatoes, cut into slivers

½ cup pitted Niçoise or Kalamata olives, diced

1   **Crust:** In a food processor, pulse together the flour, salt, pepper, thyme, and sugar. Slice the shortening into about 16 pieces, scatter over the flour, and pulse until the mixture looks like cornmeal, with a few lumps the size of pencil erasers here and there. (You can also use a bowl and cut in the shortening with a pastry blender.)

2   Transfer the flour mixture to a big bowl (unless, of course, it's already in a bowl). Sprinkle 5 tablespoons of the ice water over it. With a fork, lightly toss the flour and water together until a ball begins to form. If that doesn't happen, add up to 2 more tablespoons ice water, a teaspoon at a time, tossing until the mixture is a cohesive mass.

# WHY NOT JUST MAKE THEM?

3 Lightly press the dough into a disk about ½ inch thick. Wrap it in plastic and chill it for 30 minutes.

4 When time is up, preheat the oven to 400°F, with a rack in the middle. Leave the dough in the fridge while you get the other stuff ready.

5 **Topping:** Heat a large skillet over medium-high heat until hot. Add the oil and swirl it around for a few seconds. When the oil is hot, add the onions, garlic, rosemary, and salt and pepper. Turn the heat to medium-low, give everything a big stir, and cook the mixture for 30 minutes, stirring frequently. Add more oil if you need it. The onions should be very soft and beginning to brown in spots. When they're done, let them cool while you prepare the crust.

6 Break the dough into about 8 pieces and press them evenly over the bottom of a 9-inch square baking pan, pinching the seams together. Line the crust with foil and fill the pan with dried beans, pie weights, gold coins, or whatever you use to weight down piecrust dough. Bake for 20 minutes. Take the crust out of the oven, but leave the oven on. Carefully lift out the foil and weights.

7 Stir together the onions and white sauce. Spoon the mixture over the crust in an even layer. Place the sun-dried tomatoes and olives over the onions, preferably in some kind of organized, nice-looking way.

8 Bake for 25 to 30 minutes. The onions should be starting to deepen in color, and the pan should be sizzling around the edges. Let cool for at least 15 minutes before cutting into squares of any desired size.

9 Serve warm or at room temperature.

# Leek, White Bean, and Mushroom Tart

*Makes one 9-inch tart that, realistically, serves 3 or 4.*

The one place I don't miss butter too much is in piecrust. Crisco, which makes the flakiest piecrusts, is vegan! Of course it doesn't taste as good as butter; it doesn't taste like anything, really. But it gives a great texture, and you can easily fix the flavor by adding herbs and spices and grated lemon zest and so on.

This is one of my vegan-ized recipes that David likes better than the omnivore version. The omni recipe features goat cheese and Gorgonzola instead of white beans, but highly seasoned white beans give a remarkably similar effect. A peppery crust is topped with a creamy layer of pureed beans smothered in well-browned leeks and mushrooms. **Not that we should care if people don't notice that a dish is vegan, but with this tart, it would never occur to them!**

It's almost always better to cook dried beans yourself, but in this recipe, you can totally use canned. Haven't you already got enough to do, for God's sake? Plus, the three components of the tart can be done in stages: You can make the crust up to 2 days ahead of time (or freeze it for up to 2 months); you can make the white bean filling the day before; and you can cook the leeks and mushrooms a few hours ahead. ●

### PIECRUST

1½ cups all-purpose flour (6.6 ounces or 180 grams)

¾ teaspoon salt

1½ teaspoons freshly ground pepper (4 grams)

½ teaspoon dried thyme

Pinch of granulated sugar

¾ cup (but it's better to weigh it) Crisco or other vegetable shortening (5.4 ounces or 154 grams)

4 to 5 tablespoons ice water (2 to 2.6 ounces)

**FILLING**

Two 15-ounce cans white beans (such as cannellini or navy beans), drained and rinsed

3 tablespoons Dijon mustard

3 tablespoons olive oil or vegetable oil (don't use coconut oil)

2 tablespoons dry white wine

Salt and freshly ground pepper to taste

**TOPPING**

1¼ pounds white mushrooms

1 pound leeks

About ¼ cup olive oil or vegetable oil, plus 2 teaspoons for drizzling

1 teaspoon dried thyme

Salt and freshly ground pepper to taste

Coarse or kosher salt

1 **Piecrust:** In a food processor, whiz the flour, salt, pepper, and thyme until well blended. Dot the top of this mixture with the Crisco, perhaps 8 chunks in all. Pulse the mixture until it has the texture of coarse cornmeal with maybe a few pea-sized bits here and there, about ten pulses.

2 Transfer the mixture to a medium bowl and sprinkle 4 tablespoons of the ice water over the top. With a pastry blender (preferable) or a fork, toss together until it just begins to form a dough. Add up to another tablespoon of ice water if necessary. Gently knead the dough a few times until it actually is a dough. Don't overwork it, though, or it may get too stretchy and tough. (Crisco is wonderfully impervious, but we can't expect it to perform miracles.) Pat the dough into a disk about 1 inch thick, wrap it in plastic wrap, and chill it for at least 30 minutes, and up to a day.

3 **Filling:** Wipe out the food processor bowl with a paper towel. (You don't need to wash it.) Dump the filling ingredients into the bowl and process until smooth and lump-free. Check the seasoning.

4 Preheat the oven to 400°F, with a rack in the lower third.

5 **Topping:** Stem the mushrooms. Instead of slicing them, cut them into lovely photogenic quarters. Remove the leeks' stem ends and tough tops and slice them into ½-inch rounds. Rinse them in a colander to remove the grit lurking at their centers.

6 Heat a large, heavy skillet over medium heat until hot, then add 3 tablespoons of the oil and heat until it shimmers. Add the quartered mushrooms and cook, stirring, until they give up their liquid. Then keep cooking them until all the liquid has been reabsorbed

and the mushrooms are brown. Dump them onto a rimmed baking sheet and spread them out to cool.

7 Add another tablespoon or so of oil to the skillet. Add the leeks, thyme, and salt and pepper to taste and cook, stirring frequently, until the leeks begin to brown — 8 to 10 minutes. Check the seasoning, adding more salt and pepper if you want.

8 Add the leeks to the mushrooms on the baking sheet and toss the two vegetables together. They should be as cool as possible when you assemble the tart, so put them in the refrigerator if there's room — not easy with a baking sheet, I know.

9 On a well-floured surface, with a well-floured rolling pin, roll out the chilled pie dough into a rough circle about 14 inches in diameter and ⅛ inch thick. Carefully transfer the rolled-out pastry to a second rimmed baking sheet and chill it for about 15 minutes to relax the gluten.

10 Carefully spread the bean filling over the dough, leaving a 2-inch border. Spread the cooled leek-mushroom mixture over the bean filling, observing the same 2-inch border. Drizzle the remaining 2 teaspoons oil over the vegetables.

11 Now you'll do the free-form crust. Even *more* carefully, lift a segment of the "border dough" and fold it up over the vegetables. Repeat this step every 2 or 3 inches, pinching the dough into sort-of pleats all the way around. Only the edges of the tart will be covered; the center will be open to the skies. When you're done, sprinkle the whole thing with coarse salt.

12 Bake the tart in the lower third of the oven for 25 minutes. Then turn the oven temperature down to 375°F and move the tart up a notch, to the middle of the oven. Bake for about 20 more minutes, or until it's all well browned. Let the tart cool for 15 minutes before cutting it into wedges.

*NOTE* A cup of chopped toasted walnuts makes a nice addition once in a while.

# Panfried Giant White Beans with Kale

*Serves 2 or 3.*

This is an adaptation of a Food52.com "Genius" recipe that would need no adaptation except that it calls for Parmesan. Since we can't have Parm, I've tinkered a bit.

Oh, the beans? Order them from RanchoGordo.com. Everyone should know about this place. Dried beans are beautiful to begin with, but the ones from Rancho Gordo . . . ! **You owe it to yourself to try their gigantes or coronas, which are the size of babies' ears.** Wait, that sounds unvegan. Let's say dried apricots. ●

3 tablespoons vegetable oil

1 cup cooked giant white beans (cook them according to the package directions, but use vegetable stock, homemade [page 177] or store-bought, not water)

6 ounces kale, stems removed

¼ teaspoon salt, plus more to taste

⅓ cup chopped walnuts, lightly toasted

2 garlic cloves, minced

Pinch of freshly grated nutmeg

1 tablespoon finely grated lemon zest

1 tablespoon fresh lemon juice, plus more to taste

1 cup Bread Crumbs Treated Right (page 113; optional)

KALE! KALE! KALE! KALE! KALE! KALE! KALE! KALE!

1 Heat the oil over medium-high heat in the biggest skillet you have. When the oil shimmers, add the beans and stir to coat them. Spread them out in a single layer and cook, without stirring, for 4 to 5 minutes, until they're browned and crunchy in several places. Use a wide spatula to turn them over and repeat the process.

2 Add the kale and salt to the skillet. Panfry the kale with the beans for about 2 minutes; you want it to wilt but not melt. Add the walnuts and garlic and stir-fry for 30 seconds. Stir in the nutmeg, then stir in the lemon zest and lemon juice. Check the seasoning. If you're using the bread crumbs, sprinkle them over all and serve.

# Baked Potatoes
## with Mushroom Ragout

*Serves 4.*

If this recipe were in an old *Betty Crocker Cookbook*, it would be in the Man-Pleaser section. It's robust, cheering, and richly flavored — a perfect winter dish, which is no reason not to serve it at other times of the year.

As with all dried mushrooms, a half-ounce cellophane bag of porcini can seem ridiculously expensive. **But porcini are the beef of the dried-mushroom world.** That little packet will work very hard for you, and so will the liquid you soak the mushrooms in — which is virtually a stock in itself. ●

One ½-ounce package dried porcini mushrooms

1 cup vegetable stock, homemade (page 177) or store-bought

4 large russet potatoes (about 2 pounds)

7 tablespoons olive oil

1 small onion, finely chopped

2 garlic cloves, minced

1½ pounds white or cremini mushrooms, trimmed and sliced

Salt and freshly ground pepper to taste

1 tablespoon tomato paste

½ cup dry white wine, dry sherry, or dry vermouth

½ teaspoon dried thyme

1 teaspoon fresh lemon juice, or to taste (optional)

1 tablespoon minced fresh chives or parsley, if you've got some around

1　Preheat the oven to 425°F, with a rack in the middle.

2　Put the porcini in a heatproof bowl. Bring the vegetable stock to a boil, pour it over the mushrooms, and let them steep for 30 minutes. Line a sieve with a coffee filter or a paper towel, set it over a bowl, and drain the mushrooms. Save the precious steeping mixture! Yank the filter or paper towel right out from under those mushrooms, leaving them in the sieve, then give them a quick rinse under cold water. Drain them, squeeze them dry in another paper towel or clean dish towel, and coarsely chop them. (By the way, there's no reason not to do this early in the day if it will save you some stress.)

3   Viciously stab the potatoes all over with a fork and rub them with 1 tablespoon of the oil. Microwave them on a microwave-safe plate at 100% power for 4 minutes, then carefully turn them over and give them another 4 minutes at 100%.

4   Carefully transfer the *hot!* potatoes to the oven rack. Bake them for 20 minutes or so, until their skin is crisp and their insides are soft. (If in doubt, slightly overbaking is always better than slightly underbaking.)

5   Meanwhile, let's get back to the sauce: In a large deep skillet, over medium-high heat, heat 4 tablespoons of the oil until it shimmers. Add the onion and cook over medium heat, stirring occasionally, until soft, about 5 minutes. Stir in the garlic and cook for another couple of minutes. Turn the heat to high; add the *fresh* mushrooms, remaining 2 tablespoons oil, and salt and pepper to taste and cook until the mushrooms release their juices. Then continue to cook them, stirring, until all the liquid has gone back into them. The total cooking time will be 10 to 15 minutes.

6   Lower the heat to medium-high and add the chopped porcini and tomato paste to the skillet. Add the wine or its alternative and cook until it has evaporated, scraping up any browned bits that stick to the pan. Then add the thyme, along with about ½ cup of the mushroom soaking liquid. Cook for another minute and check the seasoning, adding the lemon juice if you think the taste needs a bit of brightening.

7   Carefully slice the potatoes in half. Use a fork to tumble their insides about and fluff them with a fork. Ladle some mushroom sauce over each potato and sprinkle with the chives or parsley, if you're using them. Serve the rest of the sauce on the side.

IF THIS RECIPE WERE IN AN OLD *BETTY CROCKER* COOKBOOK IT WOULD BE IN THE MAN-PLEASER SECTION

# Bubble and Squeak

*Serves 6 as a main dish.*

Bubble and squeak is the kind of dish that would be served at Malory Towers, the Brit boarding school where Darrell Rivers learns to be a nice girl in the six-book series by Enid Blyton. Every Malory Towers book is basically the same.

Darrell (the heroine) takes the train to school, where she catches up with all her old friends and with Matron. They take stock of the new girls, who are either spoiled brats or circus gypsies. How on earth will those girls fit in? Then there are a few chapters that might as well be called The Term Goes On. A big lacrosse game is in the offing. The school begins to be troubled by mysterious thefts, a ghost, kleptomania, or the accusation (false, of course!) that Darrell broke Mary-Lou's fountain pen. Someone sprinkles sneezing powder all over the French classroom — poor Mam'selle! Miss Grayling, the school's majestic Headmistress, has a serious talk about what she expects from Darrell. Suddenly the looming crisis is resolved, and Summer Term is about to start. Good-bye, Malory Towers! See you next term!

As my friend Miranda pointed out, the Harry Potter books share this general plot. But back to bubble and squeak, which is a traditional dish made from cold leftover boiled potatoes and other leftover vegetables. Sounds Brit, doesn't it? Luckily, we're not at Malory Towers. **We're allowed to make food taste good — even nursery food.** *Our* bubble and squeak has freshly cooked vegetables, not leftovers, and much more flavor than Darrell is used to. ●

8 ounces Brussels sprouts, trimmed and halved

6 medium carrots, scrubbed and cut into ⅛-inch-thick coins

2 medium parsnips, scrubbed and chopped

½ cup plus 2 tablespoons extra-virgin olive oil

A boatload of salt and freshly ground pepper

2 pounds russet potatoes, scrubbed and cut into ¾-inch cubes

6 to 8 cups vegetable stock, homemade (page 177) or store-bought

1 medium onion, minced

2 garlic cloves, minced

2 tablespoons whole-grain mustard

1 Preheat the oven to 400°F, with a rack in the middle. Line a rimmed baking sheet with foil.

2 Spread the Brussels sprouts, carrots, and parsnips out on the baking sheet. Toss with 5 tablespoons of the olive oil and salt and pepper them lavishly. Bake for 30 to 45 minutes, stirring every 10 minutes; the vegetables should be tender and beginning to brown.

3 Meanwhile, put the potatoes in a large pot and add enough vegetable stock to cover them. If the stock is salt-free, add salt to taste. Bring the stock to a boil and cook the potatoes until they're truly tender, about 30 minutes. No itty-bitty crunchy spots in the middle! Bubble and squeak is not about being crisp-tender.

4 Measure out ¼ cup of the potato cooking water, then drain the potatoes and just forget about them for now. Wipe the pot dry, then add 2 tablespoons of the oil to the empty potato pot. When the oil is hot, stir in the onion and cook over medium-low heat until beginning to brown, 12 to 15 minutes.

Throw in the garlic for the last 3 minutes and stir it around too. Take the pot off the heat and add the reserved potato water and the potatoes. Using a potato masher or the bottom of a heatproof glass, smash those tates good.

5 Thoroughly mix the roasted vegetables and mustard into the potatoes. Check the seasoning, adding more salt and pepper if you want.

6 In a 12-inch skillet, heat the last 3 tablespoons olive oil over medium-high heat. Add the potato-vegetable mixture and press it down. Cook for 10 minutes. Hear that bubbling and squeaking? (I don't.)

7 Peek at the underside of the dish to see if it looks brown and crusty enough to use a pancake turner or wide spatula to turn the whole thing over. The original recipe says to "flip" the contents, but I've never dared to try that. I just make sure that the browned part on the bottom gets reversed so that the light part can cook for another 10 minutes. Serve right out of the skillet.

NOTE

Although Miss Grayling would belt me for saying this, I see no reason not to add a little ham- or bacon-flavored TVP to this dish. Say ¼ cup TVP, soaked in 2 tablespoons hot water for 15 minutes and added to the onions for the last couple of minutes. Would that bother anyone? Good, because I'm going to do it. Pepperoni TVP would also be good, but that seems sacriligious even to me.

# Cauliflower Steaks
## (but Let's Not Go Nuts Here)

*Serves 4.*

You can cut a cauliflower into thick slices and call them steaks, but they are not steak and will never be steak, no matter how brown and caramelized they get. So why not call them slices? Well, because "steak" is a sexier word. And also because in vegan cooking, there are very few main courses that come in a big slab, have a decent chew, and require a knife along with a fork. So go ahead and call them steak, but don't dig out the A.1. from your previous life. **Instead, make one of the life-changing sauces in this book** (see pages 167 to 174). Or dress the cauliflower up this way. ●

### CAULIFLOWER

**1 large cauliflower**

**¼ cup olive oil**

**2 tablespoons fresh lemon juice**

**1 garlic clove, minced**

**¼ teaspoon red pepper flakes, or to taste**

**Pinch of granulated sugar**

**Lavish amounts of salt and freshly ground pepper**

### RELISH

**½ cup oil-packed black olives, pitted and chopped**

**4 sun-dried tomatoes, thinly sliced**

**3½ tablespoons olive oil, plus more if necessary**

**3 tablespoons chopped fresh parsley**

**2 teaspoons fresh lemon juice**

**Salt and freshly ground pepper to taste**

**3 garlic cloves, halved lengthwise**

**2 plum tomatoes, cut into quarters**

1   Preheat the oven to 400°F, with a rack in the middle. Line a rimmed baking sheet with parchment paper.

2   **Cauliflower:** Use a big, meaningful knife to cut the cauliflower vertically into four slices (oh, all right, steaks). Hang on to the little florets or bits that fall off.

3   In a small bowl, whisk together the oil, lemon juice, garlic, red pepper flakes, sugar, and salt and pepper to taste. (We'll call this

the marinade.) Arrange the cauliflower slices on the baking sheet and brush half the marinade over them. Bake for 20 minutes. The slices should be firm yet tender, like a good boyfriend.

4 **Meanwhile, for relish:** Gather up the stray florets and bits until you have about ½ cup of them. Chop them fine and put them into a small bowl, along with the olives, sun-dried tomatoes, 1 tablespoon of the oil, the parsley, and lemon juice. Add salt and pepper to taste.

5 As if you didn't have enough to do already, heat a small skillet and add 1 tablespoon of the olive oil. When it shimmers, put in the halved garlic cloves and plum tomatoes, cut side down. Cook over medium heat until the cut sides of the tomatoes begin to brown, then transfer the garlic and tomatoes to a small baking dish (or use the skillet, if it's ovenproof). Bake for 12 minutes, until the tomatoes have collapsed.

6 When the first 20 minutes are up, take the steaks out of the oven. Gently turn them over with a wide spatula. Brush them with the rest of the marinade and return them to the oven. Bake until brown and tender, about 20 minutes. Don't forget that the garlic and tomatoes will be cooking for only 12 minutes! Better set two timers if you have them.

7 When the tomatoes and garlic are done, transfer them to a blender, add the last 1½ tablespoons oil, and blend until smooth.

8 When the steaks are done, spoon an equal amount of tomato sauce over each. Then spoon one quarter of the relish onto each tomato-sauced slice. Serve warm or at room temperature.

# Roasted Thai-Like Vegetables

*Serves 4.*

I say "Thai-like" because sometimes **I wonder about all the Thai recipes out there.** Looking at some of them, you'd think that adding peanuts and sugar turns any dish Thai, which can't be true. But it *is* true that you'll find some of the ingredients you need for this dish in the "Thai" section of the supermarket.

It's also true that you can substitute other vegetables in this recipe, or use canned tomatoes instead of fresh. You can also sprinkle toasted almonds on top — which I guess would allow you to call it 1950s-Style Curried Vegetables, Except Using Curry Paste Instead of Powder. Speaking of which, you could use green curry paste in this, but it makes for an ugly result. Red is best.

Anyway, it's delicious.

1 head cauliflower, cored and cut into florets

2 large red bell peppers, chopped

2 carrots, scrubbed and cut into coins

1 medium zucchini or summer squash, sliced

8 ounces green beans, trimmed

1 large onion, chopped

4 garlic cloves, thinly sliced

4 tablespoons vegetable oil (not olive oil — it's horrible in Asian food!)

Salt and freshly ground pepper to taste

2 or 3 large tomatoes, halved, deglopped, and sliced

1 cup frozen tiny peas — no need to defrost them

2 tablespoons Thai red curry paste

One 13- or 14-ounce can coconut milk (*not* light, which tastes soapy)

½ cup smooth or crunchy peanut butter

2 tablespoons fresh lime juice, or more to taste

1 tablespoon soy sauce, or more to taste

For garnish: chopped peanuts, toasted sliced almonds, chopped fresh cilantro, chopped fresh mint, or chopped fresh basil, or a mixture

1  Preheat the oven to 450°F, with a rack in the middle. Set a 10-by-15-inch baking dish in the oven to heat.

2  In a very large bowl, toss the cauliflower, peppers, carrots, zucchini, green beans, onion, and garlic with 3 tablespoons of the oil. Sprinkle with salt and pepper and toss again. Spread them out in the hot baking dish and bake for 30 minutes.

3  Add the sliced tomatoes and peas and stir the vegetables gently, then return them to the oven and bake for 20 to 30 minutes more, stirring every 10 minutes or so.

4  Meanwhile, in a small saucepan, heat the last 1 tablespoon oil over low heat. Whisk in the curry paste and then the coconut milk. Whisking constantly, add the peanut butter, lime juice, and soy sauce and beat until smooth. Taste the sauce to see if you want more lime juice or soy sauce.

5  Pour the sauce "atop" the vegetables and mix it in thoroughly. Serve hot or warm, sprinkling the garnish(es) "atop" at the last minute.

YOU'D THINK THAT ADDING PEANUTS AND SUGAR TURNS ANY DISH THAI

# Endive Tarte Tatin

*Makes 4 magnificent servings that would be perfect for lunch.*

What a good idea it was to Tatin-ize a vegetable. **There's no reason these tarts should be limited to apples!** You don't have to peel or core endive. And for this version, you don't have to make a crust either. It's waiting for you in the freezer section — see, next to the puff pastry shells? We'll use those another time.

You can't use your puff pastry the second you get it home; you'll need to put it in the refrigerator a day ahead. Thawing puff pastry — even the industrial-strength Pepperidge Farm kind — is a process that shouldn't be rushed.

No one is saying you actually have to flip the finished tarte over in classic Tatin style. If you leave it as is, with the crust on top, it will still look great.

What should you serve with this? A chopped salad, maybe — anything leafy would be redundant. Or a fruit salad if you wanted to go in more of a brunch direction. And then maybe a nice loaf of Chipotle Bread (page 96). ●

**6 medium Belgian endives**
**3 tablespoons olive oil**
**1 tablespoon honey**
**Salt and freshly ground pepper to taste**

**3 tablespoons balsamic vinegar**
**Grated zest of 1 lemon**
**1 sheet Pepperidge Farm (or other vegan) frozen puff pastry, thawed (see headnote)**

1  Preheat the oven to 400°F, with a rack in the upper third. Lavishly grease a 9-inch round cake pan. Have ready a set of tongs and a round, heavy plate that's at least 12 inches in diameter.

2  Cut each endive in half lengthwise. Trim the bottoms, leaving on as much as possible. Remove the outer leaves and save them for your rabbits and parakeets.

3  Put the oil and honey in a skillet that's big enough to hold all the endive halves in a single layer. Over medium heat, whisk the mixture together until it's hot and glaze-y looking. When it reaches that point, add the endives facedown — cut side down, I mean — and cook them for 2 to 3 minutes, or until they begin to change color. Using tongs, carefully turn each half endive over. Cook for another 2 to 3 minutes, then turn the endives

onto their sides. Do you see where I'm going with this? That's right: Cook each side for 2 to 3 minutes. Then carefully arrange them cut side down again.

4  Turn the heat to medium-low. Generously salt and pepper the endive halves. If the skillet has a lid, put it on; otherwise, use foil or a baking sheet. In any case, cover the skillet. Cook the endives for about 20 minutes; they should be very soft. After 20 minutes, uncover the skillet. Cook the endives, uncovered, for a few more minutes to let them brown, but watch to make sure they don't get too dark.

5  Now take up that well-greased cake pan and sprinkle the vinegar evenly over its surface. Use the tongs to transfer the endive halves to the pan — this time, cut side up. When the endives have been packed into the pan, pour/scrape any skillet juices over them. Evenly sprinkle half the lemon zest over the whole surface. Once again, salt and pepper the endives. Let them cool for 15 to 20 minutes so their steam won't gunk up the pastry.

6  Your patience with the puff pastry's long thawing time is about to be rewarded. Lightly flour a rolling surface and let the pastry rest there for 5 minutes. (This will help it adjust to what's going to happen.) With floured hands, gently unfold the pastry. With a floured

rolling pin, roll out the pastry until it's about 1/8 inch thick and about 10 inches across. With a pastry brush or a piece of paper towel, gently sweep any extra flour before you tuck the pastry over the endives. Pinch the pastry all around the edge of the cake pan; then use scissors to trim away any untidy overhang. (Those bits are fun to bake for your own sweet self.) Then snip the pastry in eight to ten places so that steam can get out.

7  Bake for 10 minutes. Lower the heat to 350°F and bake for another 25 minutes. The pastry should be both well browned and well puffed.

8  Time up? Here comes the slightly scary part. Lift the tart out of the oven. Instantly place a serving dish over the cake pan, then *carefully* upend the dish so the endives are on top. *Carefully,* I said! With a wooden spoon, bang on the bottom of the cake pan to release the endives.

9  Now gently sliiiiiiiide the cake pan up off the endives, mentally crossing your fingers. Make any necessary repairs before sprinkling the rest of the lemon zest over the endives. Serve warm or at room temperature. Assuming you're going to finish the tart over the next couple of days, it doesn't need refrigerating.

# Pasta with Roasted Vegetables *for Our Times*

*Serves 6.*

It seems only about ten seconds ago that we all noticed the greatness of roasted vegetables. To me they still seem novel enough that I almost included recipes here for *plain* roasted vegetables. How embarrassing that would have been! Everyone knows about *those*. **Using roasted vegetables as an ingredient — that's what all the cool kids are doing now.**

½ teaspoon salt

4 tablespoons extra-virgin olive oil, plus a little more for the pasta water

1 pound Brussels sprouts, trimmed and cut in half the long way

1 small head cauliflower (about 1 pound), cut into bite-size florets

2 large carrots, scrubbed and cut into coins

3 large shallots, finely chopped

1 large onion, chopped

½ teaspoon red pepper flakes (optional)

8 ounces fusilli, broken into smaller lengths, or rigatoni, penne, or orecchiette — or, really, whatever shape you like

¾ cup panko crumbs

½ cup fresh parsley, chopped

Freshly ground pepper to taste

Juice of 1 lemon, or more to taste

¼ cup Tofu "Feta" (page 187), crumbled

1  Preheat the oven to 450°F, with a rack in the middle. Fill a large, heavy pot with water and bring it to a boil. Add salt — 1 tablespoon per gallon is standard — and a few drops of olive oil to keep the water from boiling over.

2  Meanwhile, dump the vegetables and red pepper flakes, if using, into a big bowl. Add 3 tablespoons of the oil and toss to coat the vegetables evenly. Add ½ teaspoon salt

and toss again. Spread the vegetables out on a rimmed baking sheet in a single layer. (If there are too many to fit, dig out another baking sheet for the excess.)

4  Roast the vegetables for 25 to 30 minutes, stirring every 8 to 10 minutes. When they're done, they should be nicely softened and brown in many places.

5   While the vegetables roast: Following the directions on the package, cook the pasta in the boiling water. When it's done, carefully scoop out ½ cup of the pasta cooking water, then drain the pasta well.

6   Heat a small skillet over medium heat and add the remaining 1 tablespoon oil. When the oil shimmers, add the panko crumbs and stir them over medium heat until they're golden, about 5 minutes. Put them into a little bowl and toss with 2 tablespoons of the chopped parsley.

7   In a large serving bowl, toss the pasta with the roasted vegetables and the remaining 6 tablespoons parsley. Add salt, pepper, and lemon juice to taste. If you want the pasta a little "saucier," add some of the reserved pasta water a tablespoon at a time. (I never do this.)

8   Scatter the panko crumb mixture and the crumbled tofu feta over the tossed pasta. Give everything a light toss and serve.

NOTE   Panko withers fast. This recipe is even better at room temperature, but if you plan to serve it that way, add the panko mixture at the last minute.

PASTA WITH ROASTED VEGETABLES

CARROTS!

ONIONS!

BRUSSELS SPROUTS! OH MY!

# Vaguely Asian Curried Rice Noodles
## *with Peanuts* ------▷ *Serves 4.*

**Please accept the traditional apologies for the fact that this is not a genuine curry,** if anyone still believes such a thing exists. It's a quick, easy, light, and intensely flavored dish, and infinitely variable. It's a curry for the twenty-first century. ●

Two 13-ounce cans coconut milk (*not* light)

2 tablespoons vegetable oil

1 large onion, chopped

2 tablespoons minced fresh lemongrass

1 tablespoon grated fresh ginger

1 garlic clove, minced

Salt and freshly ground pepper to taste

2 teaspoons turmeric

½ teaspoon ground coriander

½ teaspoon ground cumin

½ teaspoon ground allspice

⅛ to ¼ teaspoon cayenne

Grated zest and juice of 1 lime, or more lime juice to taste

1 tablespoon soy sauce or Bragg Liquid Aminos (see page 15), or more to taste

12 ounces rice noodles

1 pint cherry or grape tomatoes, halved

1½ cups roasted salted peanuts

4 scallions, thinly sliced

A handful of chopped fresh herbs: cilantro, basil, or mint, or a mixture

1   Pour the contents of one of the cans of coconut milk into a 2-cup measure. Spoon in enough "coconut cream" from the second can to bring the level to a full 2 cups. (Do your best to avoid the "coconut water" in the second can.)

2   Heat the oil in a large skillet over medium heat. When it's shimmering, stir in the onion and cook over medium heat, stirring frequently, for 6 to 8 minutes, until it's softened and translucent. Scatter in the lemongrass, ginger, and garlic and cook, stirring, for 2 minutes.

3   Add salt and pepper to taste, then add the spices and stir until the onion mixture is coated. Add the lime zest and juice, the soy sauce or liquid aminos, and the coconut milk–cream mixture. Lower the heat and simmer for 5 minutes.

4   Meanwhile, prepare the rice noodles according to the package directions. Drain them in a colander, rinse with cold water, and drain thoroughly.

5   Stir the tomatoes into the skillet and cook for about 1 minute, until they're heated through. Add the rice noodles and flop them around in the sauce. Check the seasoning, adding more soy sauce or liquid aminos, or lime juice to taste. Scatter in the peanuts and toss the mixture to distribute them evenly. Repeat the procedure with the scallions and fresh herbs. Okay, now you're good to go.

# VAGUELY ASIAN CURRIED RICE NOODLES

PEANUTS!

GRAPE TOMATOES!

# *Those Yummy*
# Curried Tofu Wraps

So good and so messy, those wraps that I buy at Trader Joe's. Why do I always buy them to eat in the car? Surely trying to take a bite and showering my lap with dollops of curried mayo and carrot shreds is riskier than texting would be. But wraps are more interesting than bread, and car-eating has been grandfathered in (I hope), so I'm not going to stop until it's against the law.

**Tofu in a regular sandwich can be discouraging, but in this wrap it's a pure positive** — a smooth, almost cheese-like contrast to the crunchy vegetables. Making sure the tofu's been well salted is one of the secrets. So, of course, is using a good-quality curry powder. (And that's not an oxymoron! We don't need to concoct our own curry seasonings for *everything*.)

It's best to make the filling a few hours in advance so that the flavors can get acquainted and the raisins can plump up. ●

One 12- to 14-ounce package firm or extra-firm tofu

4 teaspoons soy sauce

3 tablespoons vegan mayonnaise (I use Vegenaise)

1 tablespoon curry powder, or to taste

1 tablespoon fresh lemon or lime juice, or to taste

2 large carrots, grated

½ cup finely shredded romaine

1 red bell pepper, minced

2 scallions, thinly sliced

½ cup golden raisins

½ cup chopped salted peanuts (optional)

Salt and freshly ground pepper to taste

Four to six 10-inch wraps — preferably whole wheat, spinach, or another flavor

# I'M NOT GOING TO STOP UNTIL IT'S AGAINST THE LAW.

1 Slice the block of tofu into four slabs. Set them on a few thicknesses of paper towels (or a clean dish towel) and cover them with more paper towels (or, yes, another clean dish towel). Press down gently to extract as much moisture as possible. Replace the towels and repeat the process. Paint each side of each slab with ½ teaspoon of the soy sauce. Then let the slabs stand on *even more* toweling for at least 30 minutes. If you want to let them stand for longer than that, refrigerate them.

2 In a little bowl, whisk together the mayo, curry powder, and citrus juice.

3 Crumble the tofu into a medium bowl. Add the carrots, romaine, bell pepper, scallions, raisins, and chopped peanuts, if using, and toss everything together well. Mix in the mayonnaise-curry sauce, making sure all the ingredients are coated. Season the mixture to taste with salt and pepper, then wrap-ify it.

# Crispy Tofu *with Peanut Sauce*

*Serves 4.*

This is the perfect vegan recipe because **almost no one — vegan or non — has ever tasted anything like it.** Besides saying that it's tangy, I don't exactly know how to describe it myself. But everyone I've made it for loves it.

My husband says it's because the tofu is deep-fried. "*Anyone* would like deep-fried tofu." I said no, no, baked tofu would work just as well, and I baked the tofu in just a little oil, and it was nowhere near as good. So yes, the deep-frying is important (though easy), but I think the reason this tastes so good is that almost every "active ingredient" in the sauce has a strong, distinct flavor of its own.

The original version of this recipe contained dried shrimp paste — just half a teaspoon, but it was important. The best substitute I've found is Marmite, that weird brown British spread. If you buy a little jar, it will last forever, unless you're British. The other odd-ish ingredient called for is tamarind paste, which — like Marmite — is easy to find online. ●

Two 14-ounce packages extra- or super-firm tofu

¾ cup plus 2 tablespoons soy sauce

2 tablespoons grated fresh ginger

¼ cup corn oil or canola oil, plus more for deep-frying (6 to 8 cups)

1 cup roasted salted peanuts

1 medium onion, quartered

2 large shallots, halved

3 garlic cloves

2 teaspoons Sriracha, or to taste

½ teaspoon Marmite

½ cup water, plus ⅔ cup very hot water

1 tablespoon tamarind paste

2 tablespoons plum sauce

1 teaspoon granulated sugar

Rice for serving

## THIS IS THE PERFECT VEGAN RECIPE.

1   At least 2 hours and up to 24 hours ahead of the time you'll start cooking, place the tofu blocks between clean dish towels or several sheets of paper towels. Press out as much moisture as possible, either by hand or by putting a weight on top of the towel-covered tofu. I use a small baking dish with, like, two big cans of tomatoes in it. When you've gotten out as much liquid as you can without smushing the tofu, cut each block horizontally in half into two thinner sheets (not two smaller blocks).

2   In a nonreactive baking dish big enough to hold the four tofu slices, mix together ½ cup of the soy sauce and the ginger. Marinate the tofu in this mixture, gently turning the slices from time to time. If you'll be marinating it overnight, it will need to be chilled; if you're just doing it for a couple of hours, you can leave it at room temperature.

3   At cooking time, preheat the oven to 250°F.

4   Remove the tofu from the baking dish and gently pat dry with paper towels. Cut it into 1-inch cubes. Cover a rimmed baking sheet with a thick layer of paper towels, or do what I do and line it with a newspaper section covered with a single layer of paper towels.

5   In a deep saucepan or pot (so as to avoid spattering), begin heating 2 to 3 inches of oil over low heat.

6   **Meanwhile, make the sauce:** In a food processor, chop the peanuts as fine as you can without turning them into peanut butter. Dump them into a bowl. Put the onion, shallots, garlic, Sriracha, Marmite, and the ½ cup water into the peanutty food processor and process to a smooth paste.

7   In a small bowl, stir the tamarind paste into the ⅔ cup hot water, mashing it with the back of a spoon to extract as much flavor as possible.

8   Heat a large, heavy skillet over medium-high heat. When it's hot, add the ¼ cup oil. Let it heat for a few seconds, then stir in the shallot paste, nimbly leaping out of the way to avoid the steam that will puff up into your face. Turn the heat to low and cook the mixture for 10 minutes, stirring frequently. Don't forget to check the frying oil, which you'll eventually heat to 350°F.

9   Stir the peanuts, the remaining 6 tablespoons soy sauce, the plum sauce, and the sugar into the shallot paste. Pour the tamarind mixture through a sieve into the skillet, pressing with a spoon to extract as much liquid as possible. Still over low heat, and still

stirring frequently, cook the sauce for about 5 minutes, or until it's slightly thicker. Take it off the heat.

**10** Increase the heat under the frying oil to medium-high. When it's reached 350°F, fry the tofu cubes in two or three batches. The cubes will immediately try to clump together; do your best not to let this happen. Turn each cube a couple of times. When the cubes are golden-brown — which always takes longer than you'd expect — carefully take them out of the oil and set them on the paper-toweled baking sheet to drain. Keep the finished batches warm in the oven.

**11** When you've finished frying the tofu, leave it in the oven while you reheat the sauce.

**12** Once the sauce is hot, add the tofu cubes to the pan and gently move them around until they're coated with sauce. Serve immediately, with rice.

# Tofu "Chorizo"

- - - - - - -▷ *Serves 4.*

Mark Bittman is a brilliant vegan cook. He's also a brilliant nonvegan cook, but that's not the point right now. As far as I know, Bittman was the first person to publish a recipe where you crumble fresh tofu and then **fry the hell out of it until it's no longer tofu but a pile of browned bits lying back in the skillet and cooing, "Do with me what you will."**

One day, Bittman answered, "Okay, I'll make you into fantastic chorizo and serve you in corn tortillas." The tofu agreed, and everyone was happy. (This recipe is an adaptation of one that he wrote for the *New York Times*.)

Warm corn tortillas or rice are a nice go-with. ●

2 blocks firm tofu

3 tablespoons Crisco or other solid vegetable shortening

1 medium onion, chopped

½ teaspoon salt, or more to taste

3 garlic cloves, minced

1 canned chipotle pepper in adobo, minced

1 tablespoon chili powder

2 teaspoons white miso

1 teaspoon freshly ground pepper, or more to taste

1 teaspoon ground cumin

½ teaspoon dried oregano

Pinch of ground cinnamon

Pinch of ground cloves

Pinch of granulated or brown sugar

1 tablespoon apple cider vinegar, or more to taste

Chopped fresh cilantro and scallions for garnish (optional)

1 Cut the tofu into four slabs. Press the slabs between paper towels or clean dish towels to extract as much moisture as you can.

2 Heat a large, heavy skillet over medium-high heat. Add the Crisco and heat until it shimmers. Add the onion, sprinkle with the salt, and turn the heat down to medium. Cook, stirring occasionally, until the onion softens, about 5 minutes. Add the garlic and cook for 2 to 3 minutes.

3   Crumble the tofu into the pan. Stir/scrape the tofu, stirring frequently, until it's as brown and crisp as you like. Use a wide spatula to scrape up the good bits from the bottom of the skillet as the tofu browns. The cooking can take from 10 to 40 minutes, depending on how brown and dried-out you want the tofu to be; I do it for 40 minutes.

4   Sprinkle the tofu with the minced chipotle, chili powder, miso, cumin, pepper, oregano, cinnamon, cloves, and sugar. Cook for about 5 minutes over low heat, stirring and scraping up any browned bits from the bottom of the pan. Stir in the vinegar and adjust the seasoning to taste. Garnish with the cilantro and scallions, if using, and serve.

THE TOFU AGREED, AND EVERYONE WAS HAPPY.

# Macaroni and Cheese

*Serves 4*

If I had to guess, I'd say that there are more recipes for vegan macaroni and cheese than for any other dish. Burgers are up there too, but M and C (I refuse to say "mac 'n' cheese") seems to be what vegans yearn for the most. Considering that **by the time most people come to veganism, they've already eaten vast swimming pools of the stuff,** you'd think they'd be ready to move on, but no.

Many of these recipes begin, "This tastes exactly like real macaroni and cheese!" You wonder whether the writer has ever *tried* real macaroni and cheese. The only thing "this" has in common with the real thing is that they're both orange.

You become a bitter, sour person — yes, bitter *and* sour. You grumble that at least they should have come up with a decent *instant* vegan M and C by now; isn't that boxed stuff just chemicals anyway?

**And then you try this recipe, which I've adapted from *Serious Eats,* and your husband says, "This is better than real macaroni and cheese."** At least David did. We should keep in mind that he *knew* it was vegan, so his expectations were lower than usual. Still, the first time I made it for supper, David had four helpings, and he finished the leftovers the next day.

I would never tell people that this was regular macaroni and cheese — but if I did, they'd believe me. Not that it matches the taste of the dairy version; if you pay close attention, you'll see that the two are quite different. But somehow they're a matched set. Maybe one day I'll bring a big pan of this to a potluck and then sneak around jotting down people's reactions in a little book. I'm guessing they'll love it.

If you have leftover sauce, it works well in vegan "grilled cheeses." ●

4 ounces russet potato (about ½ medium), peeled and thinly sliced

6 tablespoons solid vegetable shortening, such as Crisco, or vegetable oil (I use shortening)

1 small onion, thinly sliced

2 medium garlic cloves, minced

2 tablespoons ketchup (yes!)

1 tablespoon tomato paste

1 tablespoon Dijon mustard

1½ teaspoons paprika

1 teaspoon garlic powder (yes!)

½ teaspoon freshly ground pepper, plus more to taste

4 ounces or 113 grams (about 1 cup, but the weight is more important) roasted macadamia nuts, salted or unsalted

½ cup soy or other nondairy milk

1 cup water

2 teaspoons miso paste (yes!)

2 teaspoons hot sauce (I use Frank's)

2 teaspoons salt, plus more to taste

12 ounces elbow macaroni

1   Plunk the potato slices into a small saucepan with enough water to cover. Bring the water to a boil, lower the heat to a simmer, and cook for 5 minutes. Don't worry, the potatoes aren't supposed to be done yet. Drain and leave in the colander until you need them.

2   Melt the shortening (or heat the oil) in a medium skillet over medium heat. Add the onion and minced garlic and cook, stirring, until soft but not brown — about 5 minutes. Add the ketchup, tomato paste, mustard, paprika, garlic powder, and pepper. Cook, stirring, for a couple of minutes, until the contents of the skillet start to sizzle.

3   Add the sliced potato and the macadamia nuts and cook, stirring constantly, over medium heat for 5 minutes. Add the milk, ½ cup of the water, and the miso paste. Bring

to a boil, reduce to a low simmer, and cook, stirring frequently, until the potatoes are completely tender, 10 to 15 minutes.

4   Transfer the mixture to a blender — preferably a high-speed model like a Vitamix. Add the hot sauce, salt, and the remaining ½ cup water. Start blending on low speed and slowly increase the speed to high, stopping frequently to scrape down the sides of the blender. (It's a stiff mixture, so if you're not using a high-speed blender, you may need to stop a couple of times to let the motor cool down.) Then blend on high speed until as smooth as possible, 2 to 5 minutes, adding water a tablespoon at a time until you have the consistency you want. Season to taste with more salt and pepper. You may need to add a lot more salt; add it ¼ teaspoon at a time, though.

5  At this point, you may put the sauce through a chinois or extra-fine sieve to make it utterly smooth. I can't stand that extra step, but I feel duty-bound to mention it.

6  In a large pot, cover the macaroni with cold water by 2 inches. Season with salt; 1 tablespoon per gallon is the standard proportion. (If you like, you can add a little oil to keep the water from boiling over; I spray the surface of the water with vegetable cooking spray.) Bring to a boil over high heat, stirring, and cook, stirring occasionally, until the macaroni is just tender (the timing will vary by brand).

7  Ladle out ½ cup of the pasta cooking water. Drain the macaroni well, then return it to the pot.

8  Add the sauce and cook for about a minute, stirring, until the macaroni is evenly coated with sauce. Thin with pasta water as needed. Serve.

# NOTES

Until I found this recipe, I always thought that russet potatoes were the smooth, thin-skinned red kind. Doesn't "russet" mean "brownish red"? Ignoring the fact that red potatoes aren't a bit brownish, I always used new potatoes whenever a recipe specified russets.

How wrong I was. When it's applied to potatoes, russet means Idaho, or baking, potatoes. You know: regular potatoes with brown, webby skin. Only russets have the high starch content needed to make the sauce the right consistency. Yukon, red, and "new" potatoes won't work.

# Fusilli with Melted Broccoli Rabe and Vegan Sausage

*Serves 4.*

It seems so bold to say "vegan sausage" right out like that. A fake ingredient? Yet if I were to say just "sausage," vegans would jump all over me. Anyway, this is one recipe where vegan sausage works great. **We've got to have *something* extra if we can't have Parmesan.** As long as you treat vegan "meats" as condiments, they won't bother anyone.

Does broccoli rabe have any flaws? Maybe one: You can start out with a bunch the size of a wastebasket and end up with about enough to put into a thimble-sized wastebasket. Like spinach, broccoli rabe shrinks waaaay down as it cooks. This is an asset when it comes to pasta: Instead of a green vegetable, you will have a deep-green sauce that will coat the pasta instead of clumping at the bottom.

**4 tablespoons vegetable oil, plus a little more for the cooked pasta**

**2 bunches broccoli rabe (about 2 pounds), chopped into 1-inch pieces**

**Salt to taste**

**2 garlic cloves, minced**

**½ teaspoon red pepper flakes, or to taste**

**4 ounces fresh vegan sausage (I use Gimme Lean)**

**1 pound fusilli or similar-sized pasta**

1   Heat 2 tablespoons of the oil in a large lidded skillet or saucepan. Meanwhile, rinse and drain the broccoli rabe, but not obsessively; you want to leave a little water on the leaves.

2   When the oil shimmers, add the broccoli rabe to the pan and give it a big stir. (An annoying job because there's so much of it, but do your best.) Sprinkle some salt over it. Stir in the garlic and red pepper flakes, cover the pan, and cook for 20 minutes, stirring

occasionally. Meanwhile, cook and drain your pasta, stirring in a little oil so it won't clump.

3   Also meanwhile, cook your sausage: Cut that ¼-pound hunk into pieces that are ½ inch or smaller. (We're basically using this as seasoning, not trying to persuade Dave that he's eating real sausage.)

4   Heat a large skillet and add the remaining 2 tablespoons oil. When it shimmers, scatter in the sausage pieces. Cook until well browned and crusty, stirring frequently. This will take at least 10 minutes.

5   After the broccoli rabe has cooked for 20 minutes, use a spoon to press a piece of it against the side of the pan. If it smooshes easily, it's ready; if not, cook it for a few more minutes.

6   When the broccoli rabe is perfectly soft, dump in the drained pasta and the cooked sausage. Toss the mixture well (I use tongs for this). See how the broccoli rabe is greening up the pasta? Broccoli rabe is so juicy that you don't need to add any liquid to the sauce.

7   That's it!

# AS LONG AS YOU TREAT VEGAN "MEATS" AS CONDIMENTS, THEY WON'T BOTHER ANYONE.

# Vegan Lasagna

You can make perfectly good vegan lasagna quite easily — or as easily as you make regular lasagna, anyway. I recently made it with mushrooms and spinach, and it was fine. **But isn't part of eating lasagna the fun of *finding* things in it?** Things like meatballs or shrimp or sausage? Exclamation points, sort of? Not every bite needs to contain a treat, but some of the bites do. Otherwise, the lasagna will seem too uniform and side-dish-y.

This is where I bring in Gimme Lean Meatless Veggie Sausage. Gimme Lean comes in tubes, like Jimmy Dean. (Get it?) It's one of the most common vegan foods that supermarkets carry, if they carry any vegan items. You'll generally find it hanging out at the fresh tofu section, which — at least around here — is usually located in the produce section. Because these things are "fresh," I guess. As of this writing, there are two varieties: beef-flavored and sausage-flavored. I've never tried the beef, but I often use the sausage.

A lot of people who won't eat TVP ("too processed!") will eat Gimme Lean because it's "fresh." Well, kind of. Luckily, the taste of sausage is easy to duplicate with proper seasoning. Gimme Lean's texture is slightly troubling, but that's easy to fix. You just fry the hell out of it.

The rest of this recipe is pretty basic, although — like many vegan entrées — it requires a few more steps than regular lasagna. So I won't tell anyone if you use purchased pasta sauce. I also won't tell you whether I do or not. ●

4 tablespoons vegetable oil

4 ounces fresh vegan sausage (I use Gimme Lean)

8 to 10 ounces white or cremini mushrooms, trimmed and sliced

Salt and freshly ground pepper to taste

4 cups tomato-based pasta sauce

10 to 12 "no-boil" lasagna strips (aren't these the *best*?)

1 batch Béchamel/Velouté Sauce (page 181)

3 cups any chopped, cooked green vegetable, seasoned with salt and pepper (I generally use broccoli or asparagus)

1 container Kite Hill Ricotta

1   Preheat the oven to 375°F, with a rack in the upper third. Grease a 9-by-13-inch baking pan or a dedicated lasagna dish.

2   Heat 2 tablespoons of the oil in a 10- or 12-inch skillet over medium-high heat. Flatten the sausage into rough patties about ¼ inch thick. (It doesn't matter how many patties; you'll be cutting them up.) When the oil is hot, put in the patties, flattening them a little more with a wide spatula. Cook for 4 to 5 minutes, until the bottoms of the patties are brown and crisp. Flip the patties and give the tops the same treatment.

3   Cut the patties into ½-inch pieces. Any bigger, and they'll give away the secret. Wipe out the skillet. Put in the remaining 2 tablespoons oil and heat it. When it shimmers, add the sliced mushrooms. Sprinkle salt and pepper over them and give them a few big stirs. Then, stirring occasionally, cook the mushrooms until the liquid they exude at first has been reabsorbed into them. They should be good and brown.

4   Put a dollop of tomato sauce — about ⅓ cup — on the bottom of the prepared baking dish. Use a rubber spatula to spread it thinly over the surface. Put 3 lasagna noodles over the bottom of the pan, arranging them according to the package directions. Spread about one quarter of the white sauce over the noodles. Spread half the green vegetable, half the veggie sausage, and half the mushrooms over the white sauce. Dollop random spoonfuls of pasta sauce — maybe ⅔ cup — over the top.

5   Arrange another 3 noodles over the vegetables. Scatter the rest of the vegetables, sausage bits, and mushrooms evenly over the noodles. Cover with the other half of the white sauce. Dollop ⅔ cup of pasta sauce over the white sauce.

6   One more layer of noodles! Spread the reserved 1 cup white sauce over them to cover the top as best you can. Spoon the rest of the pasta sauce randomly over the white sauce, then flick marble-sized bits of the "ricotta" all over the sauces.

7   Bake for about 30 minutes, until the lasagna is bubbling and the "ricotta" has browned. (It won't really melt.) Let the lasagna cool for 10 to 15 minutes before you cut it. Please. It needs time to settle down.

# Panfried Dumplings
## *(Pot Stickers)*

*Makes 24 pot stickers. The traditional appetizer serving is 4 to 6 per person, but I've seen people eat way more than that as a main course.*

**I like to begin all recipes for panfried dumplings by reminding people that I once ate thirty-six of them at a sitting.** And that was back when I still cooked with pork! I could probably eat seventy-two of the vegan kind.

Five-spice tofu is precooked — baked, usually — and adds a meaty note you can't get with regular tofu. It's becoming more widely available, even in my 3,500-person town.

You totally need a lidded nonstick skillet for these. Don't say I didn't warn you!

**DUMPLINGS**

1¼ cups finely diced cabbage

½ cup grated carrot

½ cup finely diced five-spice tofu

2 scallions, minced, with some green

2 tablespoons minced garlic

1 tablespoon soy sauce

2 teaspoons Asian sesame oil

½ teaspoon granulated sugar

¼ teaspoon salt, or to taste

½ teaspoon freshly ground pepper, or to taste

¼ teaspoon Accent (optional)

2 teaspoons cornstarch

24 packaged round dumpling wrappers (keep tightly wrapped until ready to use)

**DIPPING SAUCE**

2 tablespoons soy sauce, or to taste

2 teaspoons Asian sesame oil

2 teaspoons rice vinegar

1 scallion, minced

2 tablespoons vegetable oil

1  **Dumplings:** Toss together the cabbage, carrot, tofu, scallions, and garlic in a large bowl. Whisk together the soy sauce, sesame oil, sugar, salt, pepper, Accent, and corn-starch in a small bowl. Pour this over the vegetables and toss extremely well. (This filling can be prepared up to 2 hours in advance. Toss it well just before using.)

2 Before you make the pot stickers, it helps to watch a couple of videos on YouTube, and make sure to put the package directions where you can easily see them. When you're ready to start, clear a big space for the following doin's:

- Line one large rimmed baking sheet with parchment paper. Line a second with paper towels, or be stingy like me and use newspaper covered with a single layer of paper towels.
- Fill a ramekin with water.
- Dampen a couple of paper towels; you'll use them to cover the unwrapped dumpling wrappers.

3 **Filling:** Using the package directions as your guide, place a scant tablespoon of filling in the center of a wrapper. Dip a fingertip into the water and use it to "paint" the edges of the wrapper. Fold the wrapper in half and pinch the edges together. Pleat the pot sticker as directed on YouTube or the package. Put the finished pot sticker on the lined baking sheet. Repeat with the remaining dumplings, making sure that — like quarrelsome kids in the back seat — they don't touch one another. What a mess they are if I'm the one making them!

4 **Dipping Sauce:** Take a quick break and whisk together the soy sauce, sesame oil, vinegar, and scallion. Set aside.

5 To panfry the dumplings, heat the vegetable oil in a large nonstick pan with a lid over medium-high heat. When the oil is shimmering, add the dumplings in batches, doing your best not to let them touch each other. Panfry, gently swirling the pan, until the bottoms of the dumplings are golden, 3 to 5 minutes.

6 Holding the lid of the pan in one hand, carefully pour ¼ cup water into the pan. Clap that lid down! Steam the dumplings for 2 minutes. Remove the lid. Most of the water should have evaporated. If there's a little remaining in the pan, it will soon vanish. Continue panfrying the dumplings, swirling occasionally, until the bottoms have crisped up and any remaining water is gone. Transfer the dumplings to the paper towel–covered baking sheet.

7 When all the dumplings are done, transfer them to wherever you want — a serving dish, a single plate just for you, or whatever. Serve with the dipping sauce.

# Jambalaya ------▷ *Serves 6.*

Simple but effective. And although this is a long ingredient list, it all pulls together pretty quickly. This is also a perfect example of what vegan sausage can do for a recipe.

Filé powder is one of those ingredients whose creation it's hard to imagine. How did the Choctaw Indians figure out that dried ground sassafrass leaves made such a great seasoning? Filé works as a thickener, too, but the jambalaya will be thick enough without it. I love the taste, but it's your call. ●

½ bag (4 ounces) Butler Soy Curls (see page 20)

2 cups water, vegetable stock, homemade (page 177) or store-bought, or vegan chicken-flavored stock

1 tablespoon soy sauce

2 tablespoons vegetable oil, plus more as needed

1 large onion, sliced

1 tablespoon Creole seasoning

3 vegan sausages (about 10 ounces) — andouille, if possible — cut in half the long way and sliced ½ inch thick

1 green and 1 red bell pepper, chopped

2 celery stalks, sliced ¼ inch thick

4 garlic cloves, minced

1½ teaspoons smoked paprika

1 teaspoon salt, or more to taste

1 teaspoon freshly ground pepper, or more to taste

½ teaspoon red pepper flakes, or to taste

½ teaspoon hot sauce, or to taste

1 teaspoon filé powder (optional)

One 15- or 16-ounce can crushed tomatoes

1¼ cups long-grain white rice

2 cups vegetable stock, homemade (page 177) or store-bought

1 Put the soy curls in a medium bowl. Bring the water or stock to a boil. Pour over the soy curls and add the soy sauce. Let soak for 10 minutes, then drain the curls and press them hard to extract as much liquid as possible.

2 Heat the oil in a large, heavy pot over medium-high heat. When it shimmers, add the onion and cook for 5 minutes, stirring frequently, or until it begins to soften. Add the Creole seasoning and sausage, stirring to coat everything with the seasoning. Add the bell

peppers, celery, and garlic. Lower the heat to medium and cook, stirring frequently, for 10 to 15 minutes, until the peppers and celery have softened.

3  Stir in the smoked paprika, salt, pepper, red pepper flakes, hot sauce, and filé powder, if using. Cook, stirring, for 2 to 3 minutes. Add the crushed tomatoes, rice, and vegetable stock and bring the mixture to a boil. Lower the heat and simmer for 20 to 25 minutes, stirring occasionally, until the rice is cooked through and the liquid has been absorbed. Check the seasoning and add more salt and pepper if necessary.

HOW DID THE CHOCTAW INDIANS FIGURE OUT THAT DRIED GROUND SASSAFRASS LEAVES MADE SUCH A GREAT SEASONING?

# Buffalo'd Soy Curls

*Serves 2 to 3, or makes 4 sandwiches.*

Let's see, let's see. Where to start with Soy Curls? **How to make you realize that no matter how unprepossessing they seem, you've got to have them?** Will the previous recipe do it? Or should I remind you how much you've been missing Buffalo chicken wings now that you're a vegan, and tell you that these are just as good and much easier to eat?

David and I have often eaten an entire batch of this by ourselves, but since the recipe isn't effortless, you can stretch it to make sandwiches and serve more people. ●

One 8-ounce bag Butler Soy Curls

5 garlic cloves, unpeeled (for easier fishing-out) and smashed

4 cups vegetable stock, homemade (page 177) or store-bought, salted to taste

¼ cup all-purpose flour

¼ cup cornmeal

1 teaspoon chili powder (any kind except super-hot)

1 teaspoon salt

1 teaspoon freshly ground pepper

½ teaspoon Accent (optional)

¼ cup vegetable oil

2 tablespoons store-bought vegan butter (homemade might separate)

¾ cup hot sauce, such as Tabasco or Frank's

Celery and carrot sticks

Vegan ranch or blue-cheese dressing (see Note)

1   Preheat the oven to 425°F, with a rack in the middle.

2   Put the soy curls into a medium heat-proof bowl with the smashed garlic cloves. Bring the stock to a boil and pour it over the curls. Let soak for 10 minutes.

3   Meanwhile, combine all the dry ingredients in a bowl.

4   Drain the soy curls. Give the colander ten to twelve brisk shakes to get out even more water. Then smush the curls down in the colander with a spoon or your hand (or hands), pressing hard so as to squeeze out as much liquid as possible. Fish out the garlic. Wipe out the soaking bowl with a paper towel. Dump the soy curls back into the bowl, sprinkle in the dry ingredients, and toss the curls as thoroughly as possible. Your

goal is to have no dry ingredients left in the bottom of the bowl.

5   Pour the oil onto a large rimmed baking sheet. Arrange the curls on the sheet in a single layer. Bake for 10 minutes. With a wide spatula, turn the curls over, to help them brown evenly. Bake for another 10 minutes. Once again, turn the curls over; then bake for a final 5 to 10 minutes, until they are well browned.

6   Heat a large skillet over medium heat. When it's hot, melt the vegan butter, then whisk in the hot sauce. Add the baked soy curls and stir over low heat until they're all well glazed with sauce.

7   Put out a pile of napkins. Serve the soy curls and carrot and celery sticks with the dressing alongside. You might want to put out toothpicks as well: easier dipping with the smaller pieces.

*NOTE*

So far, I haven't found a good blue cheese dressing because I haven't found a vegan blue cheese that I like. I've found Dr. Cow's Aged Cashew & Blue Green Algae Cheese, but that's not at ALL the same thing. Maybe something blue-ish will be out there by the time you read this; if not, use ranch dressing.

If you can't find good vegan ranch dressing where you live, here's the recipe I use. I'm sorry about the dried dill and garlic powders, but they're part of what makes ranch dressing *ranchy*.

## Ranch Dressing

*Makes about 1 cup.*

1 cup vegan mayonnaise (I like Vegenaise)
1 tablespoon chopped fresh parsley
½ teaspoon garlic powder

½ teaspoon dried dill
¼ teaspoon freshly ground pepper, or to taste
About ¼ cup "original" soy milk

In a small bowl, whisk together the mayo, parsley, and seasonings. Whisk in the milk a tablespoon at a time until you've achieved the consistency you want. It's best to chill this dressing for at least 2 hours before you serve it.

# The Sloppiest Joes

*Serves 4.*

It's embarrassing to give you such a basic recipe, but this is a good example of how to use textured vegetable protein (TVP) effectively. **While we don't want to be tricking our loved ones outright, I have no problem with their believing that a vegan dish has meat in it.** With sloppy joes, beef contributes little besides texture, so why not go straight to texture?

Using mushrooms instead of beans makes this recipe a little more grown-up than some. But if there are mushroom haters under your roof, a rinsed and drained 15-ounce can of kidney or pinto beans will work fine. ●

1 cup TVP or TSP granules (see page 22), preferably beef- or sausage-flavored

1 cup boiling water (or vegetable stock, homemade [page 177] or store-bought, if you're using unflavored TVP)

3 tablespoons vegetable oil, plus more if needed

1 red bell pepper, chopped

1 medium onion, chopped

4 garlic cloves, minced

8 ounces white or cremini mushrooms, trimmed and sliced

¾ teaspoon smoked paprika

½ teaspoon ground cumin

One 15-ounce can tomato sauce, or 15 ounces homemade sauce

2 tablespoons soy sauce

2 tablespoons ketchup or barbecue sauce

1 tablespoon light brown sugar

½ teaspoon liquid smoke

¼ teaspoon cayenne, or to taste

Salt and freshly ground pepper to taste

4 hamburger buns

1  Put the TVP granules in a small heatproof bowl and pour the boiling water (or stock) over them. Stir well, then let the granules rehydrate for 10 minutes.

2  Heat a large, heavy skillet over medium-high heat. Add the oil. When it shimmers, add the bell pepper and onion. Cook, stirring frequently, until the pepper and onion are beginning to brown, about 10 minutes; add more oil if you need to. Stir in the garlic and cook for another couple of minutes.

3   Add the mushrooms and cook, stirring frequently, for 10 minutes or so, until they have softened and given up their liquid. Stir in the TVP and spices and cook for another 2 to 3 minutes, until the mixture thickens slightly. Once again, add more oil if the mixture sticks.

4   Add the tomato sauce, soy sauce, ketchup or barbecue sauce, brown sugar, liquid smoke, and cayenne. Lower the heat to medium-low and cook the mixture for 10 more minutes, stirring frequently. Season with salt and pepper to taste.

5   Serve on the hamburger buns.

SLOPPIEST JOES

# Help Me, Lord —
# Vegan Burgers

*Makes 18 to 20 burgers.*

"Have you ever heard of goober burgers?" my father-in-law, Loyd, used to ask the servers anytime he went out for lunch. Goober burgers were hamburgers with peanut butter on top. It seemed that Loydo (as everyone called him) had tasted a goober burger once, somewhere, and the experience had been powerful. As my husband said, "The fact that there were goober burgers on the menu would not be enough to prevent my father from asking if they had ever heard of goober burgers."

I often remembered goober burgers as I began, reluctantly, to scale the immense garbage heap that is vegan burgers. Immense, and freighted with so... much... emotion. And *so... many... recipes.*

**"You could call them 'sandwich disks,' to lower people's expectations," suggested David.** I tried burgers with chickpeas or black beans as the base. Burgers coated in bread crumbs, for the requisite crust. Burgers where the main ingredient was eggplant puree and all the other ingredients were included solely to disguise the eggplant. Burgers with molasses to make them look more burger-y. And all these burgers meant to replace a single ingredient: ground beef.

So what's good about ground beef? The taste, obviously. That's the easy part. The charred, crusty exterior. And, perhaps even more important, the right texture. Pile on enough condiments and the taste will hardly matter, but no one wants a burger that smooshes down like paste when you bite into it. People want to *chew.* And that meant I needed... peanut butter.

No, wait! I meant wheat gluten. Not a lot: just enough to offer what some call "tooth resistance." Wheat gluten is like a live volcano: You need to use it sparingly.

What else? Brown rice, cooked al dente, provides a convincing texture. But *black* rice provides the same texture and a much more realistic color. It also chars up beautifully.

And then a lot of ground mushrooms for umami and juiciness. And some added fat. You can't make a good burger with all lean ingredients.

**"They're not better than regular burgers, but they're just as good," reported Judge David, who has often been seen grabbing one of them from the freezer to use for lunch.** Also, an omnivore asked me for the recipe. If that doesn't prove it!

Please read the recipe all the way through before you leap in. This is a somewhat involved procedure that makes 1,000 burgers — well, 18. Of course you can halve the recipe, but if you make the full amount, you'll have plenty of extra patties (horrible word) for the freezer. And while there's a lot going on here, I swear it's not as complicated as some of the recipes I considered. ●

7 tablespoons vegetable oil

2 large onions, chopped

2 pounds white or cremini mushrooms, trimmed and sliced

4 cups cooked black (preferably) or brown rice (use vegetable stock, homemade [page 177] or store-bought, not water)

⅓ cup soy sauce

¼ cup tomato paste

¼ cup ketchup

3 tablespoons white miso

1½ tablespoons dried basil

2 teaspoons freshly ground pepper

1 teaspoon dried thyme

1 teaspoon liquid smoke

½ teaspoon Accent (optional)

3 cups vital wheat gluten (see page 26)

1   Heat a large skillet over medium-high heat, then add ¼ cup of the oil. When the oil shimmers, add the onions and cook over medium heat, stirring frequently, until well browned, about 15 minutes. Transfer the onions to a big bowl. Set the skillet aside; don't bother to wash it.

2   Working in batches, puree the mushrooms in a food processor.

3   Add the mushrooms to the big bowl. Then add everything else except the wheat gluten and mix well with your hands. When everything is blended, sprinkle the wheat

gluten evenly over the mix. *Immediately and vigorously* mix in the gluten, again using your hands. Gluten sets up almost instantly when it comes into contact with moisture, so work as fast — and as thoroughly — as you can. The mixture will very quickly change texture.

4   Theoretically, prebaking the patties will make the burgers hold together better. In practice, it doesn't make a ton of difference. So what I do is to panfry the burgers I need for supper that night. After supper, I shape the rest into patties and bake them at 350°F for 20 minutes, then freeze them "for another time."

5   Avast, me hearties! Wipe out the skillet with a paper towel. Heat it again over medium-high heat, then add the remaining 3 tablespoons oil. When it shimmers, gently set the patties you're making for supper into the skillet. Gently, I say! Because there's one thing I haven't mentioned until now: These burgers fall apart easily. It doesn't matter — the browned crumbles taste even better than the burgers — but I'm assuming you'd like to serve burgers, not a pile of crumbles. So once the burgers are in the skillet, be careful with them.

6   Cook the burgers until the undersides are dark brown and crispy. Flip them carefully and repeat the procedure. Serve in whatever way is popular in your family. And if anyone says, "But where's the cheese," slap that person.

## NOTE

The uncooked burger mixture will keep for a week in the refrigerator and for up to a year in the freezer. Leftover cooked patties can be reheated in the microwave; you don't have to sauté them. I suppose you could try these on the grill, but I've always done them in a skillet. If you want to grill them, I suggest making a small test burger so you know what you'll be dealing with. And grease the grill very well.

A FEW LIFE-CHANGING SAUCES

— — — — — —

It's not fair that there are so few vegan options for getting a meal onto the table quickly if there's nothing defrostable in the freezer. You can't do the "Oh, let's just have chicken again" thing. Pasta with plain red sauce is disappointing. You can't even have scrambled eggs, and PB&Js are so drab. *Why, God? Why hast thou chosen us to bear this burden?*

But there are some sauces that are so good that you could get away with serving them on strips of paper bag. Served over pasta, or even with plain white rice, they make a fully honorable main course. You might even be able to make them the focus of a satay-type dip-a-thon. And of course they work beautifully as plain old dips for crudités or chips. Or, if there aren't any vegetables in the house, maybe you could just lick them off your finger, as some of us have been known to do.

— — — — — —

# Intense Peanut Sauce

*Makes about 1½ cups, enough for 1 pound of pasta or any amount of raw vegetables, depending on how you ration it.*

This is adapted from a long-ago Chinese cookbook by Irene Kuo. Its name is actually Odd-Flavored Sauce, but my editor made me change it. She seemed to believe that **oddness isn't a good selling point.** What's that all about? Anyway, the recipe is for a peanut-based sauce so hyped up with flavor that it was supposed to be used in tiny dabs on plain chicken. With our modern jaded palates, we can handle larger amounts of it. And we will!

Serve over pasta, stir into rice, or use as a dip.

**LIQUID INGREDIENTS**

¼ cup peanut butter, whisked with ¼ cup boiling water until smooth

½ cup soy sauce, or more to taste

¼ cup red wine vinegar or rice vinegar

¼ cup Asian sesame oil

¼ cup granulated sugar

**SEASONING INGREDIENTS**

¾ cup peanut or vegetable oil

5 scallions, minced (include a lot of the green part)

¼ cup grated fresh ginger

4 large garlic cloves, minced

1 teaspoon red pepper flakes, or to taste

1 **Liquid ingredients:** Put your PB-and-water blend in a medium bowl. Whisk in everything else.

2 **Seasoning ingredients:** Heat the oil in a large skillet over high heat. When it shimmers, scatter in the rest of the ingredients and stir-fry this mixture for 20 seconds. Then immediately scrape it over the liquid ingredients and whisk well. Check the seasoning, adding more soy sauce and/or red pepper if you've a mind to. Done!

# Roasted Eggplant Puree

*Makes about 2 cups.*

**Eggplant puree: Is there a worse name?** Yes! "Foot puree." But we can't always be thinking about names.

A while ago, David got a *New Yorker* assignment to write about the food on Singapore Airlines. I know — he should get hardship pay, right? One chef told David that they use eggplant puree for everything, adding ingredients like tahini, lemon zest, and chopped tomatoes, depending on what it's accompanying. "You have the base, you can go in any direction you want," the chef said. "You want to finish it with Moroccan? Indian? French?"

I'm happy to go in any of those directions, although I might have to have a few meals at that chef's restaurant to help me decide which is my favorite . . . ●

3 medium eggplants

3 tablespoons olive oil

Salt and freshly ground pepper to taste

3 garlic cloves, unpeeled

3 tablespoons fresh lemon juice, plus more to taste

3 tablespoons fresh basil leaves, minced

1 teaspoon paprika (smoked paprika's a nice touch)

1   Preheat the oven to 400°F, with a rack in the middle. Grease a large rimmed baking sheet. (This recipe won't work nearly as well if you use parchment paper.)

2   Split the eggplants in half lengthwise. Brush the cut sides with oil, using 1 table-spoon total. Salt and pepper them with

abandon. Transfer them cut side up to the baking sheet, along with the garlic cloves.

3   Bake the vegetables for 30 minutes, at which point you should take out the garlic. If the eggplant flesh (another bad name) is absolutely soft and tender and you have no trouble mushing it around with the point of a

knife, take the eggplants out of the oven too. If they haven't quite reached that stage, cook them until they have.

4   Let the eggplants cool until you can safely handle them. Then drain away any eggplant juice. Scoop the insides out with a spoon and put the mush into a food processor or blender. Don't let any flecks of eggplant skin, seed clumps, or even stray seeds get in there if you can help it.

5   Squeeze the garlic cloves out of their skins and add the roasted garlic to the eggplant. Add the remaining 2 tablespoons olive oil, the lemon juice, basil, and paprika. Process or blend the eggplant until it's a smooth puree. Taste for seasoning.

6   So now you have about 2 cups of eggplant puree. . . .

## What should you do with it?

- Side dish! Add to tomato sauce with some red pepper flakes for a quick pasta!
- Add vegetable stock (and whatever else you want) for a quick soup!

How I love bullet points.

- Cover plates with it before adding the entrée, assuming that the entrée isn't something like pancakes!
- Make it into a great dip that can *also* be a side dish (see page 55)!

# Pipián Sauce

*Makes about 2 cups.*

This is adapted from a recipe of food editor Sam Sifton's that ran in the *New York Times* magazine. It takes about an hour to make, but you end up with a pot of spicy golden-brown sauce that's interesting enough to cancel out plain baked tofu. And, as we all know, that's very hard to pull off. (This makes a great enchilada sauce too.) ●

8 dried chiles de árbol

2 cups boiling water

3 tablespoons vegetable oil

3 plum tomatoes

1 medium onion, sliced

3 garlic cloves, unpeeled

½ cup hulled raw unsalted pumpkin seeds (pepitas)

½ cup unsalted peanuts

⅓ cup hulled sesame seeds

1 teaspoon ground cumin

¼ teaspoon ground cinnamon

¼ teaspoon ground cloves

¼ teaspoon ground allspice

1 canned chipotle pepper in adobo

1 cup vegetable stock, homemade (page 177) or store-bought

1 tablespoon packed light brown sugar

1 teaspoon salt, or to taste

1 tablespoon balsamic or red wine vinegar

1   Heat a large, heavy skillet over high heat for 5 minutes. Add the chiles and toast them for 5 minutes, stirring with a wooden spoon until they've darkened a shade or two; do not burn. Transfer the chiles to a heatproof bowl. Cover them with the boiling water and let 'em soak while you go on to the next step.

2   Put the skillet back over medium-high heat. (If you have a stovetop vent, use it.) Add 1 tablespoon of the oil and swirl it around to cover the bottom of the skillet. Add the tomatoes, onion, and garlic and cook, stirring frequently, for about 10 minutes, until the vegetables are charred. Transfer them to a plate. When the garlic's cool enough to touch, peel away the charred skin.

3   Now set the skillet over medium-low heat and add the pepitas, peanuts, and sesame seeds. Stirring constantly, cook these guys for 3 to 4 minutes, until they darken and

# INTERESTING ENOUGH TO CANCEL OUT PLAIN BAKED TOFU.

smell toasted. Put them into a small heat-proof bowl and stir in the spices.

4   Put the toasted chiles and their soaking liquid, the tomatoes, onion, garlic, nut-seed mixture, and the chipotle pepper in a blender. Puree until as smooth as possible.

5   Heat the remaining 2 tablespoons oil in a large, heavy pot. When the oil is shimmering, add the puree, which will spit and sputter angrily. Cook the mixture over medium-low heat, stirring and scraping continuously. (It will remain noisy.) Whisk in the stock, then add the brown sugar, salt, and vinegar. Cook the mixture, stirring frequently, for 15 minutes. It should be about the thickness of ketchup. Remove from the heat.

6   The sauce will improve if chilled overnight before serving, and it will keep for up to 10 days in the refrigerator.

# Almond-Chipotle Sauce

*Makes about 2½ cups.*

**And now a miraculous dream of a concoction** — smooth, creamy (except for the almonds), and indescribable. Omnivores would serve this with fish or chicken. I serve it alongside some kind of rice and a big bunch of steamed, grilled, or raw vegetables. The almonds give the sauce some protein, meaning that the rice and vegetables can be served with it as a main course on a summer night. The vegetables give me plenty of places to hide the sauce so that no one can see how much of it I'm eating. ●

**4 ounces sliced almonds**

**One 16-ounce jar vegan mayonnaise (I use Vegenaise)**

**3 canned chipotle peppers in adobo, plus more to taste**

**2 tablespoons smoked paprika, or more to taste**

**2 garlic cloves**

**3 tablespoons fresh lemon juice, or more to taste**

**Salt and freshly ground pepper to taste**

1 Preheat the oven to 300°F, with a rack in the middle.

2 Put the almonds in a shallow baking dish and toast them in the oven for 10 minutes, stirring after the first 5 of those minutes. Let cool completely.

3 Put the mayo, chipotles, paprika, garlic, and lemon juice in a blender or food processor. Process for about a minute, until you have a smooth, bright-orange sauce. Check the seasoning. Another chipotle? More lemon juice or paprika? Salt and/or pepper? It's up to you.

4 Once you've perfected the taste, transfer the sauce to a medium bowl and stir in the cooled almonds. Let the sauce rest for 30 minutes before you serve it. Store it in the refrigerator in an easily accessible place so you won't forget it's there. It will keep for up to 10 days.

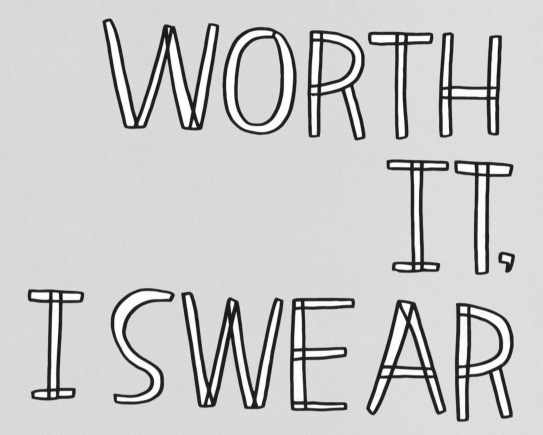

– – – – – –

When I started playing hockey, I was shocked at how much I'd have to master before it became fun. (The word "master" is approximate.) Okay, it made sense that I'd have to get used to wearing hockey skates, but then I had to learn to skate backward? And once I could do that, I had to get used to skating with a stick? And if that wasn't enough, I actually had to use the stick? Actually aim the puck in a specific direction? Skate faster? Wait, now we're doing *crossovers*? And all this when all I really cared about was getting through the practice without throwing up?

Sometimes vegan cooking feels the same. *What? I have to make my own butter?* Of course you don't have to. You don't have to grow your own tomatoes, either. But there are times when the extra work is worth it. If you can't get through the holidays without shortbread — if Christmas shortbread means a lot to you, as it does to me — you'll be much happier making it with homemade vegan butter.

Taste versus time: That's the main issue when you're cooking vegan. When taste is supremely important, come here. And be grateful that I decided there was no need to make your own tofu.

– – – – – –

## The Densest, Richest, Flavorful-est
# Vegetable Stock

*Makes about 2 quarts.*

All foodies agree: **Stock is where it starts.** You won't get anywhere without a decent homemade stock in your freezer. It must take a long time to make and it must involve many ingredients that have been roasted to a deep brown. ●

2 tablespoons vegetable oil

2 large onions, unpeeled but ends trimmed, cut into 1-inch chunks

2 large celery stalks, trimmed and sliced ½ inch thick

2 large carrots, scrubbed, trimmed, and coarsely chopped

3 garlic cloves, chopped

8 ounces fresh mushrooms, trimmed and sliced

14 cups water

1 ounce dried porcini mushrooms, rinsed to remove grit

One 4-inch piece dried kombu or ½ teaspoon Accent

12 large sprigs fresh parsley

2 bay leaves

1 tablespoon whole black peppercorns

1 teaspoon dried thyme

2 tablespoons soy sauce

Salt (optional)

1 Heat the oil in a large, heavy pot. When the oil shimmers, add the onions, celery, and carrots and cook over medium heat, stirring, until they just begin to brown. Scatter in the garlic and fresh mushrooms, stir well, and cook for another 5 minutes or so.

2 Pour the water over the vegetables. Add the dried porcini, kombu or Accent, parsley, bay leaves, peppercorns, thyme, and soy sauce. (You can salt the stock later; the soy sauce provides umami.) Bring the liquid to a boil. Turn the heat down so that the stock is just simmering and simmer for 1½ hours, or until the carrots and celery are completely tender and the liquid has reduced by about half.

3 Use a fine-mesh sieve to strain the stock into a large bowl. You can reuse the dried porcini if you want, but the rest of the vegetables should be tossed. Add salt if you want, keeping in mind that soup (and other) recipes usually call for their own salt. Cool the stock to room temperature, then refrigerate it, covered, for up to a week or freeze it for up to 3 months.

# Vegan Butter ------▷ *Makes about 1 pound.*

"So I served this cake to my friends, and none of them guessed that it was vegan!"

Maybe not. I bet, though, that a lot of them noticed there was no butter in it. Because butter is what makes most baked goods sing, and it has no equal. Not in taste, not in mouthfeel, not in the texture it imparts. Anyone who knows butter will instantly recognize its absence.

Why do so many vegan food writers ignore this fact? **When they write recipes calling for vegan margarine, which — impossibly — tastes even more horrible than regular horrible margarine, why don't they immediately beg our forgiveness?**

At this moment, the only halfway decent vegan margarine is Smart Balance. Not Earth Balance Buttery Sticks (an icky name), but Smart Balance Original. It doesn't taste offensively fake, and it has a low melting point, so it's not like chewing a crayon. Unfortunately, it's not listed as vegan because — get this! — the Vitamin D it contains is made with lanolin from sheep's wool. I can live with this, but you may not be able to.

Arguably better than Smart Balance is your own homemade vegan butter. It doesn't taste as perfect as real butter, but it imparts the same texture as butter. For things like piecrust and shortbread, that can be important, or at least as important as matching butter's texture can ever be.

**I realize that asking you to make your own butter substitute is like asking you to make your own shoes.** But it's easy to make. Remember, though, that it's specifically for baking, not sautéing. And you can't let it sit out at room temperature for too long, or it may start to separate. We're not working with industrial-grade stabilizers here. (Don't turn the page! This recipe is worth it!)

Now, what shall we name the baby? A long time ago, there was a movie called *Lorenzo's Oil* that portrayed a desperate couple's search for a medicine

# LET'S JUST HEAVE A SIGH AND CALL IT VEGAN BUTTER.

to cure their invalid son, Lorenzo. To me, this title suggested that little Lorenzo himself had been the source of the oil. No "Ann's Butter," in other words. And not a veganish name like Vutter.

Let's just heave a sigh and call it vegan butter. It's the closest we'll come to the real thing at this point until they invent a perfect substitute.

Clear some space in your freezer for whatever butter container you'll be using: wooden butter molds (yeah, right), plastic butter molds (I use these), or an ice cube tray, preferably made of silicone. The container doesn't matter much, since you'll always need to weigh the butter before you add it to a recipe. ●

½ cup "original" soy milk (4 ounces or 122 grams)

½ teaspoon fresh lemon juice

¾ teaspoon salt

1¼ cups *refined* coconut oil (9.7 ounces or 272 grams)

¼ cup plus 1 teaspoon vegetable oil (neutral olive oil works best; 2 ounces or 59 grams)

2¼ teaspoons soy lecithin granules or soy lecithin powder (10 grams; see page 27)

½ teaspoon xanthan gum (see page 27)

½ *drop* butter essence (optional; see page 16)

1 or 2 drops yellow food coloring (optional; do not use turmeric)

1 Put the milk, lemon juice, and salt into a blender. Pulse the mixture a few times. If it looks curdled, don't worry.

2 Melting the coconut oil is easy, but you'll need to focus. In a small saucepan, over the lowest heat possible, begin melting the oil. When it's about half-melted, take it off the

heat and let it continue melting on its own. You want it as to be as close to room temperature as possible while remaining liquid.

3   Pour the melted coconut oil and the olive oil into the blender along with the lecithin and xanthan gum. Blend for about 2 minutes — at the highest speed if you're using a regular blender; at a medium-low setting if you're using a high-speed one. (An immersion blender also works well for this.) After 1 minute, scrape down the sides of the blender container and then start 'er up again.

4   You only want a tiny hint of butter essence. I squeeze one drop onto a plate and dip the end of a spoon into it. Then I swish the "oiled spoon" around in the blender contents. Better too little than too much! Add the food coloring, if using.

5   If you used a regular blender, quickly pour the mixture into a medium bowl and put the bowl into the freezer. If you used an immersion blender, put the bowl of whipped ingredients into the freezer.

6   No matter how quickly it begins to freeze, the butter mixture is also likely to begin to separate. Check it after it's been freezing for about 10 minutes. If it has started to separate, take it out of the freezer and beat until smooth again. Thereafter, check the butter every 5 minutes and beat until smooth. At a certain point, when the mixture is cold enough, you won't need to do this; the ingredients will have formed a true emulsion and you'll have a beautiful lump of smooth, creamy vegan butter.

7   Stored in an airtight container in the refrigerator, this yellow gold will keep for up to 3 weeks; wrapped in plastic, it can be frozen for up to a year.

# Béchamel/Velouté —
## *The Only White Sauce You'll Ever Need*

*Makes 1 scant quart.*

Perhaps you're wondering why you need a white sauce at all. Well, because it does everything you ask it to except for dancing.

In France, béchamel and velouté are two of the "mother sauces," the five pillars underpinning classic French cuisine. (*Wait — pillars made of sauce? Don't ask so many questions!*) Escoffier invented the category for his 1903 masterwork, *Le Guide Culinaire*. How surprised he would be to know that two hundred years later, people would be making his sauces with soy milk; how even *more* surprised he would be to know that those people refused to eat dairy products for moral reasons. A friend of mine traveling in France was offered some lamb. When she said she was a vegetarian, her host looked puzzled. **"But this is *French* lamb," he protested.**

Luckily it's not our job to persuade the French how to eat. It's only our job to steal whatever useful culinary tricks they possess — and béchamel and velouté are very, very useful. Béchamel is a white sauce made with milk; velouté is a tan sauce made with stock. If you combine them, you get a nuanced sauce capable of standing in for cheese, cream, and many other things that vegans forgo.

Like Cauliflower Cream (page 183), this sauce can handle as many add-ins as you throw at it. Consider it for Lasagna (page 154) and Green Bean Casserole (page 107). ●

1½ cups "original" soy milk

1½ cups vegetable stock, homemade (page 177) or store-bought

1 medium onion, diced

6 tablespoons vegetable oil

½ cup all-purpose flour

½ cup dry white wine (or more vegetable stock)

Salt and freshly ground pepper to taste

# IT DOES EVERYTHING YOU ASK IT TO EXCEPT FOR DANCING.

1 Combine the soy milk and vegetable stock in a medium saucepan and bring to a boil, stirring frequently. Then keep them warm while you make the roux: Stir together the onion and 6 tablespoons of the oil in a large, heavy saucepan over medium-high heat. When the mixture begins to sizzle, add the flour. Cook over medium-low heat, stirring constantly, for 5 minutes. Take the saucepan off the heat.

2 Pour two thirds of the milk-stock mixture into the flour-onion mixture, whisking vigorously. Return the pan to the stove and whisk in the wine (or stock). Over medium heat, still whisking constantly, bring the sauce to a boil. Boil gently, whisking, for 4 to 5 minutes, until the sauce is thick enough to coat a spoon. If it looks too thick to you, thin it out with more of the milk-stock mixture. Season to taste with salt and pepper, not stinting on either.

# Cauliflower Cream —
## *The Other Only White Sauce You'll Ever Want*

*Makes about 1 quart.*

**Cooked foods are very rarely more than the sum of their parts.** Usually they're exactly the sum of their parts, and sometimes the sum turns out negative. Still, I'm constantly fooled by those recipes with two or three ingredients that are supposed to combine so magically that you would never, never believe how simple they were. Whisk together flour and water for amazing peppermint taffy!

So when I heard what a great white sauce you could make with cauliflower, I narrowed my eyes. But it turns out that you *can* make a thick, creamy, and complex-tasting white sauce out of cauliflower, onions, and olive oil. (Plus water and a liberal dose of salt, but they don't really count.) And although I'm *super-*suspicious of low-fat recipes where "you won't even miss the cream," Cauliflower Cream actually tastes rich and creamy. Who woulda thunk it!

Originally I thunk this book should have several white-sauce variants. Now I know that you really need only two: this and Béchamel/Velouté Sauce (page 181). ●

¼ cup olive oil

1 large onion, minced

18 ounces cauliflower florets

1 teaspoon salt, plus more to taste

2½ cups water

A grating or "shake" of nutmeg (optional)

1   Put the oil in a large, heavy pot. Turn the heat to low and add the onion, stirring to coat it with oil. Cover the pot (if you don't have a lid, use foil and put a baking sheet on top of it to help keep steam from escaping) and cook the onion for 15 minutes. It should be just beginning to brown when the time is up, but if it hasn't started browning, that's fine too.

2 Add the cauliflower florets and salt and stir to distribute the salt. Add ½ cup of the water and cover the pot again. Cook the cauliflower over medium-low heat for 20 minutes. Then add the remaining 2 cups water, once again cover the pot, and cook for 20 more minutes. The cauliflower will be falling-apart tender.

3 Using an immersion blender, a regular blender, or a food processor, puree the pot's contents until very smooth. Check the seasoning, adding more salt and a little nutmeg if you want.

## NOTE

I can't say enough good things about this sauce. As you can probably tell, the recipe is extremely adaptable. You could add a cup of vegetable stock and turn the sauce into a creamy cauliflower soup. It makes the basis of a great pasta sauce. You can use it as is in lasagna; it stays creamy when baked. It also freezes well, breaking as it thaws but requiring just a little whisking to turn creamy again.

# *"One Stop Does It All"*
# Yogurt

*Makes 1 quart.*

So many vegan recipes call for unsweetened vegan yogurt, and it's so hard to find! Even health food stores don't carry it all the time. This is probably because it tastes so terrible that the manufacturers know people will only buy the sweetened versions.

It really is awful — nothing like what you'd expect. Luckily, you can make your own lovely vegan yogurt. I bet you're thinking, "How lovely is it that now I have to make my own *yogurt*?" But it's easy, and the results are delicious whether or not you sweeten the yogurt.

**No, you don't need a yogurt maker.** Yes, you need active yogurt cultures. You can get them by adding a dollop of premade yogurt to your own batch, but as I just said, store-bought unsweetened vegan yogurt is hard to track down. So run online and order some vegan yogurt culture! (See page 25.) You stir a pinch into your soy milk mixture, put the mix to bed, and then return in a few hours to find thick, rich, photogenic yogurt.

From then on, you can use a little of the homemade yogurt to start a new batch. Or you can refrigerate the culture indefinitely and use it whenever you want. ●

⅔ cup raw unsalted macadamia nut pieces (3 ounces or 87 grams)

1 quart "original" soy milk (not "unsweetened" and *not* low-fat); no other nondairy milk will work

3 tablespoons unsweetened vegan yogurt, or 1 packet vegan yogurt culture (see page 25) — the quanity meant for 1 quart

1  Take a small saucepan, put the macadamia pieces into it, cover them with water, and bring to a boil. As soon as it boils, lower the heat to a simmer. Cook the nut pieces for 15 to 20 minutes, until they taste "cooked" and no longer feel fibrous when you chew a sample. I wish I could be more specific, but how long this takes will depend on the size of the pieces.

2  When the nuts are ready, drain them well. Put them into a blender, along with 1 cup of the soy milk. (A food processor won't work for this.) Blend like crazy, until the mixture is as smooth as you can get it. Add another cup of soy milk and do the same thing again.

3  Put the nut mixture and the remaining 2 cups soy milk in a heavy saucepan. Turn the heat to low. (If you have an electric stove, you may want to use medium-low.) Whisking often, gently bring the liquid to 110°F. Pour it into a bowl and whisk in the starter yogurt or purchased culture.

4  Cover the bowl and put it in "a warm place." This is the one time it would actu-ally be nice to have a yogurt maker. "Warm" depends on so many factors! What I do is line a big bowl with a heating pad and carefully put the yogurt bowl on top of the pad. Then I set the pad to Low and cover the whole arrangement with a clean dish towel. If you don't have a heating pad, the internet suggests lots of other ways to keep the yogurt cozy.

5  Leave the yogurt alone for several hours, though it's okay to peek at it if you want. Depending on that damn warmth, it will take the mixture at least 4 hours and possibly as many as 8, to coagulate. As it thickens, the yogurt will also become more tart. I like mine mild — it's more versatile that way — so I take it off the heating pad as soon as it's thick enough to suit me. Once again, there's no way to be specific about this, but watching the yogurt's progress is interesting (at least to me).

6  Once you decide it's ready, put the yogurt in some kind of airtight container and store it in the fridge. It will keep for at least 2 weeks.

*NOTE*  If the yogurt hasn't coagulated after 8 hours, you probably overheated the mixture on the stove. Won't you please buy an instant-read food thermometer and make all our lives easier?

# Tofu "Feta"

*Makes about 1 pound.*

**"To be perfectly honest" — why do people say that?** It suggests "To be perfectly honest *for once . . .*" — anyway, to be perfectly honest, feta's not my favorite cheese. But there are times you need it for punctuation. The Tomato-Watermelon Salad on page 92 is a good example of a dish where a bit of tang makes all the difference. Fake feta also peps up regular salads, as well as sandwiches and pizza. No, it doesn't taste exactly like feta (which isn't much of a loss), but it gives you sharply briny white crumbles that stand in perfectly.

You need to start this recipe at least 24 hours before you want to use the feta. Once made, it can marinate in the fridge for up to 5 days. In fact, it will keep improving during that time. ●

One 14- to 16-ounce block firm tofu
Salt
⅓ cup fresh lemon or lime juice
3 tablespoons flavorful olive oil
2 tablespoons water

2 tablespoons white miso
2 tablespoons rice vinegar
1 teaspoon freshly ground pepper
1 teaspoon dried basil
1 teaspoon dried oregano

1  Cut the tofu into four equal slices. Lay the slices on several sheets of paper towels, or a single sheet covering a few sheets of newspaper, or a clean dish towel. Lavishly salt them first on one side and then the other. Cover them with several thicknesses of paper towels or with another (clean) dish towel. Cover the top towel with plastic wrap. Put a magazine or phone book or something over the plastic wrap. ("Mommy, what's a magazine or phone book?") Then put several heavy things on top of the magazine. Canned goods are usually what's suggested, but if you happen to have a brick handy, that would also work. So would a pan of water. Water is heavy!

2  Press the tofu slices for at least 2 hours and up to 8. Replace the towels with fresh ones if you can see that they've absorbed all the tofu water they're going to.

3   When the tofu has been pressed, crumble it. Give the crumbles one more pressing between paper or cloth towels.

4   In a medium bowl, whisk together the lemon or lime juice, olive oil, water, miso, vinegar, pepper, and herbs. Add the tofu crumbles and stir gently to coat them with the marinade.

5   Cover the bowl and refrigerate overnight, or for up to 5 days. I'm certain that the tofu-marinade mixture would freeze well, but "to be perfectly honest," I've never tried that.

NO, IT DOESN'T TASTE EXACTLY LIKE FETA (WHICH ISN'T MUCH OF A LOSS).

— - — - — —

Every offering at a vegan bakery in Manhattan I went to recently looked like something you'd find at a middle-school bake sale. The owners had decided that a brown, thick, anonymous clump needed an inch of frosting to make it delicious. But the shop's lone customer — whose personal insulated coffee mug had a GO VEGAN sticker on it — was excited to be there. "Yaaaaaaaaaaay!" she cried thinly when her cupcake(?) arrived. *Yay! My vegan baked good is here!*

No.

If I'm making a vegan dessert, it can't be a pile of glop with icing. It needs to taste just as good as an omnivore dessert. It also needs to look just as good. With vegan desserts, presentation is crucial. It's true that the most beautiful vegan sweets on earth — the ones based on agar-agar, which look like stained glass — taste unacceptable to Westerners, or at least this Westerner. But the most delicious vegan cake on earth will taste 30 percent less good if all you've done is throw coconut on top. Presentation is key.

I wish I'd outgrown my dessert love. It seems childish to care about something sweet at the end of the meal! But the evidence suggests that won't be happening anytime soon, and maybe you're like me. If so, you're in the right place.

— - — - — —

# Chocolate Mousse

*Serves 4 to 6.*

The day of chocolate mousse has come and gone. But not for vegans who haven't been able to eat it in decades. When you serve this, you'll find that no one will say, "Isn't this kind of . . . dated?"

**It sounds slightly insulting when a recipe calls for "high-quality" chocolate.** *Not the kind* you'd *usually buy, you cheap slug.* Here, though, you should go for the best chocolate you can find; there's not much but chocolate in this mousse, so you do want the best kind. ●

**6 ounces bittersweet chocolate, chopped or grated (170 grams)**

**1 cup aquafaba (see page 14), at room temperature**

**⅛ teaspoon salt**

**⅛ teaspoon cream of tartar**

**½ cup granulated sugar**

**1 tablespoon rum (optional)**

**2 teaspoons vanilla extract**

1  Melt the chocolate and let it cool.

2  In a large bowl, preferably the bowl of a stand mixer, combine the aquafaba, salt, and cream of tartar. Whip until the mixture forms soft peaks; how long this will take is hard to predict, but it will happen. Gradually whip in the sugar. Then, using a rubber spatula, fold in the cooled melted chocolate, rum, if using, and vanilla until evenly mixed in.

3  Spoon the mousse into four to six dessert dishes or parfait glasses. Chill for at least 6 hours before serving.

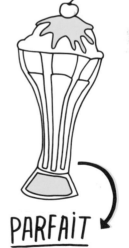

PARFAIT

# Chocolate Chip Cookies . . .

*Makes 18 to 20 cookies.*

. . . are important. **They're a staple, not an option.** Unfortunately, most recipes rely on butter and eggs. When you can't use those, it's tough to come up with a cookie that's nuanced enough. You can definitely make chocolate chip cookies that are as good as some you'd find in bakeries, but that's not setting the bar very high. And I think it's cheating to add distractions like coconut, oatmeal, and spices when the quality of the basic dough is what we're evaluating.

So we have to provide complexity of flavor in new ways — and yet not turn the cookies into a Caribbean extravaganza. Using dark brown sugar and brown rice flour helps. So does walnut oil, which is available in most supermarkets and on Amazon. Roasted walnut oil is best, but regular will also work. It would be ruinous to use a lot of butter essence, but a single drop or two adds an indefinable richness without screaming "movie popcorn." Anyway, I think we've got it down now.

Note that the dough must be chilled for at least 12 hours (and up to 72). ●

**1½ cups all-purpose flour (7.5 ounces or 200 grams)**

**½ cup brown rice flour (1.7 ounces or 50 grams)**

**1 teaspoon baking powder**

**¾ teaspoon baking soda**

**½ teaspoon salt**

**1¼ cups chocolate chips (super-accurate weight doesn't matter here, but it's about 215 grams)**

**½ cup granulated sugar (3.5 ounces or 100 grams)**

**½ cup packed dark brown sugar (3.9 ounces or 110 grams)**

**½ cup olive oil (3.8 ounces or 108 grams)**

**1 tablespoon walnut oil, preferably roasted (0.5 ounce or 14 grams)**

**2 teaspoons vanilla extract (0.3 ounce or 9 grams)**

**1 or 2 drops butter essence (see page 16; optional)**

**5 tablespoons water (2.6 ounces or 74 grams)**

**Flaky or coarse salt for sprinkling**

1   At least 12 hours in advance, toss together the flours, baking powder, baking soda, and salt. Add the chocolate chips and toss until they're coated with flour.

2   In a large bowl, whisk the sugars, oils, vanilla, butter essence, and water. Or beat them with an electric mixer. It doesn't matter, as long as the mixture ends up smooth. The oil will begin to separate out the instant you stop whisking, but don't worry.

3   Dump the flour mixture into the wet ingredients. Stir with a spoon or rubber spatula *just until the flour is mixed in.* (If you want, taste a pinch of the dough so that you can compare it to the way it tastes after chilling. There will be a difference!) Wrap the dough in plastic wrap and chill it for 12 to 72 hours.

4   When it's time to bake, preheat the oven to 375°F, with a rack in the middle. Line two rimmed baking sheets with parchment paper. You'll be baking them one at a time.

5   With your hands or a cookie scoop, form the dough into 2-inch balls, ten to a baking sheet. With your fingers or the bottom of a glass or whatevs, flatten each ball until it's about ½ inch thick. Sprinkle the cookies with a bit of flaky or coarse salt, and by "a bit," I mean "several flakes per cookie." (If you're worried about how much to use, bake a test cookie. Better than using more salt than you wanted!)

6   The total baking time is a matter of taste. Because there are no eggs in this recipe, the cookies won't brown as much as in omni recipes. Some people take them out after 10 to 12 minutes, when the bottoms are golden brown. I myself bake them for 15 minutes, until the bottoms and edges are medium brown; more browning means a more complex taste.

7   Cool the cookies on a rack. They'll taste much better when they're completely cooled and they will be better still after a few hours.

CHOCOLATE CHIP COOKIE

# Oatmeal Cookies

*Makes about 3 dozen large cookies.*

When you're converting recipes to vegan, sometimes the simplest normal recipes — sugar cookies, for instance — are the hardest to change. **If you want vegan oatmeal cookies that taste like flabby brown birdseed-based patties, that's easy.** If you want them to taste just like Mom used to make but vegan, it's a touch more complicated, but still easy enough that I don't understand why they're so hard to find.

It's okay to use purchased vegan butter here if you want. There's plenty of other stuff going on. ●

1 cup raisins, dried cranberries, or dried cherries (5.8 ounces or 160 grams)

¾ cup shredded unsweetened coconut flakes (preferred) or sweetened shredded coconut (2.8 ounces or 80 grams)

2 Flax Gel Cubes (page 203), thawed

1¾ cups packed light brown sugar (11.6 ounces or 330 grams)

2 tablespoons Lyle's Golden Syrup or honey (1.5 ounces or 42 grams)

1 tablespoon vanilla extract

4 ounces (113 grams) vegan butter, homemade (page 178) or store-bought

½ cup refined coconut oil or vegetable oil (3.8 ounces or 109 grams)

1½ cups all-purpose flour (6.6 ounces or 180 grams)

1 tablespoon ground cinnamon (6 grams)

1 tablespoon ground ginger (6 grams)

1 teaspoon salt (6 grams)

1 teaspoon baking powder (5 grams)

3 cups old-fashioned rolled oats (9.1 ounces or 260 grams)

1 cup walnuts, toasted and chopped (optional; 4.4 ounces or 125 grams)

About ½ cup raw or Demerara sugar (optional)

1 Preheat the oven to 325°F, with a rack in the middle.

*JUST LIKE Your Mom USED to MAKE... KIND OF*

2 Put whatever dried fruit you're using into a small saucepan — or a heatproof bowl, if you'll be doing this in the microwave. Cover with water and bring the water to a boil. Remove from the heat and let the fruit steep for 20 minutes.

3   Drain the dried fruit in a sieve, scatter over a couple of layers of paper towels, and dab dry with more paper towels. Let the fruit sit for now.

4   Scatter the coconut over a rimmed baking sheet. Bake it for 10 minutes, tossing it at the 5-minute mark. The coconut should be about the color of Rice Krispies. Let it cool while you do the other stuff; turn the oven to 375°F.

5   Line three baking sheets with parchment paper or greased foil. If you don't have three, just use two — you'll be baking the sheets one at a time in any case.

6   In a medium bowl, using an electric mixer, beat the flax cubes until they're entirely broken up and beginning to turn foamy. See how light the color gets! Add the brown sugar, syrup or honey, and vanilla and mix well. Next, beat in the butter and coconut oil. Looks icky, doesn't it?

7   In a very large bowl, whisk the flour, spices, salt, and baking powder together. Dump the brown sugar mixture over this, then dump the oats, soaked dried fruit, and walnuts, if using, over the brown sugar mixture. Now, with your hands, mix the whole mess together. It's a stiff dough, so this will be hard — but it's good exercise for your hands! Keep going until the add-ins are evenly distributed through the mix.

8   Still using your hands, shape the dough into balls the size of walnuts. (Want to be obsessive, like me? Then make a test ball of dough that weighs 40 grams and use it as a model for the rest of the cookies.) If you like, dip the top of each ball in raw or Demerara sugar. Then space them evenly on the baking sheets, twelve per sheet.

9   Vegan cookies always take longer to bake than you'd expect; baking a test cookie will keep you from frantically having to check them all the time. In my oven, these cookies take from 15 to 17 minutes. They still seem slightly underdone when I take them out, but they turn nice and chewy as they cool. Cool them on racks.

10   These cookies are best stored in the freezer and taken out "as needed."

# Scottish Shortbread

*Makes 16 pieces — or 15½, if you ate half of the bar you broke in two.*

I have a feeling that the Scots of yore would not appreciate the veganization of their recipe, but even the Scots of yore must change with the times. **I refuse to give up shortbread at Christmas;** therefore, it must become vegan. But is it possible to make it taste as good as the real thing?

Almost, with some tweaks. Even when your vegan butter is as good as can be, it won't have as much flavor as butter, so you'll need to add a little extra sugar to compensate. That's why the vanilla's there too, and why you sprinkle sugar on top of the dough before baking.

If you want, you can camouflage the shortbread even more by adding other flavors (see the Note). I think orange zest is the most festive. ●

**Vegan Butter (page 178; not store-bought, unless it's made by Miyako Schinner or another high-quality provider; 230 grams)**

**⅔ cups granulated sugar (135 grams)**

**1 teaspoon salt**

**1 teaspoon vanilla extract or vanilla bean paste**

**2¾ cups all-purpose flour (345 grams)**

**Demerara sugar, sugar crystals, or just regular granulated sugar for sprinkling**

1   Preheat the oven to 325°F with a rack in the middle. Line a 9-inch square baking pan with parchment paper cut to fit.

2   In a large bowl, using the paddle attachment if your mixer has one, cream together the butter, sugar, salt, and vanilla. Add the flour and mix just until a crumbly dough forms. Theoretically, overmixing could make the shortbread tough. I've never seen this

happen, but maybe that's my reward for always passing along this warning.

3   Dump the crumbly dough into the pan and pat it out so it's even everywhere. Then take a flat-bottomed glass and press it all over the dough to smush it down. This, too, is traditional, and I like doing it — but I don't see why you couldn't just press the dough down with your fingers.

# EVEN THE SCOTS OF YORE MUST CHANGE WITH THE TIMES.

4 Sprinkle the Demerara or other sugar evenly over the dough and press it into the dough's surface, using your fingers or that glass. With a sharp knife, cut the dough into 20 even rectangles. Bake for 40 to 50 minutes, or until you can tell for sure that the scored rectangles of dough can be separated without mushily falling apart. They won't be anywhere near crisp, but must be starting to develop a "crumb." This recipe takes a lot of baking!

5 Take the pan out of the oven, but don't turn off the heat! There's more baking to come. Cool the shortbread in the pan for 5 minutes before re-cutting it into rectangles. Leave it in the pan to cool for another 10 minutes.

6 Line a baking sheet with parchment paper. Carefully transfer the bars to the baking sheet, spacing them at least an inch apart. Bake for 20 more minutes, or until the cookies are completely cooked through. You should probably break one in half to check, or at least slice off the end of one.

7 When the cookies are done, carefully transfer them to a rack and let them cool completely before serving or storing them in an airtight container. It may be just my imagination, but I think they taste better after being stored overnight. (They keep for up to a week, though.)

## NOTE

If you grew up with the taste of butter-based shortbread, you may want to add a Distractor along with the vanilla. Possible options: 1 tablespoon finely grated lemon zest; 2 tablespoons grated orange zest; 1½ teaspoons *each* ground cinnamon and ginger; or 2 teaspoons instant coffee, dissolved in 2 teaspoons water. You can fool around with other stuff too, of course. Lately, I've been grinding some crystalized ginger with the flour . . .

# Better, Better, Best Brownies

*Makes one 8-inch square pan.*

The procedure for making vegan brownies probably isn't something you're used to. (*Probably?*) **But if you skate your eyes down the page, you'll see that these are just as easy as regular brownies.** And that's important: Brownies should be easy to make. It's brownies, y'all! We're not making a wedding cake here!

This recipe provides the best results for the least effort. But since aquafaba won't provide the same structure-building components as eggs would, you can't use quiiiiite as much chocolate as you could in an omni recipe — which is why the chocolate chips. Don't leave them out!

1¾ cups all-purpose flour (7.75 ounces or 219 grams)

¼ teaspoon baking soda

1¾ cups superfine or granulated sugar (see Note; 12.5 ounces or 350 grams)

⅓ cup water (2.75 ounces or 78 grams)

6 tablespoons aquafaba (see page 14)

6 tablespoons vegan butter (store-bought is fine here; 3 ounces or 85 grams), melted

2 tablespoons corn syrup (dark or light; 1.5 ounces or 41 grams)

¾ teaspoon salt

4 ounces unsweetened chocolate (113 grams), chopped

¼ cup unsweetened cocoa powder (0.7 ounce or 41 grams)

2 teaspoons vanilla extract (0.3 ounce or 9 grams)

1 cup vegan miniature chocolate chips (6 ounces or 180 grams)

1 Preheat the oven to 300°F, with a rack in the middle. Lavishly grease an 8-inch square baking pan.

2 Whisk together the flour and baking soda in a large bowl (large for easier mixing later).

3 In a small saucepan, briskly stir together the sugar, water, aquafaba, butter, corn syrup, and salt over medium heat. When everything is well blended and the mixture is beginning to reach a boil, turn off the heat and stir in the chopped chocolate and cocoa powder.

Whisk until the chocolate has melted and you've achieved a smooth mixture.

4   Add the chocolate mixture and vanilla to the bowl of dry ingredients. Don't overmix, but do stir until the batter is smooth. Fold in the chocolate chips. Transfer the batter to the prepared pan.

5   The oven's set to only 300°F because of the aquafaba, remember? — so you're going to have to bake the brownies for longer than you'd expect: 45 minutes. It's not easy to test brownies for doneness, but if you flip up a little of the top with the point of a small knife, you should be able to see that the batter has "crumbed" and is no longer gloppy-looking. Even so, the brownies will sink slightly in the center as they cool.

6   Let the brownies stand at room temperature for 6 hours before you cut them.

## NOTE

Superfine or "bar" sugar is easier to blend in, but don't drive yourself crazy if you don't have any. Just order some "Baker's Sugar" from www.kingarthurflour .com the next time you have a chance.

BETTER, BETTER, BEST BROWNIES

# Lemon Squares ------▷ *Makes 8 rectangles.*

. . . Oh, how hard this recipe was to figure out. But it was worth it.

Regular lemon squares have eggs and butter. **Replacing the butter's not much of a problem, but the eggs, my Gahd!** Working on this recipe was the first time I realized that, in addition to creating the right texture, eggs add actual flavor to baked goods. Sometimes that becomes a problem. A bakery near here sells lemon squares that we call Egg Squares in my house. But even if you don't like eggs in their egg form — and I don't — they're crucial in lemon squares.

Here's where I should archly say, "Are they really all *that* crucial?" And I would answer, "Yes, they are. But you can work around them."

Both the curd and the crust require you to dig some homemade vegan butter out of your precious hoard. You made that butter to use in baked goods; once in a while you actually have to use it. I wouldn't ask you to if it weren't important. ●

### CRUST

1 cup all-purpose flour (4.4 ounces or 120 grams)

½ cup confectioners' sugar (2 ounces or 60 grams)

Pinch of salt

¼ cup sliced or slivered almonds (1.3 ounces or 36 grams)

Finely grated zest of 2 lemons

4 ounces vegan butter, VERY preferably homemade (page 178) or store-bought (113 grams)

### FILLING

1 cup fresh lemon juice (8.6 ounces or 250 grams), from 4 or 5 lemons

½ cup orange juice or water (4 ounces or 120 grams)

1½ cups granulated sugar (10.5 ounces or 300 grams)

½ cup all-purpose flour (2.2 ounces or 60 grams)

⅛ teaspoon salt

⅓ cup nondairy milk (preferably soy milk; 2.8 ounces or 80 grams)

2 tablespoons Vegan Butter (page 178; 1 ounce or 28 grams)

1 drop yellow food coloring (optional; do not use turmeric)

**1** Preheat the oven to 350°F, with a rack in the middle. Grease an 8-inch square baking pan and line it with parchment paper (preferable) or greased foil. *For the love of God, please be sure to grease the pan before you add the foil or parchment.* In either case, leave about a 4-inch overhang on two opposite sides of the pan so you can easily pull the squares out later.

**2** **Crust:** In a food processor, process the flour, confectioners' sugar, and salt to blend. Sprinkle in the almonds and process the mixture until it's uniform. Add the lemon zest and pulse a few times until it's mixed in. Slice the vegan butter into eight pieces. Scatter the pieces over the flour mixture and pulse until the mixture looks like cornmeal.

Pat the crust mixture into the lined pan, tamping it down firmly. Bake for 15 minutes, or until it's beginning to brown. Take the pan out of the oven; leave the oven on.

**3** **Filling:** Dump the lemon juice, orange juice or water, sugar, flour, and salt into the food processor (you don't need to wash the bowl first). Blend for a minute or so, until completely smooth-ified.

**4** Pour/scrape the lemon mixture into a medium saucepan. Over medium heat, whisking pretty much constantly (sorry!), bring the mixture to a full boil. This may take 10 minutes or more (sorry again!). When it's reached a boil, allow the mixture to boil for 1 minute.

**5** Take the saucepan off the heat, add the milk and butter, and whisk the mixture until smooth. Yellow it up with food coloring if you're so inclined. There: lemon curd! Pour/scrape it onto the prepared crust.

**6** Bake for about 20 minutes, or until the top is set. Let cool to room temperature.

**7** Chill the bars for at least 2 hours to set the topping and make it easier to get the squares out. Then cut into bars. I like the bars better chilled, so I keep them in the fridge.

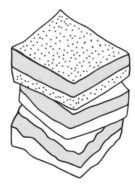

*NOTE*  If you mix the Lemon Curd with some homemade vegan yogurt (page 185), you'll produce a very good lemon pudding in 5 seconds.

# VEGAN CAKES: AGONY OR TORTURE?

It is a truth universally acknowledged that all vegan cake recipes work best as cupcakes. Cupcakes as a trend is so, so over — and yet the universal cupcake truth is still universal: Vegan cake batter simply doesn't have enough structure to rise reliably. The smaller the cake pan, the better the rise.

Which wouldn't be as much of a problem if you could use eggs. Eggs do *everything* a cake needs. When they're beaten, they come apart and then re-join into an air-trapping foam that helps keep the cake aloft. Heated, the same proteins unravel and re-form into a protein network that helps hold the cake together. As it heats further, the protein network gets stronger, and the "net" thingy of the network pulls itself tighter, stabilizing the cake's structure even more. Eggs also help emulsify a cake batter's ingredients, making the texture softer.

Yes, eggs are wonderful objects! But we can't use them, so we have to find a substitute. There are lots of those: yogurt and Ener-G Egg Replacer and homemade egg replacer and pureed bananas and applesauce and extra baking powder. In my experience, none of them are very effective in cakes. They tend to produce cakes that are overly soft and doughy. When I was tracking down cake recipes, it got so I could tell from a cake's photo whether the recipe was any good. One tip: **Never trust a picture showing an *uncut* frosted vegan cake.** If you can't see what the crumb of the cake looks like, get out of there! Anyone can make frosting and sprinkles look great. Cut into some of those cakes, though, and you'll find that what's under the frosting is more or less Play-Doh.

Since these recipes are ubiquitous, people often end up using and then rationalizing them. When you're done persuading yourself that your vegan chocolate cake is just "fudgy," that that your vegan yellow cake does not taste like banana, that people *like* their cake slushy with oil, you're finally ready for "Flax Gel: At Least It's Better Than the Rest™."

# Flax Gel Cubes

*Makes about 24 cubes.*

Flax seeds form a gel when you add water to them. This gel — if you must know — consists of a large number of monosaccharides linked glycosidically, which turns them into polysaccharides. Polysaccharides are great at holding onto water — which means a moist cake. **The polysaccharides also emulsify somewhat the way eggs do, so they help build the cake's structure.** Not as much as eggs would, true, but more than a banana could ever manage. The polysaccharides in flax gel even contain proteins and omega-3 fatty acids, just like eggs! They don't have as much of these good things as eggs do, but we really must stifle this selfish yearning for eggs.

In short, haven't you always wanted to make your own flax gel and freeze it in ice cube trays so you can pop out a couple of cubes whenever you need to replace a couple of eggs? Of course you have. And here's how to — oh, wait. You need a couple of things first, like a bulb baster or food-grade syringe. (Flax gel is too slippery and elastic to measure with a spoon.) You also need a sieve or colander that's fine enough to contain the seeds but coarse enough that the flax gel can slither its way through. Set the sieve over a bowl before you start cooking.

And you'll also need a couple of extra ice cube trays that are dedicated to holding flax gel. Not only that, but you need the kind whose "wells" hold 45 milliliters, or about 3 tablespoons. Luckily, that's the standard volume. Still, you need to be sure.

Now that you've lined up your props, let's make these lil' guys! ⬤

**6 cups water**

**½ cup plus 2 tablespoons golden flax seeds (50 grams)**

1  Put the water and seeds into a medium saucepan and bring to a boil over medium heat. Then turn the heat to medium-low and let the mixture boil slowly for 20 to 25 minutes, uncovered; stir it from time to time.

2  When the mixture has turned gelatinous and is the color of tea or cider, take it off the stove and *immediately* pour it through the sieve. Use a rubber spatula to scrape the seeds back and forth to get the last traces of usable gel. Now you have a sieve of useless flax seeds (you can compost them) and a bowl of lovely flax mucilage.

3  Whisk the gel briskly for a few seconds. Fill the syringe or bulb baster with as much gel as it will hold, then blob it into the ice cube trays, eyeballing it to make sure you're getting the correct quantity into each little compartment. Repeat the process as often as you need to, being sure to whisk the warm gel each time before syringing it up. Try to collect as much viscous gel and as little "gel water" as you can, but don't obsess over it.

4  Let the filled ice cube trays stand for an hour or so to cool, then freeze them. When they're frozen solid, wrap the trays tightly in plastic. They'll keep for 3 to 4 months.

## NOTES

A thawed flax cube is not nice-looking. Melted, it turns into a brownish hunk of jelly floating in a tiny pool of brownish water. Don't worry! As long as you mix it in thoroughly, you'll be fine. This is a lot to take in, I know. But you now have about 2 dozen flax cubes, each of which can be substituted for 1 egg. That's quite a bit of baking you'll be able to do, and you won't have to mash any bananas.

Oh! I forgot to say why vegan cakes work best as cupcakes. Flax gel isn't perfect: If you bake vegan cake batter in regular cake pans, the layers are likely to sink in the middle, or cook unevenly, or some other damn thing. Here again I must fault vegan bakers for being a liiiiiittle sneaky with cake pictures. One of the most famous photos online shows a flawless triple-layer rising triumphantly into the air. You have to read the recipe awfully closely to realize that it has a four-inch diameter. **With cupcakes (and these recipes), nothing will sag.** There *are* square cupcake holders, by the way; I own some. Their compartments hold the same amount of batter as round ones. Somehow square cakelets seem more sophisticated than cupcakes do. If you really care, you can arrange them to look like a square layer cake.

# Carrot Cupcakes

*Makes 24 cupcakes.*

**Carrot cake already seems kind of vegan, doesn't it?** After all, it was popularized back in the hippie days, and its texture is craggy and unrefined. Which I'm not complaining about! It makes adapting the recipe easier, although "easier" was an overstatement for me. When I finally tasted a good vegan carrot cake, I literally thanked God aloud. ●

2½ cups all-purpose flour (11.2 ounces or 320 grams)

1¼ teaspoons baking powder (6 grams)

1 teaspoon baking soda (4.6 grams)

1½ teaspoons ground cinnamon (3 grams)

½ teaspoon freshly grated nutmeg (1 gram)

½ teaspoon salt (1 gram)

1 cup plain vegan yogurt (see page 185 for an excellent recipe, though store-bought — preferably Kite Hill — will work too; 8.75 ounces or 245 grams)

¼ cup cornstarch (1.1 ounces or 32 grams)

1 pound carrots, scrubbed (16 ounces or 454 grams)

1 tablespoon fresh lemon juice

1½ cups granulated sugar (10.5 ounces or 300 grams)

½ cup packed light brown sugar (3.9 ounces or 110 grams)

1¼ cups olive oil (not extra-virgin) or vegetable oil (10.2 ounces or 290 grams)

¼ cup walnut oil (2 ounces or 55 grams)

1　Preheat the oven to 350°F, with a rack in the middle. Line two 12-cup muffin pans with cupcake liners.

2　In a medium bowl, whisk together the flour, baking powder, baking soda, spices, and salt.

3　Plunk the yogurt into a small bowl and whisk in the cornstarch until the mixture is as smooth as possible. Use one of those tiny

whisks if you have one; otherwise, a fork will be fine.

4　Grate the carrots with a fine grater, or do what I do: Cut the carrots into 1-inch chunks and chop them in batches in a food processor. If you use the food processor, watch carefully! Make sure to stop processing before those tiny chunks even *think* about turning into puree. When they're all grated or chopped, stir in the lemon juice and set them aside.

# WHEN I FINALLY TASTED A GOOD VEGAN CARROT CAKE, I LITERALLY THANKED GOD ALOUD.

5 Haul out a third bowl — a big one this time. Scrape the yogurt-cornstarch mixture into it and dump in both sugars. Using an electric mixer, beat these ingredients for 2 to 3 minutes, until the sugars are evenly dispersed. Gradually pour in the oil, beating until the mixture is smooth.

6 Add half the dry ingredients, mixing only until they're blended. Add the rest of the dry ingredients and repeat the process. Don't beat past the point where all the flour is mixed in. Stir in the carrots.

7 Divide the batter evenly among the cupcake papers. (An ice cream scoop is a good way to do this.) If you don't have quite enough batter to fill all 24 liners, don't worry about it!

8 Put the cupcake pans next to each other on the middle oven rack, with space between them. Bake for 10 minutes, then switch the pans and rotate them end-to-end. Bake for

10 to 15 more minutes, until the tops of the cupcakes spring back when you poke them with a finger. Let the cupcakes cool completely on a wire rack before you frost them.

9 **Frosting:** And now for the delicious cream cheese frosting! . . . well, no. Store-bought vegan cream cheese is disgusting. It looks and tastes exactly like spackling compound, though I've never actually eaten spackling compound. So I'm giving you a choice. The first frosting recipe that follows is tart and delicious. Thanks to — believe it or not! — store-bought vegan cream cheese, it has a great texture. But it doesn't taste tremendously cream-cheese–y. The second recipe tastes much more like classic carrot cake frosting, but if you don't like the taste of vegan butter, it may "trouble" you. (Our phone service has a recorded message beginning, "If you're calling to report a trouble . . . ") I like both of them JUST FINE, and either will frost 2 dozen cupcakes.

# White Chocolate–Lemon Frosting

*Makes enough to frost 24 cupcakes.*

2 ounces cocoa butter (55 grams; it must be weighed, not measured)

2 ounces refined coconut oil (55 grams; it must be weighed, not measured)

5 cups confectioners' sugar (2 pounds and 1 ounce or 950 grams), plus more if necessary

4 ounces (115 grams) Kite Hill Cream Cheese-Style Spread (in this one case, you can substitute Tofutti or Daiya)

½ teaspoon vanilla extract or vanilla bean paste

¼ teaspoon salt

3 tablespoons fresh lemon juice, or more to taste

1 In a double boiler or over extremely low heat, start melting the cocoa butter and coconut oil together. Take the mixture off the heat when it's about half melted and stir gently until the residual heat melts the rest of it. If you need to reheat it for a few seconds, that's okay. Just make sure it's no hotter than lukewarm when you put it into the big bowl you're about to use.

2 Add the confectioners' sugar, vegan cream cheese, vanilla, and salt to that big bowl and, using an electric mixer, beat. Airily dismiss your fear that the mixture looks too oily; you're about to fix that by beating in the lemon juice. Is the frosting too liquid? Add a bit more confectioners' sugar. Not tart enough? Add more lemon juice drop by drop. Tinker until it's just what you want. Then frost those cupcakes.

# More Like a Classic Cream Cheese Frosting

*Makes enough to frost 24 cupcakes.*

8 ounces Kite Hill Cream Cheese–Style Spread (227 grams), at room temperature

8 ounces vegan butter, homemade (page 178) or Smart Balance Original (227 grams)

One 1-pound box confectioners' sugar

2 tablespoons fresh lemon juice, plus more to taste

1 tablespoon vanilla extract or vanilla bean paste

Beat all the ingredients together in a large bowl for a nice long time, until they're creamy, fluffy, and spreadable. Then go to town.

# Chocolate Cupcakes

*Makes 24 cupcakes.*

This is a wonderful, wonderful cake recipe. The cupcakes come out dense but also light, with a fine crumb and an intensely chocolate flavor. The recipe's so good that when I'd finished testing it, **I thought I'd better try one more time "to make sure there aren't any problems."**

2 cups all-purpose flour (9 ounces or 250 grams)

⅔ cup unsweetened cocoa powder (2 ounces or 54 grams)

2 teaspoons baking powder

1 teaspoon baking soda

½ teaspoon salt

2 cups unsweetened "original" soy milk (16 ounces or 486 grams)

2 teaspoons apple cider vinegar

2 ounces unsweetened chocolate (see Note), chopped (60 grams)

1 cup vegan butter, preferably homemade (page 178; 8 ounces or 227 grams)

1 cup packed light brown sugar (7.8 ounces or 220 grams)

⅔ cup granulated sugar (4.7 ounces or 132 grams)

1 tablespoon vanilla extract (0.5 ounce or 14 grams)

1   Preheat the oven to 350°F, with a rack in the middle. Line two 12-cup muffin pans with cupcake liners.

2   Sift the flour, cocoa powder, baking powder, baking soda, and salt into a medium bowl. Do sift them; it makes a difference.

3   Pour the soy milk into a small bowl and stir in the vinegar. If it curdles, don't worry.

4   Begin melting the unsweetened chocolate in a double boiler or the microwave.

When it's half to two-thirds melted, take it off the heat, give it a big stir, and let the rest of the chocolate melt on its own. The chocolate should be coolish when it's added to the batter.

5   In a medium bowl, using an electric mixer, or in the bowl of a stand mixer, beat the vegan butter until it's fluffy and cohesive. Add both sugars and beat for 3 to 5 minutes, until the mixture is fluffy and cohesive again. Scrape down the sides of the bowl every minute or so, to help the ingredients get the idea.

6 Add the cooled melted chocolate and the vanilla and beat on medium speed just until combined.

7 Scrape down the sides of the bowl. With the mixer on low, add about one third of the sifted dry ingredients and beat just until combined. Scrape down the sides of the bowl. Add about one third of the soy milk and beat until just combined. Scrape. Keep alternating the dry and liquid ingredients in thirds, scraping down the bowl after each addition.

8 When everything is mixed together, *stop beating.* I'm not saying to leave lumps in the batter — I'm saying that you should stop as soon as the lumps are gone. Beating for too long will overactivate the gluten in the flour, making the cupcakes likelier to collapse.

9 The batter will be fairly stiff. Using an ice cream scoop or two spoons, dollop equal amounts into the cupcake liners.

10 Put the cupcake pans next to each other on the middle oven rack, leaving space between them. Bake the cupcakes for 25 to 28 minutes, until a toothpick inserted into the center of a cupcake comes out clean and the top springs back when you poke it with a fingertip. Cool the cupcakes on a wire rack, and make sure they've truly finished cooling before you even *think* of frosting them.

HECK YEAH! CUPCAKES!

# NOTE

You might want to try the excellent *un*sweetened chocolate chips made by Pascha. Yes, they're vegan. And "allergen-free," whatever that means. But the main point is, unsweetened chocolate chips — how cool — and you don't have to chop them! You can order them at www.paschachocolate.com. Now all they need to do is come up with miniature unsweetened chips.

# Stoutly Gingerbread Cupcakes

*Makes 18 to 20 cupcakes.*

This was the first vegan dessert I produced that David liked — loved, even. It's like gingerbread squared: deep, spicy, and moist. Thanks to the Guinness, it's not too sweet. Its only (slight) fault is that we can't serve it with real whipped cream, and I suppose we can't blame that on the gingerbread itself. But these are delicious with Whipped Coconut Cream (page 222) to which you've added a little grated orange zest, or with vanilla Ermine Frosting (page 216).

No need to limit yourself to Guinness, by the way! There are lots of interesting stouts out there, though who knows what I mean by "interesting?" I guess I mean "they taste like delicious stout." **Here stout adds a darkly grown-up quality to the cake without making it taste too beery.** ●

1 cup stout (8 ounces or 240 grams)

1 cup light or medium molasses (i.e., not dark or blackstrap; 11.9 ounces or 337 grams)

4 teaspoons baking soda (0.6 ounce or 32 grams)

2 cups all-purpose flour (9 ounces or 250 grams)

2 tablespoons ground ginger (0.4 ounce or 10 grams)

1½ teaspoons baking powder (0.25 ounce or 7 grams)

1 teaspoon ground cinnamon (0.1 ounce or 3 grams)

¼ teaspoon ground cloves

¼ teaspoon freshly grated nutmeg

¼ teaspoon ground cardamom

2 Flax Gel Cubes (page 203), thawed, or 6 tablespoons aquafaba (see page 14)

½ cup granulated sugar (3.5 ounces or 100 grams)

½ cup packed dark brown sugar (3.9 ounces or 110 grams)

¾ cup vegetable oil (5.8 ounces or 164 grams)

1 tablespoon grated fresh ginger (0.2 ounce or 6 grams)

1 Preheat the oven to 350°F (or 300°F, if you use aquafaba), with a rack in the middle. Line two 12-cup muffin pans with 20 cupcake liners (you may only need 18 or 19).

2 In a large saucepan, mix the stout and molasses over medium-high heat and, stirring frequently, bring to a boil. Take the pan off the heat and stir in the baking soda. Whee! Look at it foaming! Wait until it stops foaming and then give it another big stir. Set aside.

3 Sift the dry ingredients into a large bowl and whisk them until they're well combined.

4 Put the flax cubes or aquafaba, sugars, oil, and fresh ginger in a food processor or blender. Blend until smooth. The mixture will probably start to separate the minute you turn off the machine, but don't worry. Add

the stout mixture and blend well. Add this gross concoction to the dry ingredients and beat until everything is combined. I use an electric mixer, but you can use a big whisk if you like that idea.

5 Pour/scrape the batter into the prepared pans, filling halfway. Put the cupcake pans next to each other on the middle oven rack, with space between them. Bake the cupcakes for 30 to 40 minutes (45 to 55 minutes, if you use aquafaba), or until a toothpick inserted into the center of one comes out clean and the tops spring back when you press them lightly. Don't open the oven door until at least 30 minutes are up, or the cupcakes may sink. Cool the cupcakes in their pans on a wire rack; after 15 to 20 minutes, you can remove them from the pans to finish cooling.

# GINGERBREAD CUPCAKES

STOUT

# Orange–Olive Oil Cupcakes

*Makes 24 cupcakes.*

When did all that olive oil work its way into baking? **I'm not sure I approve. But this cake —!**

This will make about two dozen cupcakes.

2 cups all-purpose flour (8.8 ounces or 240 grams)

¾ teaspoon salt (0.5 ounce or 4.5 grams)

½ teaspoon baking soda (0.2 ounce or 5 grams)

½ teaspoon baking powder (0.2 ounce or 5 grams)

6 tablespoons fresh orange juice (3.3 ounces or 94 grams)

2 tablespoons Triple Sec or more orange juice (1.1 ounces or 31 grams)

½ teaspoon citric acid (see page 16) (0.1 ounce or 2.5 grams)

1¾ cups granulated sugar (12.5 ounces or 350 grams)

1¼ cups olive oil (9.6 ounces or 273 grams)

1¼ cups soy or other nondairy milk (10.7 ounces or 303 grams)

3 Flax Gel Cubes (page 203), thawed

2 tablespoons finely grated orange zest (0.4 ounce or 12 grams)

1  Preheat the oven to 350°F, with a rack in the middle. Line two 12-cup muffin pans with cupcake liners.

2  In a small bowl, stir together the flour, salt, baking soda, and baking powder. In another small bowl, stir together the orange juice, Triple Sec (or more juice), and citric acid.

3  Put the sugar and olive oil in a blender and blend for 2 minutes to make them nicely, uh, blended. Add the milk, flax cubes, orange zest, and orange juice mixture and blend the hell out of them. Seriously, blending them for a good long time will help with the cake's texture.

4  Pour the blender contents into a large bowl; use a rubber spatula to scrape out the

blender's interior assiduously. Gradually beat in the flour mixture, using an electric mixer set on medium, until the batter is smooth. The batter will be fairly stiff.

5   Pour/scrape the batter into the prepared muffin cups. Bake the cupcakes for 25 minutes. An inquisitive fingertip poke at the top will bounce back without leaving an "I pressed here" dimple.

6   Let the cupcakes cool completely in the pans, on a rack. This cake is best served naked, without frosting.

ORANGE-OLIVE
OIL CAKE

# Is This the Best Vegan Vanilla Cake?

*Makes three 6-inch layers or 18 to 20 cupcakes.*

I'm still not sure. I *am* sure that this is the recipe I'm stopping with. It fulfills all my vegan-vanilla-cake requirements. I don't ask much of a vanilla cake, but I do expect it not to collapse or taste like cornbread. It can't coat the mouth. It can't be bouncy. It can't reek of baking soda. It can't look like a raggedy household sponge full of big holes.

I'd give a lot to find the perfect vanilla cake recipe. By "I'd give a lot," I mean "I'd sit here forever waiting for someone to bring me that recipe." Because I've already scoured the galaxy. Most of the recipes I found began with a disclaimer — something like, "This isn't as good as omni vanilla cake, but I guess it's okay."

Well, this isn't *quite* as good as omni vanilla/white/yellow cake. But it's very good, which in the vegan baking world is kind of remarkable. **"I like this cake," David reported after I'd tested a sample layer. "Look — it's gone."**

And notice that word — "layer"! This recipe can be made into three layers that *won't collapse*. Granted, they need to be 6 inches in diameter, but that's a respectable size — especially for a three-layer cake. Of course you can also make cupcakes. ●

1 tablespoon fresh lemon juice (0.5 ounce or 15 grams; don't worry — it won't result in a lemony cake)

1½ cups "original" soy milk (no other kind will work as well; 12 ounces or 365 grams)

2 cups all-purpose flour (8.8 ounces or 240 grams)

3 tablespoons cornstarch (0.8 ounce or 24 grams)

1 teaspoon baking powder (0.16 ounce or 4.5 grams)

¾ teaspoon baking soda (0.1 ounce or 3.5 grams)

¾ teaspoon salt (0.1 ounce or 4.5 grams)

1 cup plus 2 tablespoons superfine sugar (9 ounces or 254 grams)

4 ounces Vegan Butter (113 grams; page 178; no substitutes), at room temperature

1 tablespoon vanilla extract or vanilla bean paste

Frosting (pages 216 to 225)

1  Preheat the oven to 350°F, with a rack in the middle. Grease and flour three 6-inch round cake pans and line each with parchment paper cut to size. (Trace around one of the pans with a pencil.) Or line two 12-cup muffin pans with cupcake liners.

2  Stir the lemon juice into the soy milk in a small bowl. Set it aside. Sift the flour, cornstarch, baking powder, baking soda, and salt into a medium bowl.

3  In a large bowl, using an electric mixer, cream together the sugar and butter until light and fluffy. Beat in the vanilla extract or paste. Add one third of the dry ingredients and beat until combined. Scrape down the sides of the bowl and beat in half the soy milk. Repeat these steps, scraping down the sides each time, then add the last third of the flour mixture. Beat only until the flour mixture is incorporated into the batter. Don't stand there with a dreamy smile imagining that you're improving the cake the longer you mix it.

4  If you want a layer cake, divide the batter among the three prepared pans. (A scale is the best way to make sure you've divided it evenly.) If you're making cupcakes, fill the cupcake liners two-thirds full. (I use an ice cream scoop for this.)

5  Bake layers for 35 to 40 minutes. The cake should be starting to pull away from the sides of the pans and the layers should pass both the toothpick and fingertip tests. Or bake cupcakes for 25 to 28 minutes. They should be light gold — the batter doesn't change color all that much — and should spring back if you poke them with a fingertip.

6  Cool the layers or the cupcakes on racks for 20 minutes. Then turn out the layers or take the cupcakes out of the pans. In either case, keep them on the racks until they've cooled completely, then frost.

yes! yes! YES! YES! YES!

# Ermine Frosting

*Makes enough for 24 cupcakes.*

Ermines don't get a lot of play these days, but back when this frosting was created, ermine coats, or mantles, or tippets, or muffs, or whatever must have seemed the ultimate in smooth, elegant luxury. It was called boiled frosting before someone came up with the word "ermine," but it's unlike any other cooked frosting. I didn't expect much before I tried it, and now I'm a complete convert.

Ermine frosting was popular back when eggs and butter were comparatively more expensive than they are now. Thrifty housewives would boil flour, milk, and sugar into a sort of pudding, then whip in a hunk of solid shortening. Mm-*mm!* But the technique itself creates a velvety texture that you can't achieve any other way. Replace the shortening with butter, and —

Oh, wait. We can't. But with our delicious homemade Vegan Butter (page 178), we can produce a remarkably smooth and delicious frosting. **Almost as delicious as . . . ermine fur.**

**5 tablespoons all-purpose flour (1.5 ounces or 40 grams)**

**1 cup granulated sugar (7 ounces or 200 grams)**

**½ teaspoon salt, plus more to taste**

**1 cup soy milk, preferably "original" (8 ounces or 243 grams)**

**8 ounces homemade Vegan Butter (page 178; 227 grams), at room temperature**

**2 teaspoons vanilla extract (0.3 ounce or 9 grams)**

1 Have a heatproof platter or shallow bowl ready. If you want, chill the bowl for half an hour to cut down on cooling time later.

2 In a small saucepan, whisk together the flour, sugar, and salt. Gradually whisk in the milk until you've got a smooth, pasty liquid. Ick! Over medium heat, whisking constantly but gently (so as not to create too many bubbles), bring it to a boil. Still whisking constantly, boil for a minute or two, until the mixture thickens to a puddinglike consistency.

3 With, ideally, a heatproof rubber spatula, pour/scrape the mixture onto the platter. All the recipes I've seen say you should immedi-

ately cover the mixture with plastic wrap to prevent a skin from forming. I've never done this, and it's never mattered. But if you don't like the thought of a skin forming, go ahead and cover the platter.

4 The flour mixture needs to reach room temperature before you can use it, so stick it in the fridge if you've got room in there. While the mixture cools, put the butter into a medium bowl and beat it with an electric mixer until light and fluffy.

5 When the flour mixture has cooled thoroughly, beat it into the butter 1 tablespoon at a time. Beat thoroughly after each addition and scrape down the sides of the bowl before you add the next tablespoon. When all of the flour mixture has been incorporated, add the vanilla. Beat the frosting (because now it's frosting) for 2 to 3 minutes, until it's light and fluffy.

6 Almost all vegan confections need more salt than you'd imagine, and this recipe is no exception. If you're planning to keep the frosting vanilla-flavored, you'll need to be especially careful that it's not too sweet. So taste it and add more salt a few grains at a time until it seems right.

## Variations

Flavoring the frosting is also a good way to take care of a too-sweet taste. You can make an excellent Coffee Buttercream by dissolving 1½ teaspoons instant coffee in the vanilla before you add it.

For Lemon Buttercream, dissolve ½ teaspoon citric acid (see page 16) in the vanilla before adding it, and add 1 tablespoon or so finely grated lemon zest.

We already have two chocolate frosting recipes in this book, but why not one more? For a very light, mild Chocolate Buttercream, add 2 tablespoons unsweetened cocoa powder to the flour, sugar, and salt. Whisk thoroughly before adding the milk and proceeding as directed above.

NOTE  When red velvet cake became popular at the turn of the twentieth century, it was originally iced with ermine frosting. To me, that combo is way too sweet. But the vanilla version of this frosting is great on Chocolate Cupcakes (page 208) as well as on Stoutly Gingerbread Cupcakes (page 210).

# Swiss Meringue Buttercream

*Makes about 8 cups.*

Yes, it can be done! **With aquafaba, you can make professional-caliber buttercream.** I raved about aquafaba on page 14, so I'll spare you more raving here. I wish I could also spare you the purchased vegan butter, but it's so much more stable than homemade that I'm honor-bound to call for it. If you're going to go to the trouble of making a cooked buttercream, you don't want it sweating or separating. When, oh, when will someone invent a high-end vegan butter? It's not as if the world has any other problems that need solving.

It's likely that Swiss meringue buttercream made with vegan instead of dairy butter will not cause too many complaints. Even the vegan version of this recipe is miles ahead of most frostings. But if you're worried, add a tablespoon or so of rum, brandy, or other alcoholic disguiser along with the vanilla. Or turn it into chocolate buttercream. Go to YouTube.com if you want to know more about Swiss meringue buttercream before you make it.

You'll need a candy thermometer for this recipe. You already have one, right? Good. ●

1 cup aquafaba (see page 14)

⅛ teaspoon cream of tartar

⅛ teaspoon salt

½ cup cold water (4 ounces or 118 grams)

2¼ cups granulated sugar (15.9 ounces or 450 grams)

5 sticks Smart Balance vegan butter (20 ounces), at room temperature

2 teaspoons vanilla extract or vanilla bean paste (0.3 ounce or 9 grams)

1 tablespoon rum, brandy, Cointreau, or other liquor (0.46 ounce or 13 grams; optional)

1 Put the aquafaba, cream of tartar, and salt in the bowl of a stand mixer fitted with the whisk attachment.

2 In a medium saucepan, stir the water and sugar constantly over medium-low heat until the sugar has dissolved and the mixture

reaches a boil. Then cover the pan for 2 minutes; this will wash errant sugar crystals off the sides of the pan.

3  Once the lid is on the pan, start the mixer on low speed. When the 2 minutes are up, remove the lid of the pan, clip a candy thermometer onto the side, and raise the mixer speed to medium. From here on in, you'll be watching two things at once. When the syrup reaches 234°F, turn the mixer to high. You want the aquafaba to be as stiff as possible. Dart back to the stove and check the syrup, which you want to cook until it's reached 246°F. Ideally, this will happen when the aquafaba has achieved maximum volume. If the aquafaba becomes stiff enough before the syrup is hot enough, turn the mixer speed to low.

4  When the syrup reaches 246°F, take it off the stove. It will reach 248°F, which is what you want, by the time you get it over to the mixer.

5  Turn the mixer up to high again. Add the syrup very gradually and *very carefully,* doing your best to aim it so that the whisk doesn't fling bits of syrup onto the sides of the bowl. Don't worry too much if that happens; worry instead about keeping the super-hot syrup off your hands and arms. With the whisk attachment, whip the meringue — because that's what it is now, a meringue — until

it's smooth, glossy, and cool. This may take 10 minutes or more, but the meringue must be at room temperature before you start adding the butter.

6  Beat in the vegan butter 2 tablespoons at a time, keeping the mixer speed high. The meringue will start to decrease in volume a bit, which is fine. If at any time the mixture starts to "break" and look curdled, don't panic! Just beat it, without adding more butter, until it's smooth again; if that doesn't happen, turn off the mixer and put the bowl and whisk attachment into the refrigerator for 5 minutes or so. (If that doesn't work, start whipping the mixture again and add 1 or 2 tablespoons of boiling water. But most likely, the first step — extra beating — will do the trick.)

7  When all the butter has been added, add the vanilla and liquor, if using, and beat for a few seconds.

8  I'm assuming you've already baked whatever you want to frost. If not, the buttercream can stay out at room temperature for a few hours; you may need to whisk it by hand at intervals to keep it from turning spongy. You can also chill the buttercream, but you must return it to room temperature and rebeat it before it will be spreadable.

# Bake-Sale Chocolate Frosting
*Makes enough for 24 cupcakes.*

You know, the *American* kind — not too dark, not too smooth, not too highfalutin. **Just good regular chocolate frosting.**

You can get away with Smart Balance Original vegan butter here; the chocolate disguises it very successfully. ●

4 ounces homemade vegan butter (page 178) or store-bought (see headnote; 113 grams)

4 ounces unsweetened chocolate (113 grams), chopped

One 1-pound box confectioners' sugar, plus more if needed

2 tablespoons nondairy milk, plus more if needed

1 tablespoon vanilla extract

½ teaspoon salt, plus more to taste

1  In a double boiler or microwave, heat the butter and chocolate until the chocolate is half melted. Remove from the heat and gently whisk until it's all melted and the mixture is smooth. (This is the best way to cool melted butter-chocolate mixtures: let the chocolate finish melting away from the heat.)

2  In a large bowl, beat together the confectioners' sugar, milk, vanilla, and salt. Beat in the cooled chocolate-butter mixture and continue beating until everything is smooth. If the frosting seems too thick, gradually add more milk; if it seems too thin, add more confectioners' sugar. When the frosting reaches the consistency you want, it's ready to use.

# Rich Chocolate Frosting

*Makes enough for 24 cupcakes.*

**This frosting is dark, smooth, and shiny** — almost like a ganache. If you want a less intense recipe, more like what Mom used to make, you'll find it opposite. ●

8 ounces bittersweet chocolate (230 grams), chopped

8 ounces vegan butter, *very* preferably homemade (page 178; 227 grams)

1⅓ cups confectioners' sugar (8.9 ounces or 297 grams)

¼ teaspoon salt

¼ cup unsweetened cocoa powder (0.7 ounce or 20 grams)

3 tablespoons nondairy milk, preferably "original" soy milk (1.6 ounces or 45 grams)

1½ teaspoons vanilla extract (0.2 ounce or 7 grams)

1   In a double boiler or the microwave, heat the chocolate until half to two thirds of it is melted. Then take it off the heat and let the rest of the chocolate melt under its own power. Stir it occasionally to help things along. The chocolate should be completely melted but cool when you add it.

2   In a large bowl, using an electric mixer, beat the vegan butter until it's fluffy and cohesive, 3 to 5 minutes; scrape down the sides of the bowl once every minute or so. With the mixer speed on low, add the confectioners' sugar and salt, then turn the mixer speed up to medium-high and beat for another 3 to 5 minutes, again scraping down the sides once a minute or so.

3   With the mixer back on low, add the cooled melted chocolate. Turn up the speed again and beat until the mixture is uniform. Add the cocoa powder, milk, and vanilla. Beat on low speed until everything is combined, stopping to scrape down the bowl. This frosting starts out somewhat liquid and gradually becomes stiffer as you whip it. When it has achieved a spreadable consistency, spread it!

# Whipped Coconut Cream

*Makes about 1 cup.*

In a letter to my mother, my grandmother listed a few ways to make whipped cream more cheaply, without relying on heavy cream. You could add a little gelatin to light cream. If you chilled it, evaporated milk sometimes whipped okay. **Grandma Donna didn't suggest whipping coconut cream, which turns out to be the most successful nondairy whipped cream out there.** Its mouthfeel is almost exactly like that of heavy cream. It holds its shape well and keeps well — up to 2 weeks. Really, the only trouble with whipped coconut milk is that it tastes a little canned and coconutty.

That's not much of a problem for me. I like coconut. Even so, I don't want it sneaking in *everywhere*. I wouldn't put this on pumpkin pie, for instance, or on strawberry shortcake — not without disguising the taste a bit — but I would, and do, frost Stoutly Gingerbread Cupcakes (page 210) with it. I often add coffee extract, rum, or grated orange zest to the bowl; I always add vanilla and a few grains of salt.

Trader Joe's and many other natural-foods stores sell canned coconut cream, which can be whipped straight out of the can. When you chill the can, the cream will become so stiff that it's helpful to remove the lids from both ends. There will be a tiny bit of liquid along with the cream; just let it drain away.

Whipped coconut cream won't become stiff enough to pipe, but it's perfect for spreading between cake layers or dolloping onto various desserts. The can of coconut milk needs 18 to 24 hours of chilling before you can whip the cream, so be sure to allow for that. And always use full-fat coconut milk. **"Lite" won't work.**

A 14- or 15-ounce can of unsweetened coconut milk contains about ⅔ cup coconut cream, producing about 1 cup whipped cream. So you may want to multiply this recipe from the get-go. Anyway:

Chill the can overnight. Chill the beaters from your electric mixer as well, and — if there's space in the refrigerator — chill or freeze the bowl you'll be using.

When the coconut milk has chilled for 18 to 24 hours, lift it carefully out of the refrigerator and gently turn it upside down. Use a "church key"–bottle opener to pierce four holes in the top of the can, which is now actually the bottom. Now upend the can and allow all the coconut water to drain out.

Open the can and spoon out the thickened cream. Plop it into the (preferably chilled) bowl. Beat it at high speed for about 30 seconds, until it breaks up and becomes creamy. Add ½ teaspoon vanilla extract, a pinch of salt, and ½ cup confectioners' sugar, or to taste. Whip the cream for about 30 seconds, or until it's fluffy.

You can use the whipped cream right away, or you can chill it for later. It won't "water out" like whipped heavy cream.

A little freshly grated orange or lemon zest makes a good addition to coconut whipped cream. It will also muffle the coconut taste slightly. Pinches of cinnamon, ginger, nutmeg, and other spices will do the same thing.

To make your own coffee extract, mix 1 tablespoon warm water into 1 tablespoon instant coffee. Add the resulting syrupy liquid to the whipped cream to taste. (Believe it or not, people will ask you if the coffee you used was decaffeinated. Just tell them it was.)

Other good add-ins: grated semisweet chocolate; 1 to 2 tablespoons rum or bourbon; crushed peppermint candy, if you're using the cream for a holiday recipe; crushed chocolate wafers. Really, almost any food that can be pulverized. ●

# Easy Vanilla Buttercream

*Makes enough to fill and frost two 9-inch layers or four 6-inch layers or to frost 18 to 24 cupcakes.*

Ann's World of Food doesn't run smoothly without buttercream, so I was worried about veganizing it — especially the uncooked kind, which I knew most people would rather make. One recipe I tried swore that using soy milk powder would produce a deliriously smooth result, but what I got was a penuche-textured blob that crumbled when I tried to spread it. I'm assuming that the frosting on Chelsea Clinton's vegan wedding cake was better, but I haven't yet found out how to reach that level.

It turns out that the basic confectioners' sugar version is your best bet for an uncooked buttercream. Most vegan recipes keep it simple by using confectioners' sugar mixed with solid vegetable shortening, just like the A&P used to make. This dead-white paste is unacceptable to me. Unacceptable, do you hear? (How can so many people use it on their *wedding* cakes?) **I'm just glad to have found one that tastes good.** •

One 1-pound box confectioners' sugar

4 ounces vegan butter (page 178; 113 grams)

¼ teaspoon salt

About ¼ cup nondairy milk, preferably "original" soy milk (2 ounces or 61 grams)

2 teaspoons vanilla extract or vanilla bean paste

1 In a large bowl, beat the confectioners' sugar, vegan butter, and salt until as smoothly blended and light as possible. Add the milk 1 tablespoon at a time, beating until the frosting has the consistency you want, then beat in the vanilla.

2 Use the frosting as soon as you can, before the confectioners' sugar starts to set up. You can spread it, swirl it, or pipe it just as you would regular frosting.

# NOTES

Because I'm never sure there will be enough frosting for piping decorations, I always make a bigger batch for layer cakes. In my own parlance, I "once-and-a-half it." Result: There's always tons of leftover frosting, and people sometimes complain that my cakes are overfrosted. Are these actual problems for anyone?

For Chocolate Buttercream, whisk in 3 to 4 ounces of melted and cooled unsweetened chocolate along with the vanilla. For Mocha Buttercream, use less chocolate — maybe just 2 ounces — and add 1 tablespoon extremely concentrated coffee syrup. (This is made by dissolving a few tablespoons of instant coffee in a tablespoon of boiling water.)

## TMI

### Sweeteners

Sugar is sugar. Refined sugar is sugar. Organic sugar is sugar. Molasses is sugar. Agave syrup is sugar. Maple syrup is sugar. Corn syrup is sugar. Brown sugar is sugar. Palm sugar is . . . well, you see where I'm going with this. When you're talking nutrition, there's not enough difference between sugars to worry about. We all know already that we're not supposed to eat a lot of sweet stuff; when we *do* eat it, it should taste good.

In terms of nutritional value — which isn't saying much — a cookie made with corn or beet sugar (they're identical) is just the same as a cookie made with agave syrup. It also tastes better. It gives a consistent result and observes the rules of the recipe. It isn't gloppy. And it doesn't make you feel as though you've been tricked by Chicken Little.

# I Was Going to Call This "Best-I-Can-Do" Vanilla Ice Cream — *What Happened Next Will Blow Your Mind!!!*

*Makes about 1 quart.*

There's *so* much waiting when it comes to vanilla ice cream. You need to start a day before you plan to serve it. Once the ice cream is made, you'll need to freeze it for at least 4 hours. And even before that, you'll need to have soaked or cooked the macadamia nuts. Oh, when will it ever end! But when you bring David a spoonful to try (because vanilla ice cream is "in his wheelhouse") and it turns out that he's on the phone, **so he eats the ice cream silently and gives you a thumbs-up sign — and then does a Daffy-Duck-level double-take and gives you a REALLY BIG thumbs-up sign** — it will all have been worth it. ●

2¾ cups vanilla soy milk (22 ounces or 668 grams)

2 tablespoons tapioca starch or cornstarch (tapioca works better; 0.56 ounce or 16 grams)

1.75 ounces or 50 grams raw macadamia nut pieces, soaked in water for 12 hours in the refrigerator or simmered in water for 15 minutes, drained well

¼ teaspoon salt

1 vanilla bean, split lengthwise

1 cup plus 2 tablespoons granulated sugar (8.8 ounces or 225 grams)

⅓ cup light corn syrup (3.85 ounces or 109 grams)

1¼ cups refined coconut oil, at room temperature (9.7 ounces or 272 grams)

2 teaspoons vanilla extract (0.3 ounce or 9 grams)

1 teaspoon fresh lemon juice (0.18 ounce or 1.5 grams)

¼ teaspoon instant coffee or instant espresso powder or granules

1 drop yellow food coloring (optional)

1   Pour 2 tablespoons of the milk into a little cup or ramekin. Whisk in the tapioca starch. Set aside for now.

2   Put 1 cup of the milk into a blender. Add the macadamia nuts and salt. Blend until the mixture is as smooth as possible. Add the remaining 1½ cups plus 2 tablespoons milk and blend it in.

3   Transfer the milk-macadamia mixture to a medium saucepan. (Rinse and dry the blender.) Scrape the vanilla seeds from the vanilla bean and stir them into the saucepan. Cut the vanilla bean crosswise in half and add the pieces to the saucepan. Add the sugar and corn syrup. Bring the mixture to a boil over medium heat, stirring frequently.

4   Take the saucepan off the stove. Add a few tablespoons of the hot liquid to the milk-tapioca mixture and whisk them in, then whisk that into the saucepan. Over medium heat, whisking, bring the mixture to a boil. Turn the heat to low, let the mixture reduce to a simmer, and simmer, whisking constantly, for 30 seconds to 1 minute, until it has thick-ened. (From here on in, we'll refer to it as a custard.) Turn off the heat.

5   Fish the vanilla bean pods out of the custard, but don't throw them out! Pour/ scrape the custard into the blender. Add the coconut oil, vanilla extract, lemon juice, coffee, and food coloring, if using. Blend on high for 3 minutes, scraping down the sides halfway through the process.

6   Pour/scrape the mixture — which, if you care, is now called a "base" — into a clean bowl. Drop in the vanilla bean pods again — we're going to get every bit of use out of them. Let cool to room temperature; then chill, covered, for at least 12 hours.

7   The next day, fish out the vanilla bean halves yet again. Their task is done. Freeze the base in your ice cream maker according to the manufacturer's directions. When it's done, rush it into an airtight storage container, pop on the lid, and stick the ice cream into the coldest part of your freezer for at least 4 hours and up to 2 days.

NOTE   For this recipe, I think it's important to use a vanilla bean along with vanilla extract. The flavor will be even better than with vanilla bean paste, and seeing the vanilla seeds gives the ice cream credibility. I also add the merest tiniest hint of yellow food coloring; without it, the ice cream looks a little wan.

# Chocolate Ice Cream

*Makes 1 scant quart.*

In our family, "I can't stand it" is final. If you announce that you can't stand something — open cupboard doors, a particular sports announcer's voice, the tortoise's repeated nipping of your ankles — you will no longer be subjected to that thing. This rule only applies to the parents, of course. What, give kids that kind of power?

Anyway, two things I couldn't stand to let the kids have when they were little were ice cream cones and chocolate ice cream. If they were getting ice cream, it had to be nonchocolate and it had to be in a cup. *Nothing* takes out chocolate ice cream stains, and nothing is more terrible than the instant when children bite off the end of the cone and ice cream starts to drip down their tiny heedless arms. And that always happens, no matter how many times you forbid it.

If I had had this recipe back then, would the children have been allowed to try it? Of course not. But I would have eaten a lot of it after they went to bed. It's intense, rich, and beautifully textured — almost chewy. **No omnivore in the world will find fault with it unless s/he hates delicious foods or recipes where you have to weigh the ingredients.** Or recipes that need to be started a day in advance. But except for those things, it's perfect. ●

½ cup strong (brewed) coffee — decaf is fine (1.8 ounces or 52 grams)

½ cup granulated sugar (3.5 ounces or 100 grams)

¼ teaspoon salt

5 ounces unsweetened chocolate, finely chopped or grated (140 grams)

1½ cups coconut cream (see page 223; 15 ounces or 400 grams)

1 cup chocolate soy milk (8 ounces or 243 grams)

¼ cup light corn syrup (3 ounces or 85 grams)

1 tablespoon vanilla extract (0.5 ounce or 14 grams)

½ teaspoon xanthan gum (see page 27)

1  Put the coffee, sugar, and salt in a medium saucepan. Whisking frequently to dissolve the sugar, bring to a boil over medium heat. Reduce the heat to low, add the chocolate, and whisk constantly until the chocolate is all melted. Then switch from the whisk to a heatproof rubber spatula and stir the mixture constantly; be careful not to let the bottom of the saucepan scorch. Let the ingredients bubble slowly until they've thickened into a definite syrup — one that's smooth and glossy and tastes like something you could actually use over ice cream. This may take as long as 15 minutes, but it *will* happen! Take the pan off the heat.

2  In a large saucepan, stir together the coconut cream, soy milk, and corn syrup. Bring to a boil over low heat, stirring frequently. Add the chocolate syrup and stir until it's all incorporated.

3  Pour/scrape the hot mixture into a blender. Blend for a minute or two, until the mixture is as smooth as possible. Add the vanilla and xanthan gum and blend until the mixture is smooth, scraping down the sides occasionally. What do I mean by "smooth"? You've probably noticed that every time you turn off the blender, a tiny bit of the contents clings filmily to the sides. At first that film will be speckled with tiny opaque dots — a sign that the mixture's not ready, and the reason you should keep scraping down the sides. The mixture is ready when the tiny speckles have disappeared and the film on the sides looks evenly creamy and translucent. How fast the transformation takes place depends on your blender. In my high-speed model, it takes 3 to 5 minutes. If your blender is not a high-speed one, you may need to turn it off periodically so the motor can cool down.

4  Once the necessary smoothness has been achieved, pour/scrape the mixture into a bowl. Set the bowl in the refrigerator until it's stopped steaming, then cover it and chill it for 12 to 24 hours. The mixture will become much stiffer as it chills — practically a pudding. Don't worry, and don't serve it as a pudding, even though it would be good that way!

5  Freeze the mixture in your ice cream maker according to the manufacturer's directions. Because the mixture's so thick, the dasher may clog before the ice cream has frozen evenly. If that happens, use a rubber spatula to clear the dasher and mix the lumps into the more liquid mass swirling around in the churn. (You may have to repeat this process rawwwwther a lot.)

6  When it's ready, transfer the ice cream to an airtight container. Freeze it for at least 4 hours before eating. Sorry about all this waiting around!

# Salted Caramel
# Ice Cream

*Makes 1 lavish quart.*

I used to say that ginger was the black pepper of the 1990s. These days, **I say that salt is the ginger of twenty-first-century desserts.** Actually, I don't say it, but it's true. As soon as people figured out that salting something sweet enabled you to eat more of it, they started adding more of it to desserts. Some people even like it on watermelon, those dopes.

Extra salt actually helps some sweets, though. Caramels are a good example; whether chocolate-dipped or plain, their intense sweetness is usually improved by more salt. The same trick works for ice cream. Salted caramel ice cream may seem like a cliché at the moment, but I predict that it will stay in the repertoire forevermore. This recipe is a miracle.

2¾ cups vanilla soy milk (22 ounces or 668 grams)

2 tablespoons tapioca starch (0.6 ounce or 16 grams; see Note)

1.75 ounces or 50 grams raw macadamia nut pieces (see page 19), soaked in water for 12 hours in the refrigerator or simmered in water for 15 minutes, drained well

½ teaspoon salt

1½ cups granulated sugar (10.5 ounces or 300 grams)

⅓ cup light corn syrup (3.9 ounces or 109 grams)

1¼ cups refined coconut oil, at room temperature (9.7 ounces or 272 grams)

1 tablespoon vanilla extract (0.5 ounce or 14 grams)

1 teaspoon instant coffee or instant espresso (6 grams) powder or granules

1   Pour 2 tablespoons of the soy milk into a little cup or ramekin. Whisk in the tapioca starch. Set aside for now.

2   Put 1 cup of the milk into a blender. Add the macadamia nuts and the salt and blend until the mixture is as smooth as possible.

3   Put 1 cup of the sugar in a large, heavy saucepan. Over medium-low heat, without stirring, melt the sugar. After melting, it will begin to brown and bubble. You still shouldn't stir, but you can rotate the pan to swirl the contents around. BE VERY CAREFUL: Melted sugar is extremely hot and horrible!

4   When the sugar has reached the color of a cello, take the pan off the heat. *Carefully and gradually* stir in the remaining soy milk. (The steam when a liquid is added to melted sugar is also hot and horrible!) Some of the caramel may "seize" — harden and clump up — but don't worry; it will all melt into the milk sooner or later. If it has seized up so much that you're having trouble stirring, like maybe the spoon is stuck to the bottom of the pan, just go away for half an hour to let the mixture come to its senses. If there's still a lot of hardened caramel after that, return the pan to the stove over very low heat and stir until the caramel has all dissolved into the milk.

5   Stir the macadamia-milk mixture into the caramel mixture along with the corn syrup and the remaining ½ cup sugar. Rinse and dry the blender container. Over medium heat, stirring frequently, bring the contents of the saucepan to a boil.

6   Take the saucepan off the stove. Add a few tablespoons of the hot caramel liquid to the milk-tapioca mixture and whisk well. Then whisk that stuff into the saucepan. Over medium heat, whisking, bring the mix-ture to a boil again. Turn the heat to low, let the mixture reduce to a simmer, and simmer, whisking constantly, for 30 seconds to 1 min-ute, until it has thickened. (From here on in, we'll refer to it as a custard.)

7   Pour/scrape the custard into the blender. Add the coconut oil, vanilla, and instant coffee. Blend on high for 3 minutes, scraping down the sides halfway through the process.

8   Pour/scrape the mixture — which, if you care, is now called a "base" — into a clean bowl. Let cool to room temperature, then chill, covered, for at least 12 hours and up to 24. The mixture will become very stiff.

9   The next day, freeze the base in your ice cream maker according to the manufactur-er's directions. When it's done, rush it into an airtight storage container, pop on the lid, and stick the ice cream in the coldest part of your freezer for at least 4 hours.

10   This recipe makes about 5 cups. That's slightly more base than my ice cream maker can handle, so I still-freeze about a cup of the mixture and eat it secretly; it's very chewy and delicious.

NOTE   Tapioca starch may seem like the absolute last straw, but it works so well in frozen desserts that I'm afraid I must request it here. It's increasingly easy to find in the Baking Supplies, Gluten-Free Mixes, and Scary Weird Grains section of supermarkets.

# Magic Cape

*Makes about 2 cups.*

If you mix coconut oil with chocolate, the combination stays liquid at room temperature but hardens almost immediately when it comes in contact with ice cream. Yet its low melting point means that it will instantly become lusciously melty in your mouth, which in turn means that it makes a very entertaining ice cream topping.

One great thing about making a chocolate coating topper at home is that you can use really good chocolate. Either bittersweet or semisweet will work, but the bittersweet will make a crisper coating when it touches the ice cream. **Though I often disapprove of bittersweet chocolate, I use it in this recipe.**

8 ounces high-quality bittersweet or semisweet chocolate (240 grams), finely chopped or grated

1 cup refined coconut oil (7.7 ounces or 200 grams)

2 tablespoons light corn syrup (1 ounce or 30 grams)

Pinch of salt

1 Put the chocolate, coconut oil, corn syrup, and salt in a double boiler set over simmering water or a microwave-safe bowl. If you're using the double boiler, stir the mixture until it's melted. With the microwave, blast the mixture for 15 seconds at 50% power. Stir it and return it to the microwave; repeat the process two or three times for a total of 45 to 60 seconds. That's it!

2 It's fun, especially for children, to squeeze this stuff out of a plastic bottle — you know, the kind restaurants use for ketchup. (Google "plastic squeeze bottle" if you don't happen to have a restaurant supply store nearby.) But ladling works just as well. Let the sauce harden on the ice cream for about 20 seconds before you dig in. If you tap it, the tap should be audible.

3 The sauce will remain liquid at room temperature. It will keep for months, though it may separate over time. No problem! To reuse, heat it in a microwave for a few seconds or stir it briskly.

# IT WILL INSTANTLY BECOME LUSCIOUSLY MELTY IN YOUR MOUTH.

## NOTE

To make excellent chocolate chip ice cream, first make the excellent Vanilla Ice Cream on page 226. In the last minute or so before you turn off the ice cream maker, drizzle in several spoonfuls of Magic Cape. The sauce will freeze immediately on contact with the ice cream, and the churn will break it up into bits and disperse them throughout. It may take some fooling around to figure out how much chocolate you want to use and how big you want to make the chips, but that's not the kind of experimentation anyone minds.

# Frozen Lime Cream
## with Gingersnap Crumble

*Makes 4 generous to 6 meager servings of lime cream and 6 to 8 servings of gingersnap crumble. But you'll sample so much of the crumble on your own that it will all even out.*

**For now I'm giving up on vegan Key lime pie.** In the middle of testing jillions of recipes, I got a chance to order Key lime pie in a restaurant and realized how very far I had strayed from the truth. So I decided to go with Frozen Lime Cream. Besides, when you mix in some Gingersnap Crumble, you may decide you don't need pie after all.

Regular Persian supermarket limes are better than actual Key limes — juicier, less bitter, and easier to zest. Their zest is greener too. It's bush-league to tint Key lime pie with green food coloring, but don't you still want your lime desserts a *teeny* bit green?

Unless you start this early in the morning, you'll need to make it a day in advance — a small sacrifice for a dessert that will stay creamy and scoopable in the freezer for at least a week thereafter. ●

### LIME CREAM

One 13- or 14-ounce can coconut milk, chilled for at least 4 hours

1 cup macadamia nut pieces (see page 19), soaked in the refrigerator overnight in 6 cups water or simmered for 20 minutes in 6 cups water, drained very well (4.3 ounces or 137 grams)

¾ cup granulated sugar (5.3 ounces or 150 grams)

¼ cup refined coconut oil, melted but still cool (2 ounces or 55 grams)

2 tablespoons finely grated lime zest (0.4 ounce or 12 grams)

½ cup fresh lime juice (4 ounces or 120 grams)

1 teaspoon vanilla extract

¼ to ½ teaspoon citric acid (see page 16; optional)

Pinch of salt

(continued)

**CRUMBLE**

5 ounces or 135 grams vegan gingersnaps (Nabisco and Mi-del both make good ones), crushed

¼ cup granulated sugar (1.75 ounces or 50 grams)

1 tablespoon ground ginger (5 grams)

2 tablespoons vegan butter, homemade (page 178) or store-bought, melted (1 ounce or 28 grams)

1 teaspoon vanilla extract

½ teaspoon salt, or to taste

1  **Lime Cream:** Scoop the solid coconut cream out of the can; discard the remaining liquid. Put the nuts and coconut cream in a blender or food processor, along with the sugar, and blend to a paste. Add the rest of the ingredients. Blend until the mixture is as smooth as you can get it. (If you're using a high-speed blender, you may need to stop occasionally to let the ingredients cool off.)

2  Pour the lime mixture into a freeze-able container and chill for at least 6 hours, or overnight.

3  Stir the mixture well, then stick it in the freezer for, sigh, at least 6 more hours, or overnight.

4  **Meanwhile, make the crumble:** Preheat the oven to 350°F. Line a rimmed baking sheet with parchment paper.

5  Pulverize the gingersnaps in a blender or food processor. Add the sugar and ginger and pulse a few times. Add the melted butter, vanilla, and salt and pulse even *more* times, scraping down the sides whenever you need to.

6  Dump the crumb mixture onto the lined baking sheet. Shake the sheet around a few times to disperse the mixture evenly. Bake for 10 to 12 minutes, or until — well, it's already brown, isn't it? So bake it until it's eeeeeven browner. Put the baking sheet on a rack and let the crumble cool completely.

7  Break the crumble into pieces. Store in an airtight container until you need it.

8  To serve, sprinkle the gingersnap crumble over the lime cream.

# Strawberry Sherbet

*Makes about 1 quart.*

It's traditional to say something here like "Packed with the flavor of ripe strawberries, this spectacular frozen confection will wow everyone on your list." To vary things a little, let's dangle the modifier: "Packed with the flavor of ripe strawberries, you will wow everyone on your list with this spectacular frozen confection." **Not that it's spectacular. It's just very, very good.**

1½ pounds fresh strawberries, rinsed and hulled (700 grams)

⅔ cup granulated sugar (4.7 ounces or 150 grams)

2 tablespoons light corn syrup (1 ounce or 30 grams)

2 tablespoons fresh lemon juice, or more to taste (1 ounce or 30 grams)

Citric acid to taste (optional; start with ⅛ teaspoon)

Pinch of salt

1½ cups vanilla soy milk (12 ounces or 365 grams)

1 tablespoon refined coconut oil (0.5 ounce or 14 grams)

1 tablespoon raspberry liqueur (I use Mathilde Fraise), Chambord, vodka, or crème de cassis, or more to taste (optional; 0.6 ounce or 16 grams)

1   Slice the berries into quarters or mash them with something — a potato masher, your closed fist, whatever. Put them in a bowl that's big enough to stir them with the sugar. Now what are you waiting for? Put in the sugar! Also the corn syrup and lemon juice. Also the citric acid, if using, and the salt. Give everything a big stir, then let the strawberries stand for 1 to 2 hours at room temperature.

2   Put the strawberry mixture, soy milk, oil, and liqueur, if using, in a blender. Blend until the mixture is as smooth as tiny-seed-filled silk.

3   Taste for "seasoning." Want another tablespoon of lemon juice (or a pinch of citric acid) or more liqueur? Put them in. Refrigerate the mixture in an airtight container for at least 6 hours, and up to a day.

4   Churn the mixture in your ice cream maker, following the manufacturer's instructions. Which, duh, but recipes always seem to put that in and I'm not going to break the tradition.

# TO VARY THINGS A LITTLE, LET'S DANGLE THE MODIFIER.

5 Since this sherbet has a high water content, it will melt quickly. It will also harden more than most sherbets. Solve the second of these nonproblems by serving it soon after churning or, if it's hardened in its container in the freezer, by letting it sit in the refrigerator for 20 minutes before serving. It will still melt quickly once it's served, so keep all conversation terse and business-like.

## NOTE

This makes slightly more than a quart, which is annoying if your ice cream maker only holds a quart. You could try to cram in all the mixture and see what happens — maybe it will be okay! — or you could take out 3 to 4 tablespoons of the mixture before churning.

# Chocolate Fudge

*Makes one 8-inch square pan — about 2½ pounds.*

Fudge is one thing I refuse to do without in my new vegan universe. **I'm talking about *real* fudge, the kind you can get on Nantucket and Mackinaw Island** — not some fakey version made from confectioners' sugar and carob.

This recipe is perfect except for an undisguisable hint of coconut. But maybe we shouldn't want to disguise it! After all, the only problem with the coconut is that it prevents the fudge from tasting *exactly* like the omni version — and not everyone will find that a problem.

Unless you have pure coconut cream on hand (Trader Joe's sells it, and there are several brands online as well), you'll need to chill the full-fat coconut milk for at least 4 hours before you start cooking. That will give the cream time to separate into its own layer. It's worth using the milk, at least once, for the neat little cream-separating trick I describe below.

Note that this recipe demands a food scale. There's no way to measure the chilled coconut milk by volume. ●

1¼ cups unsweetened coconut cream or two 13- or 14-ounce cans coconut milk (not light; 300 grams)

7 ounces semisweet chocolate (198 grams), finely chopped (semisweet chocolate chips are fine)

1 ounce unsweetened chocolate, finely chopped (30 grams)

½ cup unsweetened cocoa powder (86 grams)

1¾ cups superfine sugar (see page 199; 350 grams)

2 tablespoons light corn syrup (1.5 ounces or 41 grams)

¾ teaspoon salt (0.4 gram)

2 teaspoons vanilla extract (0.3 ounce or 9 grams)

2 tablespoons dark rum (optional, but adds good depth of flavor; 1 ounce or 28 grams)

¾ cup chopped walnuts, toasted (3 ounces or 88 grams)

1 Grease a heavy 2½-quart saucepan. Lightly grease an 8-inch square baking pan.

2 If you're using coconut milk, refrigerate the cans for at least 4 hours. Then, when it's time to make the fudge, upend each can. Using a "church key"–type can opener, poke four triangular openings into the bottom (now the top) of each can. Then turn each can over and drain away all the clear coconut liquid, leaving the solid fat in the can. Open the cans and scoop 300 grams of the chilled solid coconut cream into a small bowl, then transfer 50 grams of that to another bowl. You'll have a little extra cream to save and use for something else if you want.

3 In a large bowl, toss both chocolates with the cocoa.

4 Put the sugar, 250 grams of the coconut cream, the corn syrup, and the salt in the greased saucepan and use a rubber spatula to stir these ingredients until the sugar is mixed in as well as you can get it. Scrape down the sides of the pan frequently.

5 Over medium heat, stirring constantly, bring the coconut cream mixture to a boil.

When it boils, cover the pan and let it cook, undisturbed, for 3 minutes. Then uncover the pan and clip on a candy thermometer. Stirring occasionally, bring the syrup to 250°F. This may take up to 30 minutes; the syrup will hover at 220°F for ages.

6 When the syrup reaches 250°F, immediately pour it — without scraping the pan — into a clean metal bowl. Whisk in the remaining 50 grams coconut cream, the vanilla, and the rum, if using. Wash off the candy thermometer and put it back into the coconut cream mixture, which you must now cool to 210°F.

7 When the mixture is at 210°F, add the chocolate and cocoa powder and stir with a wooden spoon until the mixture is smooth. Add the walnuts with your hands, kneading them in gently. Then turn the fudge into the prepared pan, pat it down evenly with your hands, and let it stand, undisturbed, for 2 hours before cutting.

8 Store the fudge in an airtight container at room temperature for up to a week or freeze for up to 6 months.

# Pure, Rich, Great
# Vegan Caramels

*Makes one 8-inch square pan — about 1¼ pounds.*

In my *Beat This! Cookbook,* I had a recipe called Pure, Rich, Great Caramels. A woman wrote me complaining that you had to stir the caramels for 2 hours. **Didn't I understand how valuable her time was?** David said I should tell her, "Okay, just stir them for 2 minutes."

"Be that as it may," I can't go for long without caramels. These have cheered me mightily.

About 2 tablespoons refined coconut oil, melted (1 ounce or 27 grams), plus more for cutting the caramels

One 13- or 14-ounce can coconut milk (not light)

¾ cup light corn syrup (9 ounces or 256 grams)

½ teaspoon salt

1¾ cups granulated sugar (12.5 ounces or 350 grams)

¾ cup water (6.25 ounces or 178 grams)

1 teaspoon vanilla extract (4.3 grams)

½ teaspoon instant coffee granules, dissolved in the vanilla (optional, but it adds richer flavor without "reading" as coffee)

**OPTIONAL ADD-INS**

1 tablespoon finely ground coffee (8 grams)

2 teaspoons finely grated orange zest (4 grams)

1 teaspoon coarsely ground pepper (3 grams)

1 cup chopped walnuts, lightly toasted (4 ounces or 117 grams)

1   Line the bottom and sides of an 8-inch square baking dish with parchment paper. Brush the parchment with coconut oil.

2   Combine the coconut milk, corn syrup, and salt in a 4-quart saucepan and heat over medium heat, stirring constantly, for 2 to

3 minutes, until the mixture is just warm and any coconut milk clumps are dissolved. Remove the saucepan from the heat.

3   Grease the interior of an 8-quart pot with, yes, more coconut oil, or spray it with baking spray. Add the sugar and water and

stir until the sugar is wet. Over medium-high heat, stirring constantly, cook until the sugar is dissolved and the mixture reaches a boil. Then turn the heat to medium-low and cook the syrup, without stirring, until it turns a light amber color and the candy thermometer reads 310°F. Immediately remove from the heat and pour in the coconut milk mixture. Be careful! It will spit and hiss all over the place, and it's very hot.

4 Return the pot to the stove. Stir over medium-low heat until all the hardened caramel has dissolved. Raise the heat to medium and, stirring constantly (this mixture scorches easily), cook until the candy thermometer reads 240°F.

5 Immediately remove the pot from the heat. Carefully stir in the vanilla (or coffee liquid), again being careful not to get spattered. Add any (or all!) of the optional ingredients. Pour the mixture into the prepared pan. Let the caramels cool for 6 hours.

6 Grease kitchen scissors with coconut oil and cut the caramels into 1-inch squares. (You may have to regrease the scissors a couple of times.) Wrap the squares individually in waxed paper. Store at room temperature.

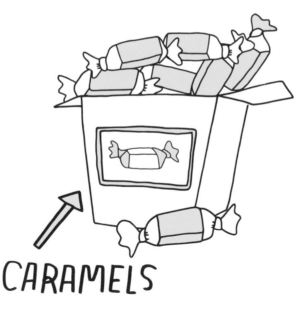

CARAMELS

# Afterword

In my return back through the passage, I heard the same words repeated twice over; and looking up, I saw it was a starling hung up in a little cage. I stood looking at the bird, and to every person who came through the passage, it ran fluttering towards the side which they approached it, with the same lamentation of its captivity — "I can't get out," said the starling. God help thee! — said I — but I'll let thee out, cost what it will; so I turned the cage about to get at the door; it was twisted and double-twisted so fast with wire, there was no getting it open without pulling the cage to pieces . . . The bird flew to the place where I was attempting his deliverance, and thrusting his head through the trellis, pressed his breast against it . . . — I fear, poor creature, said I, I cannot set thee at liberty. — "No," said the starling, "I can't get out — I can't get out."

— Laurence Sterne, *A Sentimental Journey Through France and Italy*

**Vegan food writers are generally ecstatic that you've decided to join the tribe.** "There's so much to celebrate!" they burble. Think of how pure you'll become, and how much nicer than ordinary people! Think of all the crisp, farm-fresh vegetables you're inviting into your life! Why, you've probably never even seen a Jerusalem artichoke — but once you've tried one, you'll never miss grilled cheese again.

Although I love vegetables, I prefer Peg Bracken's assessment in *The I Hate to Cook Book:*

> Facts must be faced. Vegetables simply don't taste as good as most other things do. And there isn't a single vegetable, hot or cold, that stands on its own two feet the way a ripe peach does, or a strawberry. . . . The food experts know this, too, way down deep. You can tell they do, from the reliance they put on adjectives whenever they bump into a vegetable. "And with it, serve a big bowl of tiny, buttery, fresh-from-the-garden beets!" they'll cry. But they're still only beets, and there's no need to get so excited about it.

**There's a lot to hate about veganism besides people who go on and on about the greatness of vegetables.** One hateful thing is natural foods stores. Even at shiny high-ceilinged places like Whole Foods, the vegan areas are drab. Their dispirited fake candy. Those huge open vats of anonymous grains and seeds ready to be scooped out by anyone's flu-germ-covered hands. The shelves filled with tiny brown glass jars of fir essence and Rescue Remedy. The sad little cosmetic corner, where Tom's of Maine products gleam out like rubies compared to the other offerings. The lumpy hand-knit wool goods. (By the way, what other kind of food shop sells pajamas?) The stacks of brochures and flyers everywhere, because if you're shopping there, you *must* be the kind of person who believes in rebirthing therapy.

And the customers, who have so many more questions than regular people. "So you're saying that even though there's no Sunrise Mesa Cat Treat in the pet food section — and you don't remember ever stocking it, and you've never heard of it and anyway, there's no such thing as a vegan cat — you're saying you don't sell it? Do you think you could order some?" No matter which aisle you're trying to get through — the Healthy Fig Newton aisle; the Aseptic Packaging aisle; the Gluten-Free Everything aisle — they're always already there, clopping along in their Tevas and plowing their shopping cart straight toward you.

**Vegans can be thrilled with so little, and yet they want so much.** There's an okay online recipe for vegan croissants that uses margarine instead of butter. I would never make them, but they're probably better than many commercial croissants, and at least they're flaky.

But one reader of the croissant blog has a problem: "Margarine is one molecule away from being plastic." Another wants a little tweak: "When I saw this recipe, I got very excited — but then I realized you were using regular flour. Do you think it would work with a gluten-free flour mix?" . . . "Because I'm the kind of person who's got to have everything," she should have added.

And these are the people I want in my posse?

Absolutely.

**Doing the right thing is the only thing to do, even when it steers you toward places you don't want to go.**

We've all been told that making a moral choice can be difficult. Did we think it wasn't true? Yes, we did — because for the most part, doing the right thing *is* pretty easy. Society encourages us to be patient with cranky babies, to return people's dropped wallets, and to say thank-you to bus drivers. And that's pretty much the level of moral challenge most of us face on a daily basis.

But unless you're a natural ascetic, veganism is a serious sacrifice and a drastic change. If you adopt a plant-based diet, you're most likely turning your back on your heritage. You won't know what to eat at holidays. Your restaurant choices will be limited. (Why do I suspect that the food won't be great at Bloodroot, a "vegan feminist collective" restaurant near here?) You'll have to learn words like "rejuvelac." Finding the ingredients you need may become a challenge. You'll spend a lot of time trotting around with sprouts and cheesecloth. Many of your friends and family will be hostile about your choice.

And are you sure of making a difference? I don't know.

I do know that switching to a plant-based diet won't make life easier for cows right away. Probably not for chickens or fish or any other creature either. Most likely, going vegan won't solve any problems at all, at least not in my lifetime. But I can no longer be part of the market that causes so much suffering.

**If this makes you uncomfortable, good.**

RIGHT VS. WRONG, PERIOD.

# Index

AT THE BEGINNING,
I WASN'T SURE
THERE WOULD BE
ENOUGH RECIPES
TO PUT IN A
COOKBOOK.

BUT THERE WERE!